The Men Who Gave Us Wings

Britain and the Aeroplane
1796–1914

PETER REESE

Pen & Sword
AVIATION

Dedication

To Mrs Blanche (Dabbie) Taylor who,
with her husband Wally,
gave a student their love and support.

First published in Great Britain in 2014 by
PEN & SWORD AVIATION
An imprint of
Pen & Sword Books Ltd
47 Church Street
Barnsley
South Yorkshire
S70 2AS

Copyright © Peter Reese, 2014

ISBN 978-1-84884-8481-1

Typeset by Concept, Huddersfield, West Yorkshire.
Printed and bound in England by CPI Group (UK) Ltd, Croydon CR0 4YY.

Pen & Sword Books Ltd incorporates the imprints of Pen & Sword Archaeology,
Atlas, Aviation, Battleground, Discovery, Family History, History, Maritime,
Military, Naval, Politics, Railways, Select, Social History, Transport, True Crime,
and Claymore Press, Frontline Books, Leo Cooper, Praetorian Press,
Remember When, Seaforth Publishing and Wharncliffe.

For a complete list of Pen & Sword titles please contact
PEN & SWORD BOOKS LIMITED
47 Church Street, Barnsley, South Yorkshire, S70 2AS, England
E-mail: enquiries@pen-and-sword.co.uk
Website: www.pen-and-sword.co.uk

Contents

Acknowledgements

My sincere thanks are due to the following people for their generous and skilled help in writing this book: Brian Riddle of the National Aerospace Library who from his wide knowledge gave substance to my tentative ideas and who with his colleague Christine Woodward has supported me throughout the writing; Tim Ward and the Staff of the Prince Consort's Library, who have offered me its excellent facilities over many years and, in the case of this book, especially Robert Tilley and Geoffrey Sear; Paul Vickers, head of the Army Libraries Information Services, for his inspiration with the title and help with illustrations; my long-standing friend Jennifer Prophet, for the major task of reading and improving the initial text and her detailed work concerning the Index; Dr Jim Russell for his expert reading of a subject about which he knows so much; Charles Prophet for checking and meticulously correcting any shortcomings in my technical descriptions and for his assistance with the Index; Christine Batten with her inspirational interpretation of my writing and patience with different versions of the text; the Staff of the RAF Museum Hendon who conscientiously fielded my inquiries; the Staff of Scarborough Art Gallery and Rotunda Collections; the Staff of the Yorkshire Air Museum at Elvington; Richard Gardner and all the Staff at the Farnborough Air Sciences Trust; Colonel David Bowman for his help with sources connected with RAF Upavon, Peter Capon and Staff at the Army Air Museum, Middle Wallop; The National Portrait Gallery for permission to reproduce copyright material; Jean and John Roberts for their help once again; Roger Stone and the Dickson family for help with information about Bertram Dickson and to the Royal Aeronautical Society for permission to reproduce copyright material.

I also want to acknowledge the vital assistance given by senior editor Rupert Harding at Pen & Sword and copy editor Stephen Chumbley without whose support the book would not have been published.

Finally my continued thanks go to my dear wife Barbara for her ever sound reactions and support throughout, which in this case involved standing ankle deep in water photographing Bertram Dickson's grave during a boisterous day in the Scottish Highlands.

Any shortcomings are mine alone.

Peter Reese
Ash Vale, 2014

Prologue

The extraordinary development of aeroplanes during the twentieth century has meant that air travel in them has become an established way of life, essential for inter-continental journeys and a favourable alternative for shorter international travel, even if forever associated with obligatory security checks.

Apart from the exhilarating sensation of power on take-off and the welcome thud of wheels and reverse thrust on landing, today's air travel is a relatively mundane, safe and – despite the range of on-board entertainment – tedious experience. Such flights, for instance, could hardly be more different from those of Samuel Cody, the first man to fly in Britain, in a plane constructed of bamboo and larch held together by tensioned piano wire, where his seat was open to the elements and his steering column had to be continually worked to maintain level flight. When, in 1909, he began to take up passengers, they sat directly behind (and above) him in the full force of the wind, half-deafened by the roar of the engine and menaced by the plane's large unguarded propeller whipping around at their rear.

British aviation had, in fact, commenced more than a century before Cody, but the pioneers' often inspired ideas were hampered by the lack of a suitable propulsion system. Upon the development of the internal-combustion engine, the first recorded flight came in America with the Wright brothers in December 1903, followed by Santos-Dumont in France during 1906, and after a succession of missed opportunities and false trails, by Britain when Samuel Cody – the one-time American cowboy working at the British army's Balloon Factory at Farnborough – made a flight lasting twenty-seven seconds on 16 October 1908, just six years before the outbreak of the First World War.

Following the work of the early pioneers, the present book focuses on that iconic period before the First World War with the remarkable group of individuals who drove British aviation forward against recurring and formidable difficulties. Most have been forgotten, with Winston Churchill a notable exception (although this is due more to his exploits as a wartime leader during the Second World War than to his work in the early stages of flight), and only a few names such as Rolls and Royce remain familiar. But like any other group it included born extroverts like Bristol Aircraft's Sir George White, as well as quiet and modest men such as the flying genius 'Benny' Huck. Their relative neglect can be partly explained by later massive advancement in aviation, but in Britain from the time of the early pioneers and throughout the period to the First World War there was undoubtedly disinterest – if not hostility – from influential sections within the political and scientific establishment and the armed services.

There were powerful reasons for this, since the current Liberal administration under Prime Minister Herbert Asquith was encountering major problems over the need to increase expenditure on social benefits and strengthening the Royal Navy. In 1909 the latter vote was expected to be 'gigantic' but necessary because naval supremacy was 'so essential not only to our national existence but in our judgement to the vital interests of Western civilisation'.[1] In contrast, as late as May 1911 Lloyd George was being asked 'whether with regard to the expenditure of the Board of Admiralty and the War Office upon experiments in air machines, it is contemplated by HM Government to use the air as well as land and sea for the devastating purposes of international war?'[2] At the very least, the question exhibited a lack of awareness about the positive role that air power could play for national security, but in many eyes it actually seemed the opposite. During the nineteenth century, by taking advantage of the country's insular position and its long-standing democratic traditions, Britain had been able to avoid the convulsions suffered by the rest of Europe and had built up a vast international empire. This had been achieved through the protection provided by the Royal Navy, but aeroplanes that could overfly the Channel threatened this traditional shield.

It was also indisputable that during the early twentieth century, Britain, with its much smaller army and supreme navy, was not likely to favour airpower as much as France or Germany. After France's humiliation during the Franco-Prussian War it had every reason to take advantage of its technical superiority in the new arm, which also gave its young men the chance to display the much-prized French quality of *élan*. And as an ambitious Empire, with its expansion limited by long-established powers such as Britain, France and Russia,[3] Germany was intent on strengthening its military forces, including its air capability.

Negative attitudes towards air constructors and engineers were also evident within Britain's scientific and educational circles. Despite the country's incomparable tradition of heavy engineering and past scientific breakthroughs, and the new industrial challenges being mounted by both Germany and the United States,[4] there seemed less enthusiasm for the rapidly-developing internal-combustion engine and the latest technological spurt impelled by the use of oil (and electricity) than in the industrial developments that took place in Victorian times. The advantages of speed, for instance, offered by motor vehicles were negated by a national speed limit of 20mph set in 1903 – which was strictly enforced – when Germany had no such limits.

The Cambridge historian Correlli Barnett, for one, believes that Germany's technical education was further advanced than in Britain, although this has been disputed[5] on the grounds of much instruction taking place in the emerging technical colleges that has still to receive due recognition, compared with the lack of courses in British universities. There is less debate about secondary education, especially in the case of the public schools to which many successful businessmen sent their sons, where a prevailing atmosphere of social conservatism favoured the arts and classics, and where business and new technical developments as opposed to scientific discoveries were not actively welcomed. Accounts of revolutionary air travel were left to the bumptious scientific novelist H.G. Wells or to the prophetic imagination of Rudyard Kipling who in 1904 in *With the Night Mail* described an Atlantic crossing by air, guided by radio services giving weather reports and allotting safety levels and landing priorities.[6]

Such anti-technical bias in the public schools, and the slowness of universities to take the lead, had a direct result on British aircraft engineers and designers who were forced to look for training in lesser-known technical colleges or to take up apprenticeships with the railway and motor industries. In such circumstances they needed to be both dedicated and determined, for as apprentices they enjoyed a much humbler status than as students. Prevailing attitudes also meant they needed some capital since they were less likely to receive financial support than in other countries.

In America, for instance, although the Wrights were fiercely independent, Samuel Langley received a large grant from the US Department's Board of Ordnance and Fortification for his aeronautical researches, while Louis Blériot was given preferential treatment by the French government and Count von Zeppelin received substantial funds from the Prussian General Staff and War Ministry as well as from a popular campaign promoting his airships. In contrast, the talented British aircraft designers A.V. Roe and Geoffrey de Havilland had to struggle on alone while building their planes. To an extent not seen on the continent, where German firms produced 628 aircraft between 1911 and 1914,[7] British constructors found no enthusiasm from the military authorities. When, in 1908, Roe tried to interest the War Office in his planes he was told 'much as we would like to help you by placing orders, we regret we cannot do this as we are trustees of the public purse and we do not consider that aeroplanes will be of any possible use for war purposes'.[8] It was only after being taken on by the staff of the Royal Aircraft Factory that de Havilland was able to sell his plane to them.

Such parsimony towards air power was also experienced by Samuel Cody who, during the time he was employed by the army to build British Army Aircraft No. 1, had to wait until the failure of the airship *Nulli Secundus II* before he was given the use of an engine for his aeroplane. This led to some British constructors adopting novel methods to open up a market for their machines: because the army was taking only a few of their Boxkite planes, the Bristol Aircraft Company set up flying schools through which they could demonstrate their aircraft and attract foreign markets for sales.

Whatever the efforts of British constructors, it took German sabre-rattling at Agadir in Morocco during the summer of 1911 to finally convince the British authorities about the need for an air arm and for the resulting establishment of the Royal Flying Corps (RFC) in April 1912.

Even then the aircraft constructors faced strong competition from the Government-sponsored Royal Aircraft Factory at Farnborough, that had been revitalised by the arrival of Geoffrey de Havilland. He designed their BE family of aircraft at a time when the military establishment 'put its trust so far in the ability of the Factory to design whatever would be required in time of war and the pioneers were hardly taken seriously'.[9] It took the energy and confidence of Winston Churchill, as First Lord of the Admiralty, to break Farnborough's near-monopoly by encouraging orders from private firms for the RFC's naval wing, and for parliamentary agitation during the war itself for the Factory's hold over aircraft production to be broken forever.

For today's passengers at one of Britain's major airports, seated in their sleek, air-conditioned and sound-proofed aircraft, it needs a massive thought shift to imagine a world without aeroplanes or the problems faced by the aviation pioneers. In the main they are also unlikely to be aware of those individuals who, after the coming of flight, fearful of Britain's newfound vulnerability, were committed to making the country air-conscious and encouraging the formation of an effective air force. The present book turns to that little-remembered but vital group of men, including entrepreneurs and constructors, who helped to develop the infant aircraft industry: pilots who demonstrated the aeroplanes' capabilities to spectators and purchasers alike; influential people from many quarters, including the Press, who championed the industry against other powerful vested interests and those who laid down the rules and led the RFC to France in 1914.

Theirs was to prove an epic struggle against both the physical restrictions of early flight and the equally powerful forces of caution and 'conventional wisdom' within British society. Typically British, converting their Government and countrymen into enthusiastic supporters of air – beyond its sporting appeal – proved immensely difficult, and although by 1914 the RFC was firmly established, Germany had its massive airships and far more numerous aircraft.

Ultimately, whatever was achieved prior to the war, it took the immense shock caused by the German bombing of London in 1917 for air to receive a level of funding of which previously they could only have dreamt, and before the war's end led the RAF to become the world's largest air force.

THE PIONEERS

Chapter 1

The Father of Flight

At the beginning of the nineteenth century, despite widespread scepticism in Britain towards aviation, Sir George Cayley (b. 1773) was the man generally regarded as the father of manned flight. Cayley's family owned estates in both Yorkshire and Lincolnshire, and as a strong patriot and Christian Unitarian he devoted much of his life to conducting a range of scientific enquiries and experiments more likely to bring immediate benefits to his fellow men than his groundbreaking work on aeronautics. These included a novel drainage scheme for 10,000 acres of land adjoining his Lincolnshire estates and sketching out plans for what he called 'a universal railway' for crossing rough ground – this was in effect a forerunner of the caterpillar tractor (from which the military tank emerged). In 1810 its military potential was recognised by his friend, William Chapman, who told Cayley he could be providing Bonaparte with a means of invasion.

Cayley was a handsome, kindly-looking man and throughout his life he attempted to find ways of reducing avoidable accidents. After witnessing the running-down of William Huskisson by Stephenson's *Rocket* at the opening of the Manchester to Liverpool Railway in 1830, he constructed a system for automatically applying the brakes of railway engines at the time of a collision. When a serious fire at the Covent Garden theatre caused the death of twenty-three firemen, he proposed a jointed sheet-iron curtain to close off the stage in the event of a fire, and after an accident off Scarborough where eleven men lost their lives in a lifeboat he designed lifeboats that would be self-righting. Following an accident to one of his son's tenants in which his hand was severed, he designed and built a prosthetic one for him. Such regard for safety was to have a significant effect on his future aeronautical experiments.

Cayley habitually spent much of his time tucked away in his workshop at the family seat of Brompton, near Scarborough, where he was assisted by his faithful mechanic Thomas Vick. This, together with his habit of not bothering to develop (or patent) some of his inventions, restricted wider knowledge of his work and, as far as his aeronautical researches were concerned, he faced the additional problem that they were never considered as seriously as the more conventional activities of other scientists and engineers. This was of significance when his friends included such pacesetters as Henry Bessemer, the inventor of ductile steel, George Rennie from the family of engineers who built London's Waterloo and Southwark bridges and Peter Roget, whose Thesaurus became indispensable for writers and other students of English.

Together with the very improbability of heavier-than-air flight, much of the current scepticism had arisen from the showman's tricks that had come to be

Sir George Cayley. A Yorkshire
squire with a social conscience.
(*Royal Aeronautical Society*
[*National Aerospace Library*])

associated with aerial balloons, whose technology had not advanced greatly in
more than half a century. To retain public interest a number of stunts were
embarked upon, including having the celebrated monkey, Jacopo, parachuting
from a colourful balloon. The unrealistic thinking of some balloonists was
revealed in an article in *The Mechanics' Magazine* of 1835 which suggested that a
balloon might be given the means of propulsion by putting '30 eagles, in rows,
one above the other (in an open wickerwork basket) and three abreast, supposing
them capable of flying with a weight of 180 pounds'.[1]

The lack of seriousness paid to aviation at this time was demonstrated by a
letter sent to Cayley by his friend Sir Antony Carlisle, a well-known surgeon and
fellow of the Royal Society, in which he explained he had long meditated on aerial
navigation although 'my profession excludes my taking open measures on a
subject so liable to derision and ill-natured remark'. Even so, Sir Antony freely
acknowledged the high calibre of Cayley's work telling him that 'the favourite
project of seventeen years of my life has fallen into better hands'.[2]

Whatever such contrary feelings and despite his many other interests, Cayley
never doubted the importance of aviation research. On 6 September 1809 he
wrote to the editor of *Nicolson's Journal of Natural Philosophy*[3] enclosing his
seminal essay *On Aerial Navigation* which he said 'laid down the basic principles
for the attainment of an object that will in time be found of great importance to
mankind, so much so that a new era in society will commence from the moment
that aerial navigation is familiarly realised'.[4]

Yet however strong Cayley's beliefs and powerful his message, the nineteenth century was a difficult time to spread philosophical and scientific ideas about heavier-than-air flight. Cayley attempted to disseminate his beliefs by means of contemporary journals and by conducting extensive and regular correspondence with his scientific and engineering friends, both in Britain and in Europe. More than 200 of the letters that he wrote between 1809 and 1850 still survive, as do his contributions to *Nicolson's Journal* (founded by the chemist and inventor William Nicolson[5]) that, despite a small circulation, was highly regarded both in Britain and in Europe. Cayley subsequently sent articles to its successor, Alexander Tilloch's *Philosophical Magazine* (which absorbed *Nicolson's Journal* in 1813) and which, like *Nicolson's*, set out to give the public as early an account as possible of everything new or curious in the scientific world at home and abroad. Under Tilloch it rose in stature, until by the middle of the century it was second only in prestige to the *Philosophical Transactions of the Royal Society*. It was, of course, one thing for Cayley to have his articles accepted in such publications, quite another for them to be fully understood by the magazines' readers.

Cayley also propagated his ideas on aeronautics through learned societies. During the early nineteenth century societies were set up by the new professions such as the Geological Society (founded 1807), the Institution of Civil Engineers (founded 1815), the Astronomical Society (founded 1820) and the Geographical Society (founded 1830): these bodies sponsored lectures which were subsequently published. *The Mechanics' Magazine, Journal and Gazette*, to which Cayley submitted articles, served the mechanics' institutes that had sprung up in many industrial towns, while its sister magazine in the United States had its own Patent and Registration Office for members' inventions.

In his native Yorkshire Cayley also helped establish two societies for the propagation of scientific ideas. He was a founder member and significant financial contributor to the Yorkshire Philosophical Society established in York during 1821 which aimed to provide 'science in the district by establishing a scientific library, scientific lectures and by providing scientific apparatus for original research',[6] and ten years later he took a prominent part in the founding of another society in his home town of Scarborough, again for the propagation of scientific ideas.

Above all Cayley believed in the need for a dedicated society for aeronautics, which he called The Royal Aerostatic Institution. His first attempt came in 1816 through a message to the editor of Tilloch's magazine. 'I wish to bring all those who interest themselves in this invention [his proposed aircraft] to act in concert towards its completion, rather than be jealous of each other respecting their own share of credit as inventors.'[7]

This brought no positive results, nor did a letter the following year. Cayley's second main attempt came on 23 January 1837 in a proposal to *The Mechanics' Magazine* for the establishment of a dedicated society.

Let the Friends of aerial navigation be called together by advertisement in your pages, at the instigation of a few names favourable to the project; let a place – say, the Adelaide Gallery, and some convenient day in the next month be named, and from this meeting let such revolutions emanate as may best ensure the progress of the Society for Promoting Aerial Navigation.[8]

This met with no success and in 1840 he made yet another attempt from the London Polytechnic which he had established to popularise science by demonstrating 'the most simple and interesting methods of illustrating the sound and important principles upon which every science was based'. The Polytechnic was highly popular with its workshops and working models: while its exhibits included a diving bell which was lowered into a miniature lake 10 to 12ft deep situated in its main hall; among its visitors with children were the Queen and Prince Albert, and it was there that Lewis Carroll held his first public presentation of *Alice in Wonderland*.

Using the Polytechnic as his springboard, Cayley formally proposed the founding of a Royal Aerostatic Institution 'for extending the application and improving the art of Aerial Navigation',[9] while at the same time approaching prominent individuals for their help, including Sir William Fairburn, Robert Holland and the famous balloonist Charles Green, together with his friend the 7th Duke of Argyll who, after Cayley's death, chaired the inaugural meeting of the British Aeronautical Society. As before, interest remained low.

Cayley's last public act towards establishing a society giving support for aviation came in an angry letter of 1843 which he sent to the *Mechanics' Magazine*.

I think it is a national disgrace not to realise by public subscriptions the proper scientific experiments, necessarily too expensive for any private purse, which would secure for this country the glory of being the first to establish the dry navigation of the universal ocean of the terrestrial atmosphere.[10]

In spite of his failure to found a dedicated society, Cayley's ideas and experiments on flight were to become highly regarded by the aerial cognoscenti both in America and Europe. When, for instance, Wilbur Wright wrote to the Smithsonian Institution for recommended reading into the mysteries of flight, he was directed towards the 1895 edition of the *Aeronautical Annual* by the American publisher James Means, which featured Cayley's paper *On Aerial Navigation*. And as late as 1909 Orville Wright had no doubt about Cayley's contribution to the brothers' own triumph, saying that 'he carried the science of flying to a point which it scarcely reached again during the last century'.[11]

Whatever Cayley's limitations as an aeronautical publicist, for the Wrights his aeronautical achievements were fundamental, namely as the first man after Leonardo de Vinci to be responsible for the concept of the modern configuration aircraft and to explain its main features.[12] His initial interest in aviation came by way of a toy helicopter (invented by the Frenchmen Launoy and Bienvenu) which rose in the air, while as a young man he built a helicopter consisting of two-bladed rotors of feathers stuck in corks that contra-rotated by means of a taut bow string and which apparently took him just ten minutes to construct.

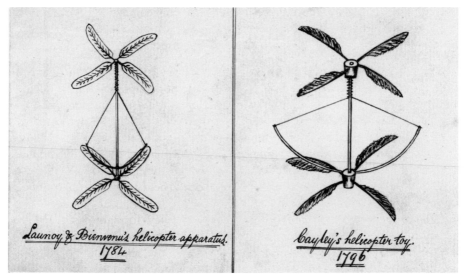

Cayley's Toy Helicopter. (*Royal Aeronautical Society* [*National Aerospace Library*])

From such rudimentary beginnings the next three years (1796–9) saw enormous advances in Cayley's knowledge. Dramatic evidence of this came by way of a silver disc one inch in diameter that Cayley had caused to be engraved on both sides and which carried his initials 'G C' and the year '1799'. Various stories surround the disc, which was presented to the Science Museum in 1935 by Mr P.H. Smith, a Scarborough shopkeeper who acquired it from a later member of the Cayley family. The air historian Charles Gibbs-Smith had no doubt it was significant and represented 'some vital stage in Cayley's thinking in order to rate such enthronement in silver'.[13] He was surely right, for despite its small size and relatively simple diagrams these showed that Cayley had already discarded previous ideas about an aircraft requiring flapping wings for a single, fixed, lift-generating wing in the form of a canopy above a seated pilot (Cayley never adopted an extended wing, although he gave his a camber and made it concave to the airflow). In addition, he divorced the forces of lift and thrust; the wing provided the upward force required, and flappers – like oars – gave the means of propulsion. Control of yaw (rotational motion from left to right) and pitch (up and down) came from a fin-like rudder set vertically and an elevator-cum-tailplane. Cayley's disc came more than a century before the Wrights' earliest designs. Its authenticity is supported by three existing drawings in the Cayley Papers[14] that might well have been made before the coin was engraved and which demonstrate the same ideas, if for a full-size aircraft with a wheeled under-carriage.

Cayley's aeronautical researches took place over two phases of his life. The first (including the disc) was from the 1790s until 1817 when he was forty-four and after an extended interruption of twenty-six years, the second stretched from 1843 to 1855, between Cayley's seventieth and eighty-second years.

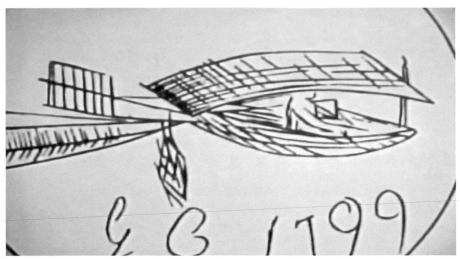

Cayley's aeroplane engraved on his disc. (*Photograph from the 2011 Exhibition at the Yorkshire Air Museum, Elvington*)

His first formal essay on flight was dated 6 October 1804, and entitled *Upon the Mechanical Principles of Aerial Navigation*. Only a fragment survives and it ends in mid-sentence but, incomplete as it is, it reveals Cayley's ideas at the time on both balloons and aeroplanes, with the latter his prime concern. Initially he considered balloons and dirigibles, saying that the latter should be in the form of 'a very oblong spherical of a streamlined nature', then came suggestions for a semi-rigid airship below which 'a long and narrow car [which] must be suspended by fixed stays'.[15] For steering he envisaged a cruciform tail unit (already evident on his disc) attached to the rear of the balloon, a development which became a reality in Britain more than 100 years later when Samuel Cody attached it to the army's airship *Nulli Secundus*.

Moving, as Cayley expressed it, 'from pleasing dreams to heavier-than-air flight'[16] he dismissed any attempt to fly by muscular strength, which he declared would always fail, in favour of using steam engines or other prime movers. Any details, which conceivably could have applied to a calorific (hot air) engine or Cayley's (somewhat unsatisfactory) gunpowder motor, were denied by the essay's abrupt ending. In any case, the current aviation authority Professor John Ackroyd has estimated that such engines' power-to-weight ratios needed to improve by a value of forty or so before powered flight could have become possible.[17]

In 1804, Cayley's calculations were assisted by his use of a whirling arm apparatus (first invented by Benjamin Robins in 1747) to measure wing lift more accurately. Using this, he discovered that the lift force increased both with a plane's forward speed and its wings' angle of incidence. He put his findings into practice when he built a small model glider with a single paper wing set in a bamboo fuselage with a cruciform tail unit operated by a universal joint[18] Air historian Gibbs-Smith described this as 'the first modern configuration aeroplane in history',[19] with fixed main plane an adjustable rear rudder and elevator (set at a positive incidence)'.

In contrast to such inspired ideas, Cayley continued to support the use of flappers rather than an airscrew, which the pilot controlled directly or through a general system of cords over pulleys. From 1807 his notebooks contained different power sources for driving the pulleys. He had already rejected the steam engine on grounds of its weight and 'cumbrousness' and instead considered the use of a hot air engine (of which he was generally recognised as the inventor) 'that sucked in air, passing it under pressure through a fire and thence – expanding with the heat – into a cylinder where it thrusts down the piston'.[20] In 1807 he also made a diagram of a small gunpowder engine (which he subsequently came to realise was not a practical proposition either) where a set amount of gunpowder was exploded to thrust a piston upwards on its working stroke.[21] The technology needed for such engines was as yet beyond him and although, from time to time over the next fifty years, Cayley attempted to perfect his ideas about different propulsion systems, it was without notable success.

He was, however, far more successful with other requirements for heavier-than-air flight and in 1808 he invented the tension wheel that was to form the basis for both cycle wheels and aircraft undercarriages. This did away with the heavy wooden spokes of the traditional wheel with its firmness depending on a rim the tension of which was achieved by strong cords which could be tightened by a rudimentary handle. Cayley calculated that in this way iron ¼in in diameter could bear 15,100lbs.[22] Characteristically he failed to patent the invention and it was left to Theodor Jones to submit it in 1826.

Together with considerations regarding weight reduction, Cayley paid close attention to streamlining, which he described as 'a solid of least resistance'. He considered the shape of boats' hulls and fish, particularly trout and dolphins, and went on to advocate that in order to reduce drag a plane's rear should also be streamlined. One of his notebook entries contained a detailed illustration of a trout's body[23] and when this was examined in 1954 by the eminent US aeronauticist Theodore von Karman he realised that its profile 'almost exactly coincided with certain low-drag aerofoil (wing) sections of contemporary aircraft'.[24]

All Cayley's major findings so far were contained in his essay *On Aerial Navigation*, which featured in the November 1809, February 1810 and March 1810 issues of *Nicolson's Journal*. Like some of his writings, it tended to be provoked by external events, in this case by the inaccurate report of a purported flight made in a man-powered machine by the Viennese clockmaker Jacob Degen, when in fact Degen was lifted into the air by a hydrogen balloon. Cayley's essay addressed the main areas relating to manned flight by a fixed-wing aircraft. Starting with propulsion, he again dismissed the use of steam engines unless their power to weight ratio could be increased tenfold. He also deserted such propelling devices as hot air or gunpowder engines for ones using the expansion of air by a sudden combustion of inflammable powders or fluids[25] – in other words internal-combustion engines. Although he did not proceed with the development of such

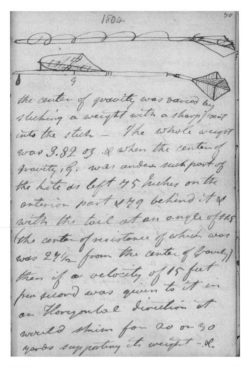

(*Left*) 'The first modern configuration aeroplane in history'. (*Royal Aeronautical Society* [*National Aerospace Library*])

(*Below*) Cayley's Gunpowder Engine. (*Royal Aeronautical Society* [*National Aerospace Library*])

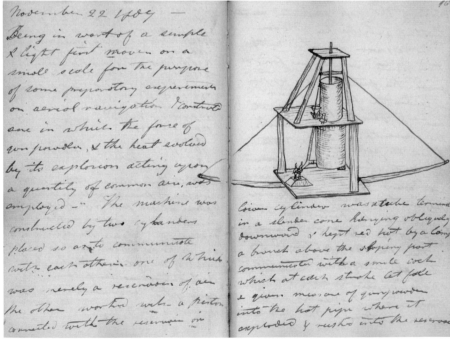

(*Right*) The tension wheel combining lightness with strength. (*Royal Aeronautical Society [National Aerospace Library]*)

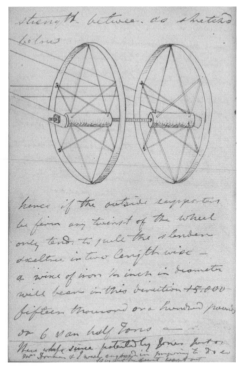

(*Below*) Streamlining. (*Royal Aeronautical Society [National Aerospace Library]*)

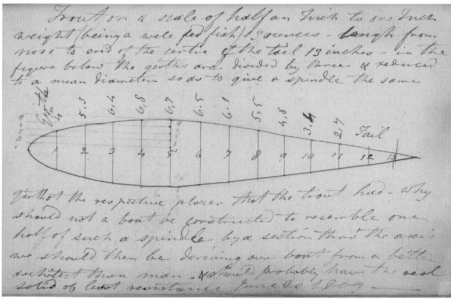

engines, he was confident a plane with such propulsion would be able to transport passengers and goods with a velocity of from 20 to 100mph.

Turning to the plane's structure, Cayley favoured wings of a short span constructed of hollow tapering tubes, enhanced with diagonal wire bracing. As for their lifting qualities, which he summarised as making 'a surface support a given weight by the application of power to the resistance of air',[26] he observed that the camber of a bird's wing gave it better lifting ability because at its leading edge the air's upward motion over the surface's convexity created a slight vacuity.

Such considerations were followed by an incomplete description of an aircraft which he reputedly tested in the summer of 1809. This was probably the world's first full-scale glider with a wing surface of 300ft^2. Cayley wrote that:

> It was very beautiful to see this noble white bird sail majestically from the top of a hill to any given point on the plain below it, according to the set of its rudder, merely by its own weight, descending in an angle of about 18 degrees with the horizon.[27]

Frustratingly, he failed to give any details about his tests.

In the second part of his essay Cayley turned to questions of stability and control. He re-affirmed that a wing set at a dihedral would give more lateral stability, and pointed out that the wing's centre of pressure should be forward of the wing's mid area. By using his crude elevator (which he called a rudder) he maintained he could control a plane's pitch (movement up and down) and, with a vertical tail plane, its yawing movement from left to right. As yet he did not seem to understand the additional control needed for a banked turn.

Cayley's interest now lapsed for about twenty-five years, although he made interventions from time to time, particularly in *Tilloch's Philosophical Magazine*. In 1816, for instance, he referred to the aerial navigation (of an airship) being 'of great importance to mankind and worthy of more attention than is bestowed upon it' and in revelatory fashion described the sky as 'an uninterrupted navigable ocean; that comes to the threshold of every man's door, (that) ought not to be neglected as a source of human qualification and advantage'.[28] Two years later Cayley despatched a long letter to Lord George Campbell, later Duke of Argyll, with details of a proposed kite-winged glider including sketches

However, it was not until 1843, close to his seventieth birthday, that Cayley's interest in the aeroplane fully revived and he entered upon the most intensive and fruitful period of his aeronautical researches. Once again this came as a reaction to other initiatives, in this case to a frontispiece design in *The Mechanics' Magazine* featuring the aircraft designer William Samuel Henson's Aerial Steam Carriage. Cayley's response came in two papers which he submitted during 1843. The first contained an alternative in the form of a convertiplane based on an idea of Mr Robert B. Taylor. This was a somewhat fantastical project, with lifting surfaces provided by four circular wings set in pairs at a dihedral, and slightly cambered 'like a flat umbrella on each side of a wheeled car'. For ascent or descent the circular surfaces opened into eight-bladed rotors that contra-rotated. In anticipation of a Harrier-type aircraft, they could be driven (by a means not yet

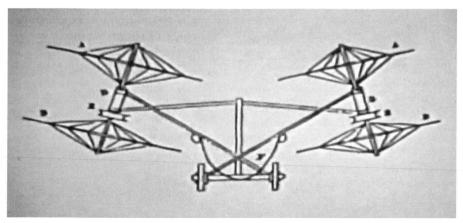

The Convertiplane. (*Photograph from the 2011 Exhibition at the Yorkshire Air Museum, Elvington*)

decided) in forward motion or for upwards or downwards flight. The converti-plane had a tail plane-cum-elevator and above that a separately hinged rudder.[29]

Cayley criticised Henson's design for its excessively long wingspan, which he thought could not be made strong enough, but he concluded that 'if therefore, so large a surface be contemplated ... would it not be more likely to answer the purpose to compact it into the form of a three-decker'.[30] Cayley's proposal therefore anticipated the biplanes and triplanes which would be used extensively during the early twentieth century.

From 1848 onwards, following a further series of tests with his whirling arm apparatus, Cayley decided to construct a full-size triplane glider. He tested this aeroplane ('The Old Flyer') during 1849, both with and without a pilot.

> The balance and steering were ascertained and a boy of about ten years of age was floated off the ground for several yards on descending a hill and also for about the same space by some persons pulling the apparatus against a very slight breeze by a rope.[31]

Some indication of his claims came in a congratulatory letter dated 12 June 1849 from his friend, Charles Clark.

> I have never been able to meet with such success as you appear to have met with experimenting with the boy. Poor Fellow! I dare say he feared the fate of our early aeronauts. I should much like to learn the principles by which this was accomplished.[32]

Well over a century later Gibbs-Smith consulted the leading aerodynamist J.L. Nayler about the feasibility of Cayley's claims at this time. Nayler concluded that he saw no reason why – in still air conditions – the machine should not have glided successfully, with or without the boy. Although Nayler observed that the gaps between the wings (constructed of cloth stretched between two spars and set at a dihedral angle) were small, their total area of 338ft[2] seemed adequate.

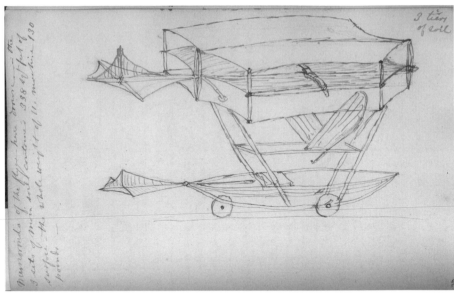

The Old Flyer. (*Royal Aeronautical Society* [*National Aerospace Library*])

One frustrating aspect of such tests for later authorities was Cayley's caution when the lightweight boy – likely to have been Cayley's grandson – was on board, in preventing the plane from moving in free flight.

The Mechanics' Magazine carried a full-page illustration and a written explanation concerning Cayley's next aerial vehicle, a man-carrying glider ('The New Flyer'), where, like the Wrights, its pilot operated controls. Cayley called it a governable parachute in which a pilot regulated its descent to earth, after it had been taken aloft and released from a balloon. Gibbs-Smith went so far as to see this vehicle as having five of the six features of a modern aeroplane, namely:

(1) main wings set at an angle of incidence with dihedral for automatic lateral stability
(2) an adjustable tail plane and fin (combined) for automatic longitudinal and directional stability
(3) pilot-operated elevator and rudder (combined)
(4) a fuselage in the form of a car, equipped with a seat for the pilot, and a three-wheel undercarriage of cycle-type wheels, with the car's position also providing pendulum stability
(5) a tubular beam and box beam construction.[33]

The vital features still lacking were, of course, wing-warping, or ailerons, to give it genuine lateral control and, most important of all, an effective means of propulsion.

There are reports that during the summer of 1853 Cayley launched his coachman – or another employee – on a flight across the dale at Brompton Hall. These

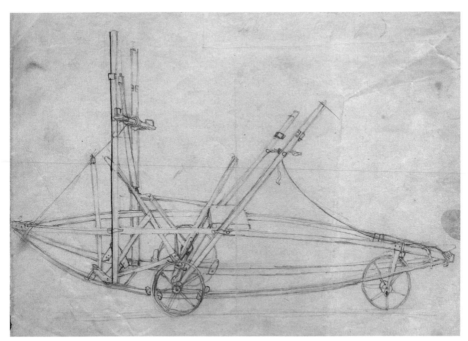

The New Flyer. (*Royal Aeronautical Society* [*National Aerospace Library*])

came from a single source, Mrs George (Dora) Thompson, Cayley's grand-daughter, who at the age of eighty, recalled events that had taken place when she was nine years old.

> I have scratched in my memory as to the date of his flying machine, which I saw fly across the dale. It was in 1852 or 1853. Of course, everyone was out on the high east side and saw the start from close to. The coachman went in the machine and landed on the west side at about the same level. I think it came down rather a shorter distance than expected. The coachman got himself clear, and when the watchers had got across he shouted, 'Please, Sir George, I wish to give notice. I was hired to drive and not to fly' (of course, in broad Yorkshire). That's all I recollect. The machine was put high away in the barn, and I used to sit and hide in it (from Governess) when so inspired.[34]

In another of her versions she estimated the flight to be roughly 500 yards and called the coachman pilot its moving element who brought about its capsize.

* * *

Cayley's aerial achievements are undeniable. Together with his keynote invention in 1799 of the fixed wing aeroplane and his identification of the elements of flight involving lift, propulsion and maintaining stability, during 1804 (the year before the Battle of Trafalgar) he reputedly built and flew the first glider, and finally, when eighty years of age, with his glider of 1853 and its cambered wing he demonstrated all but one of the basic requirements for winged flight. By means of both laboratory testing (with whirling arm devices) and flight testing (relatively limited as this was) he founded the science of aerodynamics. As historian John Ackroyd put it, 'At the time of his death (in 1857) no other person in aeronautics had acquired a grasp remotely approaching his in this field'.[35]

Following the advances in propulsion systems during the later years of the nineteenth century through gas fired and internal-combustion engines, Cayley's groundwork pointed the way for succeeding British pioneers to progress from gliders to powered aircraft. In fact, in his native land work was largely ignored, if not forgotten, for which Cayley has to bear a degree of responsibility. As an affluent man, he was able to pursue many other interests and commitments that were not nearly so difficult or materially unrewarding. He also spread his knowledge of aviation somewhat thinly, with theories about balloons and airships as well as heavier-than-air vehicles, and his actual flights were made in the seclusion of the family's rural estate in East Yorkshire, with no engine of any description. When, at eighty years of age, he conducted his last flights he was unlikely to have relished a protracted series of tests or to risk unduly the broken necks among his family or employees that he knew to be the inevitable price of progress.

Cayley also failed to establish a dedicated Aeronautical Society which, when it finally appeared nine years after his death, had only sixty-five members by the end of its first year. While there were outstanding men among them, such as Francis Herbert Wenham, William Fairbairn and Sir Charles Siemens, they did not possess George Cayley's perspicacity and, in any case, the new organisation was too small and with insufficient funds to make a strong impact in furthering the cause of British aviation. In fact, after mounting its first Air Exhibition in 1868 it tended to languish until the coming of Major Baden-Powell near the end of the century, by which time, in America, Samuel Pierpoint Langley, Octave Chanute and the Wright brothers were about to demonstrate their more advanced achievements. As a result, when writing after the First World War Walter Raleigh, the official British historian of Air Warfare, felt able to dismiss Cayley's contributions with devastatingly mild acknowledgement.

> He more than once anticipated later inventions but he put nothing on the market. His mind was fertile in mechanical devices so that if one proved troublesome, he could always turn his attention to another. He was content to enumerate a truth and to call it probable.[36]

It was not until 1955 that the then Secretary of the Royal Aeronautical Society, Captain J.L. Pritchard, during its First Cayley Memorial lecture reminded those attending how Cayley was the father of British Aeronautics, 'a pioneer and prophet (who) so far as heavier-than-air craft was concerned, and indeed aeronautical science in general, was someone far ahead of his contemporaries who (still) thought in terms of bird flight and wing flapping'.[37] In more recent years Cayley's rehabilitation has continued and has attracted regular interest in the media. In 1973, for instance, a replica of his 1853 glider, built by John Sproute and piloted by Derek Piggot, made a successful flight at Brompton Dale[38] and

Derek Piggot flying at Brompton Dale in 1973. (*Photograph from the 2011 Exhibition at the Yorkshire Air Museum, Elvington*)

twenty-five years later, on 5 July 2003 industrialist Richard Branson flew a modified replica of Cayley's glider, built by BAE Systems, across Brompton dale to mark the 150th anniversary of Cayley's first manned flight there.

Whatever the countervailing opinions about him, there is little doubt that the failure of subsequent British pioneers to give George Cayley's findings the attention they deserved was an important factor in their country losing the lead he had established in early aviation.

Chapter 2
Shape of Things to Come

By 1840 George Cayley had been joined by two further air pioneers, John Stringfellow (b. 1799) and W.H. Henson (b. 1812), whose Aerial Steam Carriage served to revive Cayley's interest in the aeroplane. Both Stringfellow and Henson were skilled engineers who operated in the lace industry, Stringfellow as a highly skilled bobbin maker and Henson as an inventor of both lace-making and knitting machinery.

It was when Henson moved from the Midlands to Chard's lace-making mills that he met Stringfellow and they discovered a mutual interest in mechanical flight. Although the younger Henson was still a bachelor, Stringfellow was married with four children and he was heavily involved in Chard's public affairs.

John Stringfellow.
(*Royal Aeronautical Society [National Aerospace Library]*)

There, like George Cayley, he founded Chard's (Scientific) Institution that aimed to provide weekly lectures covering a range of subjects (excluding religion and politics) and from 1840 he also gave lectures himself.

Such commitments affected his opportunities for aerial researches, but during a series of meetings at Stringfellow's home he and Henson considered using long wings (contrasting with Cayley's that were more or less square) for a model of a projected full-scale aircraft. They planned to propel it with a light steam engine driving two multi-blade propellers running in counter-rotation. But the partnership was interrupted in 1841 when Henson went to live in London, although Stringfellow continued to experiment with 'gliding models, constructional devices and a light steam engine'.[1]

In London Henson received advice on how to patent his ideas for a projected full-scale aircraft – his Aerial Steam Carriage – from John Chapman, a craftsman and writer on engineering developments. Chapman was known for devising an improved version of Joseph Hansom's Safety Cab, for which he received a patent in February 1841 and it is likely that he took an active part in drawing up the specifications for the aerial carriage, for Henson's biographer, M.J.B. Davy, seriously doubted that Henson would have been sufficiently capable. While Davy acknowledged Henson's ambition was 'coupled with a certain inventive genius', he felt he 'lacked that solid determination and perseverance which was necessary for even limited success in the difficult problem of mechanical flight'.[2] It is also

William Samuel Henson.
(*Royal Aeronautical Society*
[*National Aerospace Library*])

not clear, following their earlier meetings, what part Stringfellow played in the design work for the Aerial Steam Carriage, although he was certainly responsible for producing steam engines for their later models.

During 1841 Stringfellow visited Henson in London, taking with him an engine of his own making and although Henson was unlikely to have used it he subsequently asked Stringfellow to produce a lighter and more powerful one. His request came at a time when Stringfellow had very many demands on his time, including constructing a surgical instrument to prevent a surgeon making too deep an incision while taking blood, and it is not clear whether or not he built one.

Henson certainly received help with the patent for his full-size Steam Carriage from an attorney, D.E. Colombine, who drew up a grandiose prospectus for an Aerial Transit Company to build it (with Colombine as its Secretary). This did not hold back: it claimed that 'the Invention has been subjected to the severest tests and examinations and the results are most satisfactory, so much so that nothing but the completion of the undertaking is required to determine its practical operation'. It went further, saying that 'its utility is undoubted, as it would be a necessary possession of every Empire, and it is hardly too much to say of every individual of competent means in the civilised world'.[3]

The aim was to raise £2,000 in all, in sums of £100. Both Colombine and Frederick Marriott, a newspaperman and resident of Chard, undertook to buy shares. They contacted a Member of Parliament who was expected to shepherd a private bill relating to the company through the House of Commons that was laid before the House on 23 March 1843. But because of its over-optimistic prospectus, particularly in view of the inadequate research and experimental work that had been carried out so far and the massive difficulties yet to be overcome, it was greeted with the ridicule and scepticism that had dogged earlier aviation initiatives. Even so, a patent was granted for the Aerial Carriage which was published together with a full specification and drawings of the plane in *The Mechanics' Magazine* of 1 April 1843. Nothing like this complete aeroplane project had been seen before. The double-surfaced, fabric-covered wings of the huge monoplane spanned 150ft with twenty-six great ribs carried on three main spars 'for which the front and rear had been scientifically located mid-spar and (there were) central pylon trusses employing tension rods to take the wing bending strain'[4] – something which was to become standard practice with aircraft some sixty-five years later. It was to be propelled by paddle wheels, or 'pusher' propellers, and controlled by a tail that could be raised or lowered by a vertical rudder. Its wings were not only covered with fabric, but they were cambered. It had an enclosed cabin and featured a pioneering bicycle undercarriage which historian Harald Penrose writing in 1967 maintained was 'in the mode of the airliners of today'.[5]

Whatever its dimensions, in appearance the Aerial Steam Carriage leapt forward to the aircraft of over half-a-century later. Predictably publications from all over Europe reacted to it with lampoons, pictures and satirical comments,

Henson's Aerial Steam Carriage. (*Royal Aeronautical Society* [*National Aerospace Library*])

including one of it flying the world's first air routes from London to Egypt and India. In contrast, *The Times* of 30 March 1843 was notably more controlled and hopeful of manned flight before long.

> Mr Henson says he has invented a machine by which men may traverse the untrammelled regions of the air in any direction at their pleasure. This is not the first time by many that such a pretension has been advanced ... Not one has succeeded while all the world has at once longed for their success and derided their hopes ... yet we are compelled, by careful enquiry, to profess our belief that he has done so much towards simplifying the question ... that the earlier, if not immediate, possession of the long-expected pioneer of flight may now be safely anticipated.

John Chapman, who had more knowledge about the drawings for the carriage than most, was also cautiously optimistic with his submission for the 1 April edition of *The Mechanics' Magazine*. 'We have only the probabilities for guidance, but as far as we can judge them they are in favour of Mr Henson's success.'[6] In later years, when the British regulations for Patents, including Henson's, were being revised, Chapman was far more forthcoming and critical. He wrote:

> A very eccentric but observant and imaginative man of the name of Henson had made remarks on the action of the wind and on the flight of birds which

led him to conceive the idea of a machine for flying founded on principles different from any which had previously been adopted. He was far too poor to pay for a patent, model etc, and fell into the hands of a party who had neither honesty nor discretion proportional to the control which command of funds gave him.[7]

Chapman's remarks were well made for, whatever the remarkably modern features of the Aerial Steam Carriage, if a full-scale version had actually been built it could not have flown. It was likely that the original drawings had been made for a much smaller plane with a 50ft wingspan since the calculations concerning engine power and structural safety were utterly inadequate. A possible explanation is that Colombine encouraged Henson to scale up its size. If so, Henson would have fully deserved the wave of criticism aimed at his plane. In the next issue of *The Mechanics' Magazine* the critics were joined by an elderly George Cayley, who had unquestionably made more calculations on wing stresses than anyone else but remained convinced by short square-shaped ones. Cayley warned that 'the extent of leverage, however well guarded by additional braces is in this necessarily light structure terrific'. Not content with this, he revealed his own prophetic powers by putting forward the possibility of multi-winged aircraft.

Henson exhibited a model of his Aerial Steam Carriage in Cayley's Adelaide Gallery[8] in the Strand, and Stringfellow visited him in London at this time where they talked of making the model lighter and equipping it with a more powerful engine. Yet, when Henson conducted a series of tests during August and September of 1843, the Carriage's motive power still relied on an inadequate steam or a clockwork engine. Both proved unsuccessful for after the model had run down an inclined plane it 'came down flop' on its release.

On 11 November 1843 Henson wrote to Stringfellow in the hope that his outstanding talent for building miniature steam engines might provide the model Steam Carriage with the impetus it so badly needed. His approach was favourably received and shortly before Christmas, Henson went to Chard and on 29 December the two men signed a joint agreement, 'to construct a model of an Aerial Machine to be employed in such a manner as the parties above-named shall consider best and most profitable'.[9] With this agreement Henson acknowledged that the Aerial Transit Company was dead and his and Stringfellow's best hopes for success lay with their model.

In early 1844 Henson moved back to Chard where, with Stringfellow, he laid down a larger model based upon carefully scaled-down drawings of Henson's patent specification. Its wings were 3ft 6in wide and measured 20ft from tip to tip. These provided 70ft^2 of sustaining surface, with a further 10ft^2 in the tail. In addition to its tail plane and rudder the model had a fin high above its centre of gravity (like Samuel Cody's plane of 1908) to correct any rolling or side-slipping. Henson and Stringfellow worked together for several months before, at the end of 1844, Henson returned to London, leaving Stringfellow to complete the plane.

On 24 April 1845 Stringfellow wrote to Henson about making a further pair of propellers and improvements to the engine, together with the pressing need to conduct some experiments outside. Whatever Henson's reactions, Stringfellow carried these out in an unfrequented location two miles from Chard called Bewley Down (known locally as Bala), although they proved far less successful than he had hoped. He found the machine's controls wanting: it failed to support itself and, after going down a ramp, it went straight into the ground or, if it took off, as its momentum slowed it would stall and drop wing-first into the ground. After seven weeks of repeated but futile attempts, he abandoned them. Stringfellow subsequently told his friend Fred Brearey (the current Secretary of the Royal Aeronautical Society) that 'the steam engine was the best part. Our want of success was not for want of power or sustaining surface, but for want of proper adaptation of the means to the end of the various parts'.[10] At worst, such experiments provided Stringfellow with a basis for further tests, which he would make during 1848.

On 28 September 1846, Henson had become so short of money for experimental work that he took the step of writing to their arch critic, the 73-year-old Cayley.

> Although I am personally unknown to you I have taken the liberty of addressing you this letter upon Aerial Navigation knowing it to be a subject on which you, as well as myself, feel deeply interested. You probably imagined that I had long since given it up as a failure, but you will be pleased to hear that I have in conjunction with my friend Mr Stringfellow been working more or less since 1843 towards the accomplishment of Aerial Navigation and that we feel sanguine of our endeavour.[11]

Cayley's reply was courteous, if cautious, but not actively helpful towards any such collaborative venture.

> I had thought that you had abandoned the subject, which though true in principle you had rushed upon with far too great confidence as to its practice some years ago. If you have been making experiments since that time you will have found how many difficulties you have to adjust and overcome before the results you wish can be accomplished ... I like your zeal, and as you seem disposed to treat me with your confidence I can assure you that I shall not abuse it. As to new principles there are none ... Though I have not the weight of capital to apply to such matters, perhaps I might be able to aid you in some measure by my experience, or connection with other mechanical persons. I do not, however, think that any money, except by exhibition of a novelty can be made by it.[12]

In Chard Stringfellow had enjoyed no more success in raising capital for their experiments, and whatever hopes remained for their partnership ended on 4 March 1848 when Henson married 25-year-old Sarah Anne Jones at Saint Botolph's, Aldgate, following which the couple set sail on the 31st for New York. There they joined the rest of the family and Henson continued to live at Newark on the Hudson River for the rest of his life.

While Cayley was still concerned with full-size gliders, the possibility of achieving powered flight with a heavier-than-air model depended on Stringfellow. From 1846 he worked on a new and smaller monoplane with a swallow-shaped wing about 10ft from wingtip to wingtip and 2ft at its widest point, which was rigid in front and feathered at the rear. It had a tail 3ft 6in long and 22in at its widest point that was not set at the vertical. With such a conformation, the model was bound to be unstable and Stringfellow decided to attempt his first flights inside a disused lace factory, traversing a room some 22 yards long. Here his miniature steam engine confirmed Stringfellow's particular talent. Its cylinder was just ¾in in diameter with a length of stroke of 2in, with the gearing on its crankshaft giving three revolutions of the propellers for one stroke of the engine. Amazingly, the weight of his entire model, with water and fuel, was under 9lbs.[13] It was tethered to a wire, before being released for the remainder of the room's distance. After an unsuccessful attempt with the tail set at too high an angle, Stringfellow modified it and this time, after it was detached, the plane gradually rose and traversed the room before striking a hole in the canvas which he had placed at the room's farther end. With this, John Stringfellow achieved the first self-supported flight by a power-driven model, although it took place in controlled and non-hazardous conditions.

One who witnessed the flight was a Mr John Ellis, the lessee of the Cremorne Pleasure Gardens in King's Road, Chelsea. He commissioned Stringfellow to

Stringfellow's 1848 Monoplane model. (*Royal Aeronautical Society* [*National Aerospace Library*])

demonstrate his model in an open tent-like structure which Ellis had erected there, promising him a third of the profits from the expected visitors.[14] The first flight was scheduled for 22 August 1848 and on this occasion *The Times* was notably more cautious than it had been for the Aerial Steam Carriage trials.

A series of experiments were made beneath an immense hood or awning in Cremorne Gardens yesterday afternoon to test the powers of a machine invented by Mr Stringfellow to propel itself through the air. The day was most unpropitious and it would be hardly fair to pass judgement on the powers of the machine to carry out the assertions of the inventor compared with those who have witnessed it under more favourable circumstances. It certainly possesses a propelling power and it would appear that with the addition of sustaining power it might form an important aid to aerial or balloon experiments.

Like Cayley before him, Stringfellow decided to discontinue his aerial researches which, as well as proving both immensely difficult and time-consuming, appeared to offer no prospect of financial reward. Again, like Cayley, Stringfellow's interest also revived after a lengthy period, in his case with the founding, in 1866, of the Aeronautical Society of Great Britain. When the Society drew up plans for an Aeronautical Exhibition at the Crystal Palace during June 1868, the Society's Honorary Secretary, Fred Brearey, asked Stringfellow to make a contribution, and Stringfellow agreed to enter three exhibits. The first was a triplane model, possibly inspired by a paper read by Frances Wenham at the Society's first meeting at which (like Cayley) he favoured multiple wings. Second was Stringfellow's particular speciality, a light steam engine of about half a horsepower working two propellers 3ft in diameter at about 300 revolutions a minute. His final submission was a working model of an aerial steam carriage which, with its engine, boiler, water and fuel, weighed a maximum of 12lbs and was attached by a travelling pulley to a line across the Exhibition Hall.

All three featured prominently. Stringfellow's biographer M.J.B. Davy believed that by using rectangular wings Stringfellow's triplane design approached very nearly to the actual biplanes and triplanes of the early twentieth century.[15] Davy also pointed out that its propeller (of circular shape) was an advance on the previous design.

The Society's committee of jurors proved enthusiastic and considered the plane's whole design was distinguished by its neatness and elegance. However, the lack of progress achieved by British aviation since Cayley was evident from other aircraft on show: two were crude helicopters, two distinguishable aero-planes, while the remainder were still flapping-wing machines. Stringfellow's was the only model designed to be screw propelled and its steam engine producing 1hp for a total weight of only 13lbs – excluding water and fuel – was quite remarkable.

Nonetheless, the other powerplants on display showed a growing trend towards the use of internal-combustion engines – of the sixteen exhibits seven

Stringfellow's model at the 1868 Aeronautical Exhibition. (*Royal Aeronautical Society* [*National Aerospace Library*])

were to be worked by gas and explosive materials.[16] Unfortunately, their performance had to be taken on trust for only two engines, Stringfellow's and another,
designed by Camille Vert, were capable of being set in motion and Camille Vert's
engine was too small for its power to be estimated.

Stringfellow deservedly won the £100 prize offered by the Aeronautical Society
for the 'lightest engine in proportion to its power', although the Society's
shortage of funds at this time was seen in their decision to pay the prize in
instalments. During the Exhibition, Stringfellow's model triplane never flew in
free flight but ran along a wire stretching for a distance of about 100 yards when,
according to Stringfellow's son, F.J. Stringfellow, 'it showed an evident tendency
to support itself'. Following the Exhibition plans were made to set it free in open
country, but after so much inside work the engine needed major repairs. In any

case, due to its instability the plane was highly unlikely to have completed a sustained flight in disturbed air.

In succeeding years, in spite of deteriorating health, Stringfellow continued working on his models until three months before his death on 13 December 1883 but without further notable progress.

*   *   *

Following Cayley's fundamental discoveries, the contributions made by Henson and Stringfellow towards manned flight, while significant, were less outstanding. Henson's claim rested mainly on his futuristic aircraft design (where he might well have benefited from the assistance of John Chapman). Even so, his Aerial Steam Carriage helped to popularise the idea of dual and multiple wings and it incorporated modern features, including wing bracing, hollow spars and a streamlined body. Although unproven mathematically and lacking an internal-combustion engine or a means of lateral stability, the majority of its features, after due testing, would be incorporated into aircraft during the early years of genuine flight.

Stringfellow's claims centred on his highly-skilled development of a light steam engine and its attendant airscrews. However well-engineered, this method of propulsion stood no chance of long-term success and, although he also made repeated attempts with models to cure the problems of instability, he did not realise that the generation of lift came from lower pressure at the top of a wing compared with higher pressure at the bottom. In fairness, such restricted knowledge was partly due to continuing financial difficulties, which deprived both men of reliable testing equipment.

Even so – despite the neglect of Cayley's findings – when in 1868 the Aeronautical Society observed that 'with respect to the abstruse question of mechanical flight it may be stated that we are still ignorant of the rudimentary principles which should form the basis and rules for construction',[17] no other country had more advanced knowledge.

Chapter 3

Multi-Wings, Wind Tunnels and Tethered Planes

During the second half of the nineteenth century, later British pioneers were engaged in detailed studies of airframes, including wings (aerofoils), and the relative efficiency that could be achieved with the use of different shapes. They were, however, necessarily limited with their propulsion systems since the development of light but sufficiently powerful engines was yet to be achieved.

First came Francis Herbert Wenham (b. 1824), the son of an army surgeon who, after being articled at seventeen to a large engineering firm in Bristol, was present at the building of *The Archimedes*, the only screw-powered steamer afloat at that time. Such expertise in screw propulsion (together with high-pressure boilers having improved power to weight ratios) would lead him to his subsequent aeronautical experiments. Wenham designed a small steamer whose boiler pressure reached 300lbs/in^2, compared with the normal 60lbs/in^2 and also submitted patents for advanced condensing engines that greatly increased the speed of ships and were to prove useful for the blockade-runners during the American Civil War.

Another of his enthusiasms at this time was photography using the Daguerre photographic process. In 1853 he took his small steamer up the Nile to photograph the interior of Egyptian tombs, which resulted in the publication of a best-selling series of picture postcards. During the Nile journey Wenham had the task of shooting game to supplement the expedition's food supplies and his observations of bird flight aroused in him a strong interest in aeronautics that was to continue throughout his life. His observations were aided by the use of a telescope, the earlier grinding and setting of which led to him being accepted as a Fellow of the Microscopical Society at just twenty-six, while his remarkable conclusions concerning the functions of birds' wings would, in 1866, lead him to deliver the inaugural lecture to the newly-established Royal Aeronautical Society.

In spite of Wenham's obvious ability and quite remarkable energy, limitations in his early education affected the quality of his discoveries and prevented him achieving the best results. In an obituary, Edward Nelson of the Royal Microscopical Society referred to his lack of elementary mathematics, saying that 'if only it could have been lifted what an inventor he could have been'.[1] Such limitations also affected his aeronautical researches. Notwithstanding, like Cayley he quickly realised, that for manned flight, steam engines either needed a far lower weight ratio per horsepower than even his condensing boilers could achieve, or other power sources had to be used. While in 1864 he patented a hot

Francis Wenham.
(*Royal Aeronautical Society*
[*National Aerospace Library*])

air engine believed to have been the first of its kind in Britain, after building it he became concerned about a patent for a comparable invention developed by the Frenchman Lenoir, whose engine was very heavy on fuel. But in the event both Wenham's and Lenoir's engines were soon superseded by those of the German engineer, Otto.

Whatever his undoubted knowledge of engines, Wenham's principal contributions to aviation lay in his observations about bird flight and his wing testing equipment. His initial lecture to the Aeronautical Society had the rather laborious title *Aerial Locomotion and the Laws by which heavy bodies impelled through air are sustained,* in essence it concluded 'that the swiftest-flying birds possess extremely long and narrow wings and the slow, heavy flyers short and wide ones'.[2] During his lecture he also maintained that 'the wings of all flying creatures, whether of birds, bats, butterflies or other insects have this one peculiarity of structure in common; the front or leading edge is rendered rigid by bone, cartilage or a thickening of the membrane; and in most birds of perfect flight even the individual feathers are formed upon the same condition'.[3] Cayley had made similar observations upon the shapes of birds' wings and had decided that their centre of pressure should be forward of the wings' main area but by now Cayley's work was largely ignored.

Wenham went further by concluding that it was not only birds that derived most of their lift from the forward position of their wings but that the wings of man-made machines should also be given a high aspect ratio (a long and narrow conformation), a conclusion also reached by Henson. From this it seemed to follow that the most effective wing formation would be a number of long narrow wings arranged one above the other. During 1866 Wenham constructed a full-size glider with wings made up of superimposed layers, with the pilot lying in a prone position; however he neglected to calculate any mathematical proportions and his glider failed.

In 1868, during a discussion at the Aeronautical Society, Wenham and String-fellow united in favouring the screw to achieve aerial propulsion over others who retained their belief in beating wings.[4] However, they showed themselves notably cautious in continuing to favour steam as the safest means of propulsion, although they acknowledged that a proper gas engine – when built – would surely answer better. Such debate not only demonstrated the lack of progress in Britain towards genuine manned flight but led Fred Brearey, the Association's Secretary, to acknowledge a pressing need for much more scientific testing

> as to what is the actual power required to perform flight under various con-
> ditions. This, as we have before urged, may, in great measure, be determined
> by isolated experiments – by ascertaining the resistance, aerial friction and
> the lifting power of planes of various forms and angles, set in currents of air
> of known velocity. These simple and important trials have never yet been
> made; and the data to be obtained from the results, must certainly be of
> value, in aiding the construction of aerial machines, which are now
> embodied by different inventors, apparently in the most random and con-
> tradictory manner.[5]

Mr Brearey suggested that such experiments would 'require the use of a steam engine and fan blower of large size ...' which would inevitably involve a con-siderable outlay.

Wenham, therefore, built the first wind tunnel where such tests on the cambered surfaces of wings and the lift and drag relating to small models could be carried out. In 1870 he designed a long, rectangular 10ft duct with an inside cross-section in the shape of a square 18in on each side, with a steam engine powering a fan that drove air through a duct at about 40mph.[6] Unfortunately he failed to install vanes to channel the airflow, which left it uneven and there-fore somewhat inaccurate.

Nonetheless, by using his wind tunnel Wenham was able to re-affirm the results achieved by Cayley's whirling arm tests, which appeared to have been forgotten. Wenham's tests confirmed what he already believed, namely that the wing's centre of pressure was, in fact, near its leading edge causing most of the lift to come from there and subsequently led him to discover that the lift-to-drag ratios needed to be much larger than had been expected, thus underlining the need for aircraft to have more powerful and lighter engines. Unfortunately, his limited grasp of mathematics and the crudeness of his wind tunnel rendered such findings less clear-cut than they might have been.

Wenham continued to be active in the Aeronautical Society for the next ten years, until resigning in July 1882 owing to a longstanding antipathy to Fred Brearey, its Honorary Secretary. The following years were not good ones for the Society whose numbers dwindled and where continuing indifference in British society as a whole sapped its function as the official representative body of British aeronautics; nor did it change until 1896 when the enthusiastic Captain Baden-Powell became Secretary. In France the mood was considerably different, although actual progress was no further advanced. This was seen in an optimistic paper by Monsieur de Lucy of Paris (published with the British Aeronautical Society's Report for 1867) in which he concluded that 'science is ripe, industry is ready, everybody is in expectation, the hour of aerial locomotion will soon arrive'.[7]

The absence of such optimism in Britain and its effect on Wenham is seen in his protracted correspondence with the Franco/American air pioneer Octave Chanute. While Wenham's letters continued to illustrate his strong opinions and critical stance towards other British pioneers, they also showed he was not fully acquainted with the extent of progress elsewhere. It is clear from one of his letters to Chanute in 1892 that he believed the only person who had approached aeronautical success so far was Stringfellow, although in fairness Wenham also

Veteran air publicist Octave Chanute. (*Royal Aeronautical Society* [*National Aerospace Library*])

prophesied that 'if ever success is to be attained I believe America will have the credit of it; your mechanics are more ingenious and inventive than ours'.[8]

Four years later Wenham was bitingly critical of two other British figures involved in aerial matters, namely his continuing *bête noire*, the Aeronautical Society's Fred Brearey, for his ignorance of mechanical principles, and Hiram Maxim for the design of his massive flying machine which Wenham dismissed as one of 'the most clumsy ill-conceived arrangements of the kind I have ever seen'.[9]

Wenham also clung stubbornly to his belief in the superiority of the steam engine over a benzoline motor, while continuing to view effective mechanical flight as an almost insuperable aspiration. As late as 1905 he revealed how he was still not fully aware of the progress made with the internal-combustion engine when he wrote 'what we need is the adaptation of some propelling power to prolong the flight'.[10]

One can imagine his surprise when, in the same year – and however tactfully – Chanute gave him the astonishing news about the progress made by the Wright brothers. 'I think it is due to you, as the pioneer of aviation and my valued friend, to be the first to be told confidentially that the Wright brothers have been in possession of a practical flying machine for the past two years and have been improving it.'[11] In spite of Wenham's wind tunnel and his theories about high ratio and cambered wings, as he got older he lived in a partial time warp. While his findings had undoubtedly assisted the American pioneers, by the turn of the twentieth century they had moved on and, while Wenham still viewed manned flight as unattainable, two remarkable young men who relished the challenge had tackled it with relentless thoroughness.

In Britain, although there were air pioneers other than Wenham, their somewhat erratic approaches left them considerably short of attaining genuine flight. One such was Horatio Phillips (b. 1845) whose work also centred on wing technology. Born in London, on leaving school he entered his father's workshops as an apprentice to the sporting gun maker's trade, where he 'very quickly evinced considerable mechanical aptitude' and, like so many others, was attracted to the study of aviation by his observations on wild bird flight. By the age of nineteen he was making model aeroplanes and 'from that time until his death his interest in the advancement of aviation never ceased'.[12] Phillips produced his own wind tunnel, 17in square and 6ft long, into which he directed a steady current of steam from a large boiler (working at a pressure of 70lbs/in^2) through which he hoped to avoid the wind flow fluctuations that had marred Wenham's experiments.[13]

Phillips' most notable achievement was his aerial machine of 1893 which, instead of using an orthodox wing, was sustained in flight by air currents acting upon slats of wood arranged like a Venetian blind. When the machine was in motion the convex upper surface near the front of the slats deflected the air upwards, thus creating a partial vacuum which helped raise it.

Phillips positioned no less than fifty slats, each 1½in wide and 22ft long, within a frame 22ft wide and 9ft 6in high, which he mounted on the front of an aeroplane carriage in the manner of a large sail. The carriage also carried a small steam engine and boiler that worked a screw propeller, 6ft 6in in diameter, that

Phillips' Multi plane 1904. (*Royal Aeronautical Society* [*National Aerospace Library*])

Phillips' Multi plane 1907. (*Royal Aeronautical Society* [*National Aerospace Library*])

played on the slats. Phillips tethered his machine to a post around which he constructed a circular wooden track, 628ft in circumference. In a number of trials the machine – which was on wheels – reached a speed of 28mph during which its front lifted to a maximum of 3ft off the track. But Phillips' machine never progressed from this intermediate stage for, as *The Times* of 24 May 1893 rightly concluded, although

> it possesses a tendency to ascend and, this having been ascertained, it remains for the principle to be applied to a machine which shall be capable of sustained flight. And to be a success, not only must it be capable of sustained flight, but it must be capable of correctly poising itself in the air during flight, and during a gently inclined descent, should the propelling power by any accident become inoperative. This, it is claimed, the machine in question will do.

As yet, Phillip's carriage was not large enough to carry an operator and its designer had not considered the many additional problems involved with free flight. As a result, important as Phillip's work was in the subsequent development of wing shapes, and with his lower surfaces having a gentler curve than the upper ones, he made no attempt to answer the problems concerned with the threefold axes of flight, namely 'pitch', moving up and down; 'yaw', turning to the right or left in flat flight; and 'roll', or lateral control involving the raising or lowering of the wing tips. In reality, his work did not move the British pioneers much closer to genuine flight.

Phillips was followed by Lawrence Hargrave (b. 1850) whose aviation researches were far broader. Although he lived in Australia he thought of himself as British: Hargrave was born in England seven years after Phillips, and it was there he spent his early years with his mother and two younger children while his father pursued a legal career in Australia. When his father became a District Court Judge, he sent for him, having made plans for his son to follow a legal career but Lawrence, having enjoyed himself circumnavigating the country, failed the matriculation examination required for the Bar and instead became an apprentice with the Australian Steam Navigation Company, where he soon demonstrated remarkable practical ability.

By the time he was twenty-eight the adventurous Hargrave had acquired a wealth of life experience, including surviving a shipwreck and being subject to many other perils while exploring nearby New Guinea before, on his return to Sydney, he married and became an Observer (Astronomical) at the Sydney Observatory. He was interested in bird flight and in his spare time he built a trimaran propelled by paddles which he began to consider as a possible means of propelling an aircraft, an approach which, like Cayley, would seriously hamper his progress in aviation.

By 1883 a succession of gifts from his father (who had invested wisely in land) enabled Hargrave to resign from the Observatory and pursue his own interests. The study of aeronautics had become particularly important to him and towards the end of 1885 he constructed an aerial model weighing an ounce, powered by sixteen rubber bands and driven by flappers, which reputedly flew for 110ft in free flight. A larger model followed and during the first half of 1888 he built what would prove to be the first of over more than thirty different engines for flying machines. In this case it was a single-cylinder compressed-air motor whose power

Lawrence Hargrave.
(*Royal Aeronautical Society*
[*National Aerospace Library*])

to weight ratio proved quite unsatisfactory. At the time he also made drawings for a revolutionary three-cylinder rotary engine using petrol vapour, which was never built. His other main concern was with planes' wings and, after conducting a number of experiments from 1893 onwards on cambered dihedral wings, his main successes would come with those shaped like a flat box in large honeycomb form.

Hargrave was acutely conscious of his remoteness from Britain and detachment from other researchers in Europe and America. Although he had assembled a good aeronautical library, during the early 1890s he determined to start communicating with leading aeronautical figures worldwide. He sent information about his own work to Hiram Maxim in Britain, whom he knew was working on a giant aircraft, although Maxim did not reciprocate. He also communicated with S.P. Langley, the Secretary of the American Smithsonian Institution, who (like Hargrave) began a series of aerodynamic experiments with both model and full-size planes. And, like other researchers, Hargrave opened a correspondence with the retired American civil engineer and air enthusiast, Octave Chanute.

As a result of Chanute's letters to him he started experimenting during 1892 with curved wings, yet on 10 February 1893 he was back to 'a kite of three dimensions'[14] which was to develop into his famous cellular, or box, kite that offered unparalleled stability, the design of which led to the first successful aircraft in Europe built by Santos-Dumont in 1906. During a fruitful seven-week period,

Hargrave built sixteen such kites, and in 1897 William A. Eddy, the meteorologist at Bayonne, New Jersey, used a Hargrave-type box kite to reach a record height of 9,383 ft. Inspired by the hang-glidist Otto Lilienthal, Hargrave then changed tack and in 1894 adopted a monoplane construction for his first full-sized glider, but this was destroyed after being caught by a side gust of wind. Therefore during the following year he reverted to his characteristic box-like components when designing his first powered man carrier, but frustratingly, owing to the poor performance of its engine – which he assembled first – the plane was never built.

In 1896 Hargrave designed his second man carrier, a box-kite biplane with a small elevator-cum-rudder and a steam engine driving four flappers. This was intended to take off from water and was equipped with four wingtip floats.[15] But its engine turned out to be a failure and this machine was also never built, although its design bore a remarkable resemblance to the European Voisin/Archdeacon float glider of 1905, which lacked the Wrights' wing warping devices.

It was probably with mixed feelings that Hargrave received a letter from Chanute telling him that he had been experimenting with a full-size glider (whose wings appeared to owe more to the designs of Francis Wenham than Hargrave), and that during the summer of 1896 he had conducted hundreds of flights with it without the slightest accident. If this were so, he had plainly moved well ahead of

Lawrence Hargrave and James Swaine with Hargrave's box kites 1894. (*Royal Aeronautical Society* [*National Aerospace Library*])

Hargrave four-decker, compressed-air driven model. (*Royal Aeronautical Society [National Aerospace Library]*)

Hargrave. Nevertheless, Hargrave continued his work but successive versions of his steam engines proved too heavy, and by devoting so much of his time to flapper propulsion his propeller designs also made little advance. In any case, by now others had entered this field, and in 1896 the Englishman, Percy Pilcher, with whom Hargrave also corresponded – and who had earlier joined with Maxim in his aerial work – told Hargrave about a small oil engine together with a screw propeller which he proposed to fit to his own glider.

By 1 June 1898 Hargrave produced his twenty-fifth engine which still depended on steam power and which again proved inadequate, although he attempted to develop a pure jet engine as well. It was his belief that his engines were hampered by the poor quality of workmanship among Australia's small number of jobbing engineers that he commissioned to help him, although Australians such as Harry Hawker and Bert Hinkler would soon show high engineering skills.

In March 1899 Hargrave took the radical step of travelling to England with his family where he hoped to build a man-carrying flyer, only to be disappointed by his cool reception and at discovering there were no funds available for aeroplane construction. However, while in the country the Aeronautical Society invited him to deliver a paper on his kites, when Percy Pilcher took the chair. Hargrave responded by presenting some of them to the Society.

Hargrave returned to Australia where he designed his last full-scale aircraft. This was of tinplate 'with multiple main wings, (along) with a smaller multiplane tail unit with a large central float, and two smaller side floats'.[16] It had a steam engine, which again turned out to be a failure, and it was not until 1906 that Hargrave belatedly reconsidered using a petrol engine to power his flappers. This also failed.

Although Hargrave was modestly wealthy, he seemed reluctant to spend over-much on his aeronautical work. According to his journal in the twenty-eight years from 1887 to his death in 1915 he spent exactly £418 19s 1d on experimental material and was probably equally parsimonious with the amounts paid to his mechanics.[17] Finally after experiencing so many setbacks over a protracted period and conscious of the exciting progress elsewhere, in March 1906 he decided to cease full-time aviation experiments, although he remained determined to continue with his work on engines. He lived on till 1915 when he died of 'a near broken heart' after he learned of the death of his son at Gallipoli.

In retrospect, Hargrave's aeronautical career was largely unfulfilled, although his reverses could not be adequately explained by being out of touch, for he corresponded extensively with other major aeronautical figures and in 1900 when he was in England he met leading figures in British aviation. His chief disability came from the lack of an efficient engine, caused in part by his continuing misplaced reliance on steam power and in using flappers for propulsion. His biographer, W. Hudson Shaw, also believed that Hargrave's lack of a close collaborator in Australia – 'an equally dedicated fellow experimenter'[18] – was another most important factor.

The air historian Charles Gibbs-Smith is sweepingly critical about Hargrave's lack of progress. He believed he possessed some coherent disabilities – or weak-nesses – 'due to the fact that he was basically chauffer-minded; he was not a true airman in his approach to aviation',[19] and there is no escaping the fact that Hargrave only flew his 1894 glider during a small number of tests and then only a few feet off the ground. While he made almost fifty models and over thirty motors he never really attempted to master the art of flying a full-size glider.

A.V. Stephens, in an unpublished biographical paper on Hargrave, agreed with Gibbs-Smith that Hargrave's models 'had little inherent stability and for this reason he flew them just before sunrise when there was little wind'.[20] Stephens went further than Gibbs-Smith, believing that Hargrave 'wasn't an entirely sound scientist' and had 'bees buzzing in his bonnet'. Stephens cited Hargrave's first paper on flight, presented to the Royal Society of New South Wales in 1884, which bore the formidable, if impenetrable, title of *The Trichorded Plane*. Although Stephens alleged he had read the paper repeatedly he confessed he was still left 'with doubts as to exactly what he was driving at'.[21] On the other hand, the aerial commentator A.E. Berriman appeared to have no difficulty summarising the paper as 'describing inter alia, a simple mechanism for frapping and "feathering" a pair of wings' – although even he took a number of further sentences endeavouring to explain the concept itself.

Hargrave's papers did not make the easiest of reading, but however variable the nature of his researches he published them for everyone to see and refused to patent his inventions in case they hampered progress. His key contribution to aerodynamics was undoubtedly the invention of the box kite, which in its many forms gave stability and lifting power to a number of the earliest European aeroplanes. As for aeroplane engines, in spite of his repeated setbacks he drew up plans for early rotary and even straight jet engines which would subsequently be developed – and widely used – within the next half-century.

* * *

In contrast to Hargrave, who considered himself British but remained an Australian, the American, Hiram Maxim (b. 1840) arrived in the 1880s to work in Britain and remained there for the next thirty-five years, becoming a naturalised citizen. Like Cayley, before taking up aviation work this dedicated craftsman and 'chronic' inventor was responsible for a bewildering range of mechanical innovations, including apparatus to prevent the rolling of ships (he was a notoriously poor sailor), an automatic sprinkler system to extinguish fires, steam generators and wheels for both railways and tramways, carburettors for oil and gas engines, the electric light bulb (the timely patenting of which could have made his fortune), smokeless powder and his best known invention of all, the automatic machine gun where 'all the functions of loading and firing (were) performed by energy derived solely from the burning propellant powder'.[22]

Maxim's inventions had a far greater effect than Cayley's – his machine gun, for instance, came to exert a massive influence on infantry tactics during the First World War. As Basil Liddell Hart wrote, 'Emperors, Statesmen and generals had the power to make war but not to end it. Having created it, they found themselves helpless puppets in the grip of Hiram Maxim who, by his machine gun, had paralyzed the power of attack'.[23]

By 1887, although still heavily involved with marketing his gun worldwide, the bombastic and ever-confident Maxim had given considerable thought to the development of the aeroplane, which he always believed could become another potent weapon of war. In 1911 he even provided it with a bomb-dropping mechanism contained in three patents, numbered 7774, 8220 and 21722, entitled *Improvements in and relating to bombs for use in connection with aeroplanes or flying Machines*, registered in March, April and October of that year.

Remarkably, his aerial vehicle, which he estimated would cost in the region of £100,000 and require his undivided attention for five years, was strikingly unambitious.[24] Maxim began work on it by renting a large mansion at Bexleyheath called Baldwyn's Park and recruiting two American mechanics to carry out experiments on the basics of flight, the first step to which he rightly believed was to develop a fast-revving light internal-combustion engine as its power unit. But then his courage failed him, for although by 1885 Karl Benz had installed an internal-combustion engine in a three-wheeled automobile it was initially somewhat unreliable, so Maxim uncharacteristically played safe and decided upon a highly efficient steam engine instead.

An elderly Hiram Maxim with Claude Grahame-White, Guy Livingston and R.T. Gates at the 1911 Olympia Aero Exhibition. (*Royal Aeronautical Society* [*National Aerospace Library*])

He was later to acknowledge his blunder, 'for the quantity (and weight) of water consumed by [his massive plane] was very great indeed'[25] – enough water for an hour's running added 600lbs – making it impossible to compete with an effective internal combustion unit. Whatever its weight, Maxim's steam engine was undoubtedly efficient, made up of 2,800ft of copper tubing and producing 362hp at a steam pressure of 320lbs/in^2.

With typical thoroughness he went on to address the design of its propeller, using a whirling arm device (the largest built to date) and a wind tunnel to test different screw profiles,[26] the first two of which were 17ft 10in in diameter. Maxim constructed them

> of seasoned American white pine and when finished varnished them on both sides with hot glue. The blades were covered with strong Irish linen fabric of the smoothest and best make, glue was used for attaching the fabric, and when dry another coat of glue was applied, the surface milled down again and then painted with zinc white in the ordinary way and varnished.[27]

Such propellers succeeded in achieving a thrust of more than 2,000lbs.

In spite of such remarkable power Maxim never intended to run his machine free. He mounted his plane on ordinary steel rails of about an 8ft gauge outside

Maxim's Great Aeroplane. (*Royal Aeronautical Society* [*National Aerospace Library*])

which he placed another track measuring 3in by 9in made of Georgian pine with a gauge of about 30ft. He equipped his machine with two complete sets of wheels, one for running on the lower steel rails and the other for engaging the wooden track when the lower wheels had been lifted 1in clear of the steel rails.[28] For a vehicle running along a track he needed no rudder and the engine's controls were simple enough, although he designed its throttles to be operated both singly or together.

The huge flying machine had no fuselage, ailerons or tail, although its wings were 105ft long, with propellers mounted behind them. Vertical control depended on fore and aft elevators and Maxim discovered that lift-off onto the second set of wheels was achieved at full throttle at 300ft along its rails.

On 31 July 1894 at Baldwyn's Park, he declared himself ready to demonstrate the plane before the Press and a selected audience. Maxim and two crewmen were scheduled to go on board, while another was stationed behind ready to slip its tether. On the third attempt, with its engine developing 240lbs/in^2 of pressure and the screw thrust exceeding 2,000lbs, the massive craft, weighing 8,000lbs (including 600lbs of water), darted forward and rapidly reached a speed of 42mph. Rising from the ground its wheels started running on the upper track but after completing a journey of 1,000ft, one of the axle-trees doubled up and all the strain came to be placed on the other three. As a result the upper track broke and the machine moved higher into the air before a part of the broken track caught in one of its screws. At this, Maxim turned off the engine and his craft sank into the

Preparing Maxim's plane for action. (*Royal Aeronautical Society* [*National Aerospace Library*])

soft turf. The damage was considerable but Maxim's monstrous aeroplane had flown for some 600ft, the last part in (unintended) free flight.

After repairing the machine, installing stronger outriggers and replacing the damaged platform, he was ready for a further public demonstration on 3 November 1896. Admission was by ticket only, price 2/-, the proceeds of which were in aid of the local Bexley Cottage Hospital. The second test went according to plan and the plane rose to run along its upper track without incident. Following this, Maxim declared his experiments over and his great craft was subsequently broken up.

After the first test *The Daily Graphic* reported that his plane's appearance was 'as distinct from one's usual conception of a flying machine as the old "Rocket" is from the steam locomotive of to-day' but suggested that people were not unduly impressed by such an odd vehicle running along its track. Such light regard changed to the irreverence so often given to early aviation experiments when in another article entitled 'Wanted, a Sinbad', the newspaper suggested that, as Maxim's steering was rudimentary, a trial by ordeal should be revived by challenging Maxim to navigate his machine across Epsom racecourse or some other place void of houses and trees. The article concluded that 'Prisoners, jurymen and judges would find this more exciting than a trial at the Old Bailey and as science might be incidentally advanced, the proposal is worth consideration.'[29]

The Daily Graphic was plainly not prepared to recognise either the technological achievements behind such an odd vehicle, or acknowledge any significance towards the attainment of true flight. Such reactions to Maxim's plane were shared by the American air pioneer and commentator, Octave Chanute. Following the first unsuccessful test he began by stating the obvious, that '(Maxim's) machine, the result of the efforts of the highest mechanical skill of the age, and a capital enormously greater than any hitherto applied to such an enterprise, lies maimed and helpless on the ground, from which it will never ascend again.' After asking 'What have we learnt from (the tests)?' Chanute came to the bleakest of answers:

> The laws which control the action of plane and curved surfaces in mid-air are not even remotely understood ... To imagine this machine serenely pursuing its course through a gale, or even buffeting its way through a stiff breeze, is to imagine a spectacle which the mind repels as an impossibility. The successful flying machine of the future, if ever we arrive at such, must possess a self-sustaining power and a means of generating and applying it in an emergency far beyond that proposition of 6hp per pound weight which Mr Maxim has so distinguished himself in obtaining.

In fairness, Chanute reminded his readers 'that Mr Maxim claims that he has succeeded in his object which was simply the raising of an air-vessel by its own power into the air. Having achieved this, he drops it, and we think, providently, for here the real difficulties begin'. This lack of ambition plainly baffled Chanute, who believed 'that from the first, inventors concerned in aerial travel have said as of one voice "Let us first get into the air" while fully neglectful or regardless of the momentous problems that arise as soon as they achieve the point of their aspirations.'[30] Apart from its great size and cost, it was difficult to see Maxim's plane having any influence on subsequent developments, including American professor Samuel Langley's Great Aerodrome being constructed at the turn of the century (which flew free and used an internal-combustion engine).

In Britain, following the limited aerodynamic advances of Wenham, Phillips, Anglo/Australian Hargrave and Maxim, progress towards piloting and controlling an aerial vehicle depended on pioneer aviator Percy Pilcher, who would attempt to fly at the first opportunity, while in America, where aviation researches were the equal or more advanced than those in Britain, hopes were resting on Professor Samuel Langley. Meanwhile the Wright brothers, who were determined not to attempt powered flight before acquiring a full understanding of a flying machine's control system, were waiting in the wings.

Chapter 4

The British Troubadour

Percy Sinclair Pilcher (b. 1867) was not only the last British air pioneer before the coming of the twentieth century, but the most determined to get into the air whatever the difficulties and dangers. This led his biographer, Philip Jarrett, to write that he 'concentrated on flight trials almost to the exclusion of mathematical theory and scientific experiment. We have no systematic performance estimates, aerodynamic tables and calculations or even a diary or flight log.'[1] Pilcher's impatience and imperfect preparations were understandable since he had fewer resources than either Cayley or Hargrave, let alone Hiram Maxim, and had been dogged by financial problems from the beginning.

Percy was the youngest of three sons and four daughters born to Thomas Webb Pilcher, formerly curator of the British Museum's Picture Gallery in Rome, and his second wife Sophia Robinson, and by the time he was eleven he had lost both his parents. With the family acutely short of money, it was decided that Percy should be sent to join the Royal Navy, which he did on 15 July 1880. At Dartmouth as a fifteen-year-old cadet on the training ship HMS *Britannia* he experienced no undue problems with either the academic or the physical training, although as a high-spirited, independent-minded boy he found himself disciplined for several offences such as being 'very troublesome at morning drill' and 'not wearing his drawers when the order being [*sic*] given'.[2]

On 18 April 1889, after six years' service, Lieutenant Pilcher resigned from the Royal Navy at his own request and was taken on as an engineering apprentice with Randolph Elder, shipbuilders of Govan. When at the firm's Southampton works in 1890 he persuaded his employers to let him attend lectures as an unmatriculated student at Southampton and University College, London.[3]

After eighteen months Pilcher returned to Glasgow as a draughtsman with shipbuilders J. and G. Thomson of Clydebank, accompanied by his sister Ella. Here his academic aspirations were rewarded when he was seconded as an assistant lecturer to the Naval Architecture and Marine Engineering Department of Glasgow University headed by Professor John Biles, for whom he had worked at Southampton. Manned flight had been Pilcher's passion from boyhood, and as his university classes only took place during the winter months he had his first opportunity to make an intensive study of aircraft design. Pilcher was fully aware of other pioneer constructors, especially Hiram Maxim in England and Otto Lilienthal in Germany. An avid reader of anything on aviation and – like many of his contemporaries – a scrapbook collector, his notebook includes an article on Maxim from the *Strand Magazine* of 1896. Pilcher, however, did not restrict himself to printed articles, for he communicated directly with the Austrian hang-glidist Lilienthal, Hargrave and Octave Chanute, as well as Francis Wenham, who wrote to him concerning Lilienthal's flying machines.[4]

Although Maxim's 104ft multi-wingspan plane was never designed to run free, Lilienthal's inexpensive, unpowered 'gliders' were always intended to be flown, whereby he hoped to learn about the elements of flight. With Pilcher's limited funds and natural impatience to fly, he was bound to follow Lilienthal's path and,

Percy Sinclair Pilcher. (*Royal Aeronautical Society* [*National Aerospace Library*])

Otto Lilienthal and family. (*Royal Aeronautical Society* [*National Aerospace Library*])

during 1895 in his spare time he constructed his first hang glider, which he named 'The Bat'. He built it in his Glasgow lodging house, designing it to fold up so that it could be carried into the surrounding countryside for flight-testing. Although Pilcher had planned to visit Lilienthal in Germany he decided to build his glider first 'to get the greatest advantage from any original ideas I might have'.[5]

On his arrival at Lichterfelde in April 1895 he found Lilienthal flying his large biplane glider by shifting his body backwards and forwards to change the angle of its nose and speed. The intrepid Pilcher was allowed to take his turn and make several glides of his own, but when he told Lilienthal about his own projected glider, weighing 44lbs (but designed to carry 200lbs in flight) with wings of 150ft^2 set at an acute dihedral, Lilienthal was emphatic that it needed a tail plane. Pilcher was unconvinced and during July 1895, after returning to Glasgow, he began flight-testing by running his glider down a hill until he could take off. After early disappointments, he followed Lilienthal's advice by fitting a circular tail plane and lowering its wings until they were only 6in above the plane's body. During a second attempt on 12 September he rose to 20ft and landed safely after a flight lasting almost a minute. Longer glides followed, although the wing tips tended to be damaged by striking the ground.

During the summer of 1895 Pilcher built a second glider ('The Beetle') with wings set higher, into which he considered installing an engine. Bearing this in mind, he made its frame stronger by using white pine, thereby increasing its

Lilienthal in flight. (*Photograph from the 2011 Exhibition at the Yorkshire Air Museum, Elvington*)

weight to 80lbs and this, in turn, required its wing area to be increased to 170ft^2 bringing new problems of control. The Beetle's large wings were flat, supported by central bracing wires running from king posts to compensate for their greater instability compared with the those of the Bat. With such large wings, Pilcher planned to position himself much lower, with his forearms resting on the glider's lower cross-span. Testing quickly showed the Beetle to be ungainly and with his body's low centre of gravity providing very little control. He described how 'a sudden gust of wind would carry the machine backwards leaving me, because of my weight, as it were, behind, and it is only by slipping out of the machine when it was above my head that I several times avoided going head over heels backwards with it'.[6]

Such antics required great caution and, uncharacteristically, during the summer of 1895 the winds in south-west Scotland continued to be light, thereby severely restricting his number of glides. Undeterred, he went on to build a third glider which he called 'The Gull', larger but also lighter than the others. Pilcher completed this during the early months of 1896 and tested it that summer, but he found it controllable only in the calmest weather and he severely damaged it whenever he attempted to fly in a stiff breeze.

In the spring of 1896, Pilcher took the decision to resign his post at Glasgow University and become a full-time assistant to Hiram Maxim and his firm of Maxim Nordenfelt Arms and Ammunition Co. Ltd. A powerful motive for this was the opportunity to use the large hanger that Maxim had built at Eynsford in Kent, close to a hill dubbed 'The Knob' from where he could conceivably launch his gliders. He moved the Gull into the hanger, together with a fourth glider, 'The Hawk', which he built at Eynsford during the first half of 1896. By now Pilcher's progress as a constructor was becoming apparent and although smaller than the Gull, the Hawk was a clear advance on it. Built predominately of bamboo, its wings with their camber of just 5in were attached to two vertical masts set approximately 2ft 6in behind their leading edges. Its triangular tail was made from three lengths of bamboo with fabric stretched across them and it was also supported by hemp lines coming from the masts. Pilcher used two strong rods to make a body aperture between the wings, where during his attempts to fly he could pass his head and shoulders up while resting his forearms on a longitudinal cross member. Later he positioned two pads on short struts, which he designed to support his shoulders when his arms were almost straight (although this had the risk of his tumbling through and breaking his arms).

Pilcher's cavalier attitude to such vulnerability was apparent in a lecture he gave to the Military Society of Ireland the following January, when he talked of similar risks taken by Lilienthal with his gliders. Pilcher maintained that 'although it appears uncomfortable [it] is not really as bad as it seems. It allows great freedom in moving one's weight about and gives one an excellent command of the machine when standing on the ground'. He went even further, telling his listeners that 'it has often been suggested that it would be a good plan to have a pair of stirrups to fit one's feet into while in flight, to have a net to sit in or some such device to relieve the weight on the arms but ... anything of this kind would be an encumbrance and would hinder movement, fidget one, and keep one from slipping out of the machine quickly in case of accident'.[7] One can only conjecture how far his audience was persuaded by such arguments, especially as by this time Lilienthal had been killed in an air accident.

Under the Hawk's body Pilcher placed two bamboo rods suspended on steel springs, with wheels at their base. When on the ground the glider rested on this rudimentary chassis, which also took the first impact on landing.[8] The burden placed on this undercarriage was not excessive, as the Hawk weighed just 50lbs unloaded, and had an estimated weight in flight of 195lbs.

Pilcher thought more highly of his Hawk than any of his previous vehicles and he applied for a patent under the title 'Improvements in Flying and Soaring Machines', which was granted on 6 March of the following year. Although he still steered and 'balanced' the Hawk by altering the position of his body rather than fitting any controls, during the summer of 1896 at Eynsford he increased the length of his glides and the ease of his landings. But time for such experiments was limited as he was committed from May to August with Maxim at an International Exhibition of Motors and their Appliances held at the Imperial Institute in South Kensington. There Maxim displayed a model of his aeroplane,

Pilcher flying his Hawk glider. (*Royal Aeronautical Society [National Aerospace Library]*)

together with a propeller and one of his 150hp compound steam engines, while Pilcher's Hawk was also on show.

During June Pilcher found an opportunity to visit Lilienthal, and was allowed to fly a biplane glider with its wings high above the pilot. Pilcher did not rate it highly and by now their aerial objectives appeared to be diverging. Lilienthal continued to view gliding as a sport for its own sake and considered installing a small carbonic acid gas motor at his gliders' wing tips to give him ever more soaring flights. Pilcher, on the other hand, aimed to gain flying experience prior to installing a screw engine that would provide genuine horizontal flight. His apprehension about the German's latest vehicle appeared fully justified when on Sunday 9 August 1896 it stalled, dipped a wing and Lilienthal plunged to his death.

Safety was an important consideration with most of the early pioneers and during the previous June Pilcher received a letter from Lawrence Hargrave in Australia putting forward the case for the inherent stability offered by wings of box-kite construction. But Pilcher was not ready to adopt such angular construction and he bluntly told Hargrave that

> We are rather at cross purposes. With your kites you naturally aim at stability but with my soaring machines, stability, strange as it may appear, is a thing I am very much afraid of. I like to have the machines practically neutral so as to be perfectly under control or rather, more susceptible to the control movements of my body.[9]

In truth, Pilcher was far more concerned with finding a satisfactory power source than pursuing safety. On 30 November 1896 he accompanied Professor G.H. Bryan when he delivered a lecture on 'Flight, Natural and Artificial' at the Imperial Institute at South Kensington. In his concluding remarks Bryan said that he looked forward with confidence to the time when a light motor with sufficient horse power would solve the problem of flight. In Pilcher's vote of thanks to the speaker he echoed the message, by confidently maintaining that

> the rest of the way to true flight will soon be marked out, not by any one great invention but by the careful compiling of quantitative data and the elimination of errors and fallacies. We no longer grope in such utter blindness for the first essential experimental truths as the earlier experimenters, but there is a very great deal of which we still remain hopelessly ignorant.[10]

Pilcher did well to acknowledge such continuing ignorance for, undoubtedly brave and energetic as he was, he neither had the knowledge of aerodynamics, the testing equipment nor a powerful-enough propulsion unit to make the breakthrough needed. This did not stop him pressing forward as far as he could however, and during the early part of January 1897 he declared his intention to construct a small oil engine with limited endurance to drive a screw propeller about 4ft in diameter for around a minute. Pilcher intended to start it by running down an incline and he believed it would produce 4hp to give a flying speed of

30mph[11] although, with the inefficient airscrew at his disposal, his estimate of performance would prove grossly optimistic.

In addition to the risks synonymous with early flight, Pilcher needed money to continue with his work. His sketchy academic and professional background, together with his unswerving courage, worked against him and Sir John Biles, professor of naval architecture at Glasgow, said of him, 'he was one of the few men I have met who had no sense of fear ... I was deterred from helping him as much as I ought to have done by a fear of the risks that he ran'.[12]

During 1897 Pilcher continued with his aerial activities, although his achievements remained disappointing. He drew up plans to build a steam-powered glider, for which he applied for a patent but providentially it was never built. In an attempt to attract much needed financial support, at Eynsford on 20 June he used the Hawk to give a demonstration of his flying skills to a large party of scientists and others. Although still without an engine, Pilcher used a thin fishing line, 600 yards long, pulled by three boys to tow him into a light breeze and then into the air. While on his first attempt the length of his possible flight was compromised by the rope breaking, he succeeded in travelling up to 250 yards from his starting point.

On 15 September his plans suffered an unexpected setback when Vickers took over Maxim's company which not only much reduced Maxim's influence but deprived Pilcher of Eynsford's hanger and flying ground inevitably increasing his costs.

During the summer of 1897 Pilcher was involved in new moneymaking activities. He accompanied engineer Walter Wilson to Cowes, where they demonstrated a small sailboat with an oval sail resembling a pair of Pilcher's glider wings. Although only a qualified success, it helped to further a friendship between the two men that culminated in them registering a company on 9 November 1897 'capable of carrying out engineering work including some on patents and inventions'. As joint managing directors, Wilson and Pilcher stood to gain much needed funds if the company succeeded, although the energy required in establishing it during 1898 was certain to interfere with Pilcher's aerial experiments. This was confirmed in his letter towards the end of that year to Professor Fitzgerald in Dublin.

> During the last year I was not able to do anything with the flying work, as we were so busy getting our new business into going order; but the summer before when I was able to devote some time to it, the results we obtained were most encouraging.[13]

In fact, 1898 was not quite as barren aeronautically as Pilcher made out, although he must have been frustrated to learn of advances elsewhere. Octave Chanute wrote to him about his biplane and quadruplane gliders that Chanute maintained were exceedingly easy and safe to handle and, on 25 July 1898, the British Patent Office accepted a joint patent by Chanute and his co-designer, Augustus Herring, for a powered triplane. This persuaded Pilcher to build a quadruplane called 'The Duck', although it never materialised. Whatever the fate of the Duck, from the end of 1897 Pilcher's own engine was unquestionably well advanced and in 1898 he refurbished his Hawk glider which was intended to take it.

The next year, 1899, promised to be successful for Pilcher's aerial experiments, although problems with financial support and a suitable flying field remained. Early in the year Pilcher raised the question of a field (and testing ground) when he wrote to Major Baden-Powell, at the Aeronautical Society, asking whether the Society 'will really think of starting a [flying] camp and a clubhouse?'.[14] With Baden-Powell's approval he took on the role of seeking suitable sites and in a letter of 9 June suggested Taplow in Buckinghamshire. 'We could get a nice plot on the river there quite cheap – on a short lease – I believe we could get a couple of acres subject to a 6 month notice to quit – at £2 an acre per year. Or would you prefer to use Dorney Common?'[15] Whatever sites Pilcher might discover, it was clear the onus for payment remained firmly with Baden-Powell and the Aeronautical Society.

Further progress towards a flying field seemed possible when, on 10 April 1899, Lawrence Hargrave arrived in Britain with his family, bringing five of his kites and a model soaring machine. It was arranged for him to address the Aeronautical Society about his kites on 26 May at a meeting chaired by Pilcher who, in his vote of thanks to the speaker, took the opportunity to advise the members present that 'the best thing that can be done is to try and subscribe enough funds to found a clubhouse somewhere out of London at which experiments can be made'.[16]

In spite of Pilcher's many attempts, no suitable site was acquired and he was obliged to base his flying at a Midlands location offered by his friend, the Honourable Adrian Verney Cave, who had known him from their naval days. This was at Stanford Hall, near Rugby, the family home of Adrian's father, Lord Braye. Between July and September 1899 Pilcher made four flights there, covering distances of between 300 and 400 yards, with the expectation of carrying out a powered flight in the very near future.

Meanwhile, although the firm of Wilson and Pilcher was progressing well, there was understandably little spare capital for work towards powered flight and its co-directors decided to send out a joint circular to raise an additional £4,000, £2,000 of which would be issued in shares and £2,000 in cash, with Pilcher hoping to attract further backing through demonstration flights at Stanford Hall on 30 September. To raise interest he billed it as his last gliding demonstration before attempting power-assisted flights and succeeded in attracting a number of potential backers, including Henrike Heaton MP, a wealthy champion of improved navigation. This proved something of a watershed for Pilcher, for in addition to his projected flights in the Hawk he was due to display a new triplane, owing much to Chanute's designs of the previous year, in which he intended to place an engine. Although this was not yet installed, he intended to run it for the spectators, but in August it suffered a broken crankshaft while being tuned up to produce more power. As a result his flights assumed a singular importance, despite them becoming more hazardous because of heavy overnight rain soaking the Hawk glider.

Verney Cave personally overhauled the line and pulley system for launching the glider but some of Pilcher's friends tried to dissuade him from flying due to the Hawk's sodden state and because of the continuing strong and variable winds. However, he felt he could not miss the chance of performing before such influential people. Pilcher planned to rise from a level field after being towed by a light line, some 300 or 400 yards long, drawn by two horses. His first attempt took place at 4.00pm and, following a short pull, the Hawk rose to about thirty feet when the cord snapped and Pilcher descended steadily to the ground.

Although the machine was still soaked, another trial was agreed for 4.20pm. Once again the glider rose to some thirty feet travelling approximately 150 yards before a snap was heard and the Hawk's tail collapsed due to one of its mooring cables breaking. The glider somersaulted forward, causing its wings to fold up and it was brought down heavily with Pilcher under the wreckage; his rescuers found him unconscious, with his left leg broken high up the thigh. They took him to Stanford Hall, where he was examined more thoroughly by four medical men who pronounced him suffering from 'very severe concussion, a fracture of the left thigh and a fracture of the right shin bone'.

He died on Monday, 2 October, thirty-four hours after the accident and without regaining consciousness. The Coroner said all the jury could do was to return a verdict of accidental death, although they expressed their regret that Pilcher 'had lost his life in perfecting what, if he could have proved a success, would be some good to the world'.[17] He died intestate, and his depleted financial position was revealed by the gross value of his estate at £150 8s 6d, with its net value of £39 19s 0d.

Although Pilcher followed Lilienthal by building and flying a series of hang gliders, unlike Lilienthal his aim was for full powered flight. This was bound to lead to the use of larger gliders causing greater difficulties in balancing and correcting their centres of gravity in flight. Walter Wilson believed that Pilcher was, in fact, considering rudder control using auxiliary surfaces, but how close he was to installing them will never be known.

Whereas Lilienthal tended to examine the results of his flights scientifically, Pilcher kept pressing forward with new modifications, such as fitting the Hawk with wheels designed to roll along the ground prior to take-off. Before he had installed control systems, Pilcher's impetuosity and desire to succeed led him to build an engine worked by means of carbonic acid gas which, when compressed into liquid form, was reputedly capable of propelling his plane at 25 to 30mph.

Producing an engine before carrying out the calculations required for its vehicle's performance ran directly counter to the recommendations of the more experienced American air pioneer, Octave Chanute, who wrote:

> If an aeroplane endowed with automatic equilibrium has first been developed by experimenting in the wind, methods of adapting motors thereto will be speedily discovered, and we shall reach a full solution of this problem of

transportation through the air, which has been puzzling man for over 2,000 years.[18]

As a consequence, even if Pilcher had installed a 2hp engine in the Hawk it was unlikely to have flown. The same would have been true for his triplane and its projected 4hp engine, for with its propellers of 3–4ft diameter it could not have attained the 70 per cent efficiency required for horizontal flight. In the event, Pilcher had not yet installed an engine but his death (and Lilienthal's before him) sent out a powerful message to the American Wright brothers to carry out exhaustive tests on perfecting their methods of control before they proceeded to apply power.

Pilcher was the first air pioneer in Britain to construct, and make successful free flights in a heavier-than-air craft and the first to die in a fixed wing aeroplane (for which he was constructing an engine). Sadly for Britain, although the attainment of genuine flight was close, after Pilcher's death the country fell into 'a regrettable state of moribundity' in terms of air research.[19] While Pilcher was close to completing a biplane equipped with a 4hp engine and a 4ft propeller, giving it the theoretical capability of making a short flight, he had not yet developed the necessary controls nor carried out the protracted testing required. More than any other British pioneer, Pilcher flew by the seat of his pants and, given the immense risks he took and his unfortunate death, it was understandable that there should be an interval before another British aspirant attempted to add manned flight to the country's already large number of scientific firsts.

Chapter 5

Lift off in America

Across the Atlantic the attitude towards the long-elusive goal of manned flight was different. From 1886, when the powerful American Association for the Advancement of Science (AAAS) added an aeronautical programme to its other aims, theories became more credible and 'although doubters still existed and the press still glorified experiments gone awry, most engineers fully anticipated the arrival of a powered flying machine'.[1] Anticipation was one thing, achieving it another, although such dreams seemed more attainable when the two men best known in America for championing flight, Samuel Langley and Octave Chanute, were both distinguished and respected.

Samuel Pierpoint Langley (b. 1834) was generally recognised as the 'leader of American Science'[2] but, equally important, as Secretary of the country's famed Smithsonian Institution he controlled its single largest source of funds for scientific research. By 1887 he had persuaded wealthy philanthropist William Thaw to subscribe funds for a massive whirling arm device, 60ft in diameter, to test airflow over lifting surfaces[3] and he was also able to cultivate the friendship (and therefore attract the support) of both Alexander Graham Bell, the telegraph and telephone pioneer, and Albert F. Zahn who had developed his own aero-dynamic research laboratory at Washington's Catholic University where, during the last five years of the nineteenth century, he constructed the country's first wind tunnel.

Langley was attracted to the study of aviation by Octave Chanute who had brought aviation before the AAAS when Vice President. It was Chanute's lecture there on bird flight that led Langley to study the flights of Otto Lilienthal, resulting in Langley's book *Experiments in Aeronautics* that set out to prove that under proper direction manned flight was practicable.[4] Langley was determined to build both model and full-scale powered aircraft (which he confusingly called aerodromes), for which purpose he transformed the Smithsonian's carpentry and machine shops and engaged able helpers such as the machinist L.C. Mathy, gifted carpenter R.L. Reed and George E. Curtiss for general aerodynamic work. To strengthen his team further he also recruited the scientist Edward Huffaker and glider constructor Augustus Moore Herring.

In spite of such formidable financial and human assets, Langley himself jeopardised likely progress with his compulsion to micro-manage his staff when working on a research programme and also by his favoured method of approach by beginning with rough trials before seeking to concentrate on more detailed experiments. Even so, the general expectation was when, rather than if, progress could be made in America towards genuine powered flight. In reality it took five

Professor Samuel Pierpoint
Langley. (*Royal Aeronautical Society*
[*National Aerospace Library*])

years, during which time Langley's team encountered a series of major setbacks and repeated disappointments, before the No. 5 prototype of a model steam-driven, tandem-wing plane (one wing behind the other) was catapulted from the flat roof of a houseboat on the Potomac River, and flew for a total of 3,300ft, followed by a second flight of 2,300ft. Unlike the powered model launched indoors by John Stringfellow fifty years earlier, this was the first large prototype to remain in the air for any length of time. Langley followed it six months later with his No. 6 model aeroplane which travelled 4,200ft from the houseboat at a speed of about 30mph. In Britain two years earlier, Hiram Maxim had set his great flying machine in motion, but its progress on rail tracks and his plans for it to rise just off the ground while still tethered could never compare with Langley's free flights.

The other outstanding American air pioneer during the last two decades of the nineteenth century was the self-educated French immigrant Octave Chanute (b. 1832). He became one of America's most respected civil engineers, building railroads and bridges that opened up the country, and after pioneering a method of treating railroad ties to increase their lifespan he declared he was willing to spend the proceeds on his pursuit of aeronautics.

Apart from his own work on aerial vehicles, Chanute was a self-appointed proponent for aviation who not only helped to capture Langley for the cause but, in 1894, published a compendium of articles for would-be aviators entitled *Progress in Flying Machines*, by means of which he intended to account for 'past failure, clearing away the rubbish, and pointing out some of the elements of success'.[5] Through his handbook and above all his widespread personal correspondence with other air pioneers in Europe, America and elsewhere, Chanute aimed to act

Langley's Tandem Wing Aerodrome. (*Royal Aeronautical Society* [*National Aerospace Library*])

as 'an international conduit vital for the exchange of ideas and encouragement as the invention of the aeroplane evolved'.[6]

He also aimed to develop and fly his own glider and eventually 'to add a motor and two screws, revolving in opposite directions'.[7] Unlike Lilienthal he wanted it to have a form of automatic stability that required its pilot to intervene only when he wanted 'to change direction either up or down, or sideways'.[8]

Following experiments with multiple pairs of wings involving designer Augustus Herring (who left Langley to work for Chanute) and carpenter William Avery, by 1896 Chanute had produced a triplane glider with three superimposed wings anchored at their sides with diagonal wires on a box-like framework. In his hunt for stability Chanute gave his glider a cruciform tail attached to a universal joint which, when struck by a gust of wind, was designed to give way in the opposite direction, thus tending to return the craft to straight and level flight. The central section of the bottom wing was later removed to give room for the pilot who, when controlling the vehicle, had to move only two to three inches rather than the 15 to 18in needed for the Lilienthal type. Chanute maintained that scores of flights were made in this glider without mishap, and the contemporary American air historian, Tom Crouch, believes that it was the most significant and influential aircraft of the pre-Wright era – far better than any Lilienthal gliders – and one that became the basis for all externally braced biplanes.[9]

Like any aircraft of the time Chanute's Katydid glider owed much to the work of British pioneers Francis Wenham and Horatio Phillips, together with Lawrence Hargrave in Australia and the fearless exploits of the hang-glidists Otto Lilienthal and Percy Pilcher. Chanute, however, was by now an old man and he admitted to Langley that he would not be able to perfect a successful aeroplane himself, although he hoped to be remembered as one who had developed a genuine prototype that would contribute towards it.[10]

Langley's ambitions knew no such bounds and he advanced from his flying models to building a massive aircraft, which he also intended to launch from a houseboat on the Potomac River. Unfortunately his plane, confusingly called 'the Great Aerodrome', turned out to be a tragedy not only for its constructor and his team but for the American Board of Ordnance and Fortification that had supported its massive cost. Langley's opportunity to obtain over $50,000 from this source coincided with America's impending war with Spain which actually began on 25 April 1898, at which time Langley optimistically maintained that an enlarged version of his Nos 5 or 6 models would be able to carry a man in flight 'for a time and distance which would render them important factors in land and naval warfare'.[11]

To co-ordinate its construction Langley recruited Charles Manly, a graduate in electrical and mechanical engineering from Cornell University who proved to be a worthy colleague. The wings were to be set at a high camber and it was to have controls for climbing, descending and turning. The most difficult problem appeared to be the choice of a suitable engine and here Langley, somewhat surprisingly, selected a radical rotary, air-cooled, internal-combustion engine invented in 1898 by Stephen M. Balzar of New York. This had three cylinders, but Balzar agreed on 5 December 1898 to build a five-cylinder version within just ten weeks at a cost of $1,500. In addition, the Great Aerodrome required an enhanced houseboat and launcher as well as more advanced controls of its own. Despite hopes for rapid completion, Langley's plane took some three years and an expenditure of over $50,000 before it was ready. The most persistent problems occurred with the engine, and after a string of failed promises by Balzar over its completion Manley took charge, converting it into a fixed radial unit, although its power output still proved insufficient. By March 1903 it was pronounced ready but by now Langley had been compelled to draw on additional funds intended for other research.

Due to the major difficulties with the engine, less attention was paid to problems relating to stability and control and during December 1902 Langley attempted to bring the reclusive and independent Wright brothers to Washington 'to get some of their ideas on the subject'. They, however, proved unwilling to be drawn in this way.[12]

Although Langley and Manly realised the problems of stability and pitch were far from resolved they believed that their arrangements so far could keep the aircraft going for a short flight. During its first trial on 8 September one of the propellers broke and it was aborted but, after repairs, on 8 December 1903 everything was ready. Once the engine was brought up to full speed, the machine

The Great man-carrying Aerodrome on its Houseboat. (*Royal Aeronautical Society* [*National Aerospace Library*])

was released. Manley subsequently described exactly what happened. 'At the end of the launching track I experienced a slight jerk and discovered immediately that the machine was plunging forward and downward at an angle of 45 degrees … I prepared for the plunge since it seemed that nothing could be done to obviate it.'[13]

A Washington reporter who was at the scene said the aerodrome entered the water 'like a handful of mortar' and the plane was substantially damaged, although Manly was uninjured. As the eminent historian Tom Crouch concluded, 'the decision to compound the basic difficulty of getting this overly complex, structurally weak and under-powered craft into the air by boosting it from a complete standstill to flying speed in only 70 feet was, to judge the matter kindly, unwise'.[14]

After two months of frenzied repairs, they made a second attempt. This time Manly found himself staring at the sky as the aeroplane slipped into the water on its back. He was submerged in freezing water but after surfacing from under the ice sheet, managed to swim to open water and save himself.

The plane proved unsound from both a structural and aerodynamic point of view and Professor Langley was harshly criticised. Robinson, the state representative from Indiana, called him 'a professor … wandering in his dreams of flight … who was given to building … castles in the air'.[15] Langley's request for more funds from the Board of Ordnance was swiftly refused, with one of its members, Major N.W. Macomb, believing it would take years of study and work involving the expenditure of thousands of dollars before they could produce a practical aircraft.

The spectacular failure of Langley and Manly proved the most expensive setback for aviation so far since in Britain Maxim's great aeroplane had achieved its limited objectives. Remarkably, Langley's failure did not delay America's quest for manned flight, for by now two relatively unsung pioneers, whose experiments had been entirely funded from their own resources, were within days of testing their own aircraft.

As skilled bicycle makers the two Wright brothers, Wilbur (b. 1867) and Orville (b. 1870), were in the tradition already established in Europe of non-academic engiers (such as Britain's Stringfellow, Wenham and Pilcher) with a new interest in aeronautics. The Wrights, however, brought most formidable qualities to the movement. Their father, Milton, was a bishop in the American United Church, which owed much to the strict traditions of the German and Dutch reformed churches. 'Yet strict as he was in his adherence to his own ideals and principles Bishop Wright was broad-minded and tolerant and did not set rigid rules of conduct for his children.'[16] The Wright boys were encouraged to investigate whatever aroused their curiosity and this helped to set them on their path to manned flight.

Their mother's death from tuberculosis also proved very important, for with their father elsewhere on his missionary work, their eldest brothers away from home and their younger sister, Katharine, about to go to university, Wilbur and Orville were left alone in the family house. Wilbur wrote 'My brother Orville and myself lived together, played together, worked together and in fact thought together'.[17] For these reasons the Wrights brought formidable qualities of mind, sound training and temperament, and a unique closeness that would prove most advantageous in tackling problems that had proved intractable to others.

Apart from a small toy helicopter designed by the Frenchman Alphonse Penaud which their father had bought for them to play with as boys, it was probably the widely-publicised death of Lilienthal in 1896 that prompted them towards aviation. Whatever the cause, their determination was quickly revealed in Wilbur's bold approach to the Smithsonian Institution in May 1899 '(asking) for any papers it held on aviation and for a list of other works in print in the English language'.[18] When they examined the material sent them, they were astonished to learn what an immense amount of time and money had been expended in futile attempts to solve the problem of human flight.[19] Of particular interest were the accounts of flights made by Lilienthal and Pilcher in which they attempted to maintain their gliders' balance by shifting the weight of their bodies.

Orville and Wilbur Wright. (*Royal Aeronautical Society* [*National Aerospace Library*])

With remarkable self-confidence the Wrights at once set to work to devise a more efficient way of maintaining equilibrium. Like so many others, they looked for a solution by watching birds in flight and concluded that 'the bird certainly trusts its wing tips so that the wind strikes one wing on top and the other on its lower side, thus by force changing the birds' lateral position'.[20] They reasoned that if a man could only use wings in the same way his plane could be kept on an even keel and even banked on controlled turns similar to a cyclist leaning into a turn. A version of this lateral control (which came to be known as wing warping) had already been considered in Britain but had not been developed.[21] The Wrights implemented a control system by means of a model box kite with two wings, which apparently pitched up and down to their commands and, as early as 1899, they planned an aeroplane glider with controls in the form of a warping device and an elevator positioned at its front for pitch control.

They went on to seek information beyond that supplied by the Smithsonian or from reports about Samuel Langley's work. In May 1900 Wilbur decided to write to Octave Chanute explaining that for some years 'I have been afflicted with the belief that flight is possible to man ... with this general statement of my principles and belief I will proceed to describe the plan and apparatus it is my intention to test'. This proved to be the first of almost 400 letters that passed between them and it included a description of the brothers' trials so far and Wilbur's plans for a full-sized machine. Chanute replied four days later inviting Wilbur to visit him in Chicago.[22]

Another instance of the brothers' professionalism was when they contacted the Chicago weather bureau about a good location in which to test their glider. It recommended a remote area in North Carolina on the Atlantic coast called Kitty Hawk that enjoyed constant winds and, equally important, had a beach about a mile wide clear of trees and high hills.[23] On the strength of such advice they decided to take their man-lifting glider on the thousand-mile journey to Kitty Hawk. It had a wingspan of 17½ft, a width of 5ft, it weighed 52lbs and cost just $15 to build. Even so, in constructing their wings they had used the calculation tables for lift arrived at by Chanute and Lilienthal, which they rapidly suspected might be unsatisfactory. The Wrights felt sure they needed larger wings with a smaller camber, than those used by the other two, and produced a glider with two wings 5ft apart, capable of twisting or warping for roll control and a front elevator for up and down movement (pitch). As yet it had no rudder.

On 6 September 1900 Wilbur set off for Kitty Hawk and Orville joined him there. After erecting a tent as their base they started using their machine as an unmanned kite tethered to a small wooden tower, which they attempted to control from the ground with cords. When they found their wings proved deficient in lifting capability they became ever more convinced that Lilienthal's figures must be wrong, although their control of the machine in the air proved better than they had anticipated. In any case, for genuine aerial tests they knew they had to try free flight.

After moving their base to the huge sand dunes off the Kill Devil Hills and launching their glider from the brow of a large dune, it began to perform quite

Wrights' Glider – Wilbur lying prone, 1901. (*Royal Aeronautical Society* [*National Aerospace Library*])

well. On 19 October 1900 the brothers went an important stage further by launching their glider with Wilbur lying prone on it. He made a dozen descents until he was gliding from 300 to 400ft in airtimes of 15 to 20 seconds. But they were still far from satisfied and, after spending a total of barely two minutes in flight, they decided to return to Dayton to increase their craft's wingspan and adjust its camber.

While redesigning their glider, Wilbur wrote a long letter to Chanute explaining their experiments with the pilot lying prone and operating the controls for lateral equilibrium and fore and aft balance.[24] Chanute replied courteously enough but without really showing he understood the full significance of the flight control system which the brothers had created.

By May 1901 the Wrights had redesigned their glider by adding a forward elevator, extending its wings and changing their camber to that used earlier by Lilienthal. Their machine now weighed 98lbs, larger than any previously and nearly twice the size of that designed by Percy Pilcher. Following this, they moved to their testing base among the windswept and endless sand dunes of the Kill Devil Hills. There they built a wooden hanger, and after inviting Chanute to watch their impending trials reluctantly agreed to him bringing with him two engineer companions, Edward Huffaker and George Spratt. Flight trials began on 8 August 1901. Their best was a distance of 335ft, which ended with a nose-dive into the ground. This was far below the levels they expected and when they

More advanced Wrights' Glider. (*Royal Aeronautical Society* [*National Aerospace Library*])

returned home they were despondent, with Wilbur telling Orville that 'not within a thousand years would man ever fly'.[25]

Wilbur sent Chanute a lengthy technical report and, after he had delivered a lecture to the Western Society of Engineers in Chicago on their progress so far, the brothers carried out a most thorough testing of Lilienthal's wing calculations. They did so by using a rig that revolved like a horizontal windmill, together with a wind tunnel 6ft long and 16in square, to measure the behaviour of air flowing over more than 200 types of wings. As a result they discarded the earlier figures and by December 1901 had more information about the aerodynamics of wings, 'on cambered surfaces, a hundred times over, than all our predecessors put together'.[26] These revealed that it was the design of the wings – rather than the engine or propellers – that enabled a plane to lift itself because a non-powered glider could never have flown without them.

Octave Chanute was amazed at the quality of their research so far, but it was not until August 1902 that they again set off for the Kill Devil Hills. This time their machine's wings, 32ft long by 5ft across, had a higher aspect ratio with a lesser camber ranging from 1:24 to 1:30. The wings' curvature high point was a third back from its leading edge and, in addition to their front elevator, they placed a rudder on the plane's rear to correct the previous inexplicable swings in flight. They found their new wings produced far more lift than before, and in three days' flying Wilbur made 125 glides. They still faced the problem of stalling, which they solved by Wilbur's brilliant suggestion that the vertical rudder should be made movable and fixed to the warping system. This completed the essential elements of the Wrights' flight control system for pitch, bank and turn, and using it the brothers made 900 glides of over 600ft lasting up to twenty-six seconds, including aerial turns. Such successes enabled them to plan for a powered aircraft, although they omitted to patent their work on wing design and their three-dimensional control system.

By now the Wrights realised they had to protect their discoveries from competitors. Having rebuffed advances from Professor Langley they decided that Chanute's attempts to publicise their progress so far were premature, if not mischievous. They also avoided a meeting with Hiram Maxim, which Chanute had suggested, but they did receive a visit at their home in Dayton on Christmas Eve 1902 from another of Chanute's correspondents, the English aviation enthusiast Patrick Alexander. By now Chanute had also encouraged a young French army captain, Ferdinand Ferber, to build a rough copy of the Wrights' glider. Ferber had obtained a 6hp gasoline engine and was seeking a suitable propeller in an attempt to move ahead of all other pioneers, including the Wrights.

This did not mark the end of Chanute's initiatives, for at a dinner held in his honour by the Aero Club de France on 2 April 1903 he spoke of gliding experiments in the United States by himself and the Wrights, in which he gave the

Wrights' Glider turning using wing warping. (*Royal Aeronautical Society [National Aerospace Library]*)

impression that they were either his collaborators or pupils. In the illustrated lecture he also revealed their three-axis control system, although his technical descriptions lacked some clarity. Notwithstanding, French experiments with 'Wright type' gliders encouraged by Chanute would mark the re-emergence of European aviation.

Meanwhile, the Wrights were busy developing a suitable engine and propeller. They knew it would require a larger flying machine to carry the expected burden of 625lbs, and intended to increase their plane's wing area from its present 300ft^2 to 500ft^2, which they achieved by a 40ft × 6ft wingspan with the two wings set 6ft apart and having a curvature of 1:20.

The brothers estimated they needed an engine developing around 8hp but, after failing to find any firms willing to supply it, their mechanic, Charlie Taylor, took on the task with his engine which achieved 13hp rather than the original aim of 8hp. They used an aluminium alloy crankcase, but as it was without a fuel pump or carburettor it only ran at one speed. While testing during February 1903 its bearings seized and it was April before a new crankcase could be supplied. (By now a range of boat and aerial engines were being produced in France, including some with more power.)

The next and quite unexpected problem for the Wrights arose from their propellers. They found that ships' propellers only gave 50 per cent efficiency and that Maxim's and Langley's 'paddle' propellers were even less efficient. The Wrights calculated that their propellers needed at least 60 per cent efficiency, so using their wind tunnel they carried out a protracted series of tests to determine the propeller's required length, width, curvature and speed of rotation, the results of which filled five notebooks. They soon discovered that current propellers were 'all wrong and built a pair of propellers 8½ feet in diameter based on our own theories that are right'.[27] These were made from three laminations of spruce wood. Meanwhile the US Patent Office rejected the registration of their three-dimensional control system and, as a result, its acceptance in America would be delayed until 1906.

On 1 September the Wrights again set out for Kitty Hawk with their new aircraft. While they were there they received news of Langley's unsuccessful launch of his Great Aerodrome, about which Orville observed, 'whereas Langley's plane started from 60 feet in the air and landed 300 feet away we are able from the same height to make 400–600 feet without any motor at all, so that I think his surfaces must be very inefficient'.[28]

In early October the Wrights were still experiencing major problems with their engine and when Chanute arrived at Kill Devil Hills on 6 November 1903 the weather was bitterly cold. He left after six days, during which time he forecast that the brothers' lift-off power was inadequate, although they were both touched by the two pairs of gloves he gave them to help combat the increasing cold. On 20 November the sailing ship *Lou Willis* brought replacement propeller shafts which enabled them to run up their engine again, but on 28 November they encountered more trouble when they found a propeller shaft had cracked. It would now be December before they received a replacement; they were tempted to give up and try again the following year but, because another attempt by Langley was imminent, they decided to continue. On 8 December the Great Aerodrome plunged straight down into the Potomac – which cleared the way for their first attempt to fly. This took place six days later and, enlisting the help of five local lifeboat men, two small boys and a dog, they initially laid 60ft of rail track on a gentle downward slope. After tossing for pilot Wilbur won, but because of his lack of familiarity with the new elevator he climbed too steeply and the Flyer stalled, settling back onto the sand after just three and a half seconds and a 60ft journey.

On 16 December they worked to repair the plane and decided on a further attempt the following day. Although the wind registered 22–27mph and it was bitingly cold, they re-laid the track and this time Orville won the toss. At 10.35am, wearing a business suit, starched collar, tie and cap, he stretched out in his hip cradle and after covering 40 of the rails' 60ft the Flyer slowly lifted into the air. Orville also experienced difficulty with the large forward rudder, and the plane returned sharply to earth after rising to a maximum of 10ft for a journey of just 120ft, lasting 12 seconds. Yet as Orville expressed it, 'it was nevertheless the first in the history of the world in which a machine carrying a man had raised itself by its own power into the air in full flight, had sailed forward without reduction in speed, and had finally landed at a point as high as that from which it

Man's first flight, 17 December 1903 at Kitty Hawk. (*Royal Aeronautical Society* [*National Aerospace Library*])

started'.[29] At 11.20am Wilbur made the second flight of the day. He was still experiencing difficulties with the forward rudder, but he covered 175ft during a 12-second flight. Orville's second attempt achieved 200ft in a 15-second flight. Finally, Wilbur's second flight measured 852ft in 59 seconds. Following this, the Flyer was caught by a violent gust of wind, rolled over and destroyed – but the flying sequence was over and its significance, not only in America but in Britain and elsewhere, could not be exaggerated. Later in the twentieth century Orville would proudly write that 'it had more effect on the world since the discovery of America'.[30]

At the time things appeared less clear-cut, while in Britain, the country of George Cayley, the authorities would be remarkably slow in recognising the aeroplane's potential – and also reluctant to purchase the Wrights' plane and its technology.

STRUGGLE FOR AIR CONSCIOUSNESS

Chapter 6

Rejecting the Wrights' Offers

For a small, heavily-populated island that had traditionally relied on the Royal Navy for its protection and whose capital city was less than fifty miles from the coast, the threat from air power enabling an enemy to leapfrog the English Channel could hardly be exaggerated.

In fairness, the first frail aircraft could not readily pose a threat, but with Germany emerging as Britain's most likely opponent in a future war, its investment in airpower, if predominantly in large airships underlined the possible dangers. Having lost the race for manned flight it was, then, all the more remarkable that when the Wrights offered their aeroplane and its technology to Britain it would lead to a remarkable series 'of lost opportunities and missed chances'[1] by the British government.

Much of this was due to a single individual, Colonel John Capper (b. 1861), a serving engineer officer who came to occupy a unique place in early army aviation. He took over command of the Army Balloon Sections (the combatant units that undertook reconnaissance work for the ground forces) as a brevet lieutenant colonel in April 1903 and from then on his influence grew. In the same year he acted as Secretary to a Committee of Enquiry that was convened after the South African War to consider any possible improvements to army ballooning, which at the time included all forms of aerial activity: balloons, kites, airships and aeroplanes which, in military parlance, were 'flying machines proper'.

The Committee recommended the establishment of a Balloon School, a more compact military unit to replace the earlier Balloon Sections (and companies) commanded by Colonel Capper since 1902, over which Capper was appointed Commandant in April 1906. In May of the same year he was given the additional role of superintendent of the Balloon Factory (where the army's first airship was being constructed). With this went promotion to the rank of full colonel. Responsibility for military aeronautics therefore came under one officer who, from 1904, was increasingly hopeful for the work being undertaken at Farnborough, including the development of aeroplanes.

There were a number of reasons for this: one came about in September 1904 when Capper was sent to the St Louis World Fair to view displays of German, French and American aeronautical equipment. Following this, he took his wife on a visit to the Wrights' home at Dayton, Ohio, where he was highly impressed by both the family and the calibre of their aeronautical work. Due to his visit he became on close terms with them, and his wife formed a friendship with their sister, Katherine, which lasted some years. At the time he also said that whenever

Colonel Capper with members of the Aeronautical Society of Great Britain attending a kite display at Cobham Common on 1 July 1907. From left to right, Mr W.H. Dines, Colonel J.E. Capper, Hon. C.S. Rolls, Mrs Bruce, German Military Attaché, Major Baden-Powell, Mr E. Frost, Colonel Trollope, Colonel Fullerton and Mr L.S. Bruce. (*Royal Aeronautical Society* [*National Aerospace Library*])

they were ready to sell their invention he hoped they would 'give Great Britain the first chance'.[2]

Following his return to Britain, in December 1904 Capper submitted an official report on his visit to the War Office, in which he said he was satisfied that the Wrights had made 'far greater strides in the evolution of the flying machine than any of their predecessors' and if their work was 'carried to a successful issue, we may shortly have as accessories of warfare, scouting machines which will go at a great pace and be independent of obstacles of ground whilst offering from their elevated position unrivalled opportunities of ascertaining what is occurring in the heart of an enemy's country'.[3]

His report ended with specific recommendations for British military aviation which, in fact, helped to bring about his appointment as Superintendent of the Balloon Factory. He pointed out the army's 'want of a proper experimental school ... for the carrying out of such experiments as are necessary to determine the conditions which a dirigible balloon or flying machine must fulfil to be successful and for collating information on the subject'. Further, 'I would advocate the gradual formation of a Government Library at Aldershot of all works which bear on the subject of aeronautics together with the need for contact with others working in the field to save experiments being made which have proved profitless elsewhere'.[4]

From such recommendations, Capper's ambitions were clear. He wanted to create a world-class military research establishment of his own at Farnborough, towards which the Wrights had already given him a valuable start when, during his visit to Dayton, they supplied him with certain details of their flying machine and its motor, which they illustrated with photographs taken in different conditions of flight.

On becoming Superintendent of the Balloon Factory, he was able to further his plans when he took what he must have believed was a most important step in securing the services of Lieutenant John Dunne of the Royal Wiltshire Regiment, son of General Sir Hart Dunne. Dunne's father and others, notably Colonel John Winn, who was a member of the influential Royal Engineer Committee, knew about Dunne's original work with model aircraft and believed he would soon be able to produce an aeroplane superior to those of the Wrights. Dunne's aim for an inherently stable machine, rather than the Wrights' aircraft that needed its pilot to maintain its equilibrium, appealed strongly to Capper.

This was not all. Capper had already acquired the services of a brilliant, practical engineer and aerial designer in the unlikely shape of former American cowboy and playwright, Samuel Franklin Cody (b. 1867). In June 1904, before he went to America for the St Louis Fair, Capper had interviewed Cody about the possibility of him becoming an Instructor in Kites at Aldershot (kites could be

Lieutenant John Dunne, whose distinguished antecedents seemed to influence Capper unduly, with the French aviator Commandant Felix. (*Royal Aeronautical Society* [*National Aerospace Library*])

Samuel Franklin Cody.
(*Jean Roberts*)

used for reconnaissance in windy conditions when balloons were grounded). Cody was given a succession of short contracts until Capper became Commandant of the Balloon Factory, when Cody joined its permanent staff. During July 1905, the unlettered but remarkably resourceful Cody built a glider kite (apparently when he was on leave) which Capper talked about enthusiastically at a meeting of the Aeronautical Society in December of that year.

Such skills must surely have increased Capper's conviction that whatever the nature of the Wrights' activities, work towards manned flight could be carried out successfully at Farnborough. Capper employed Cody to construct the steering system for the army's first airship being built at Farnborough and when time allowed, Cody was permitted to move on from his glider kite to a powered version and then to building an aircraft.[5] Cody's plane would owe much to the Wrights' design, including a forward elevator, rear rudder and another above the upper main wing, details of which were likely to have been passed to him by Capper or less probably by Cody's (and Capper's friend), air enthusiast, Patrick Alexander.[6]

Capper's growing conviction that he could construct successful aircraft at the Balloon Factory had a direct effect on his attitude towards the army's purchase of the Wrights' plane. The Wrights' own attitudes were also fundamental towards their failure to disseminate their expertise. Following their initial success on

17 December 1903, they constructed a larger and more powerful flyer the following year, whose flight trials were conducted at Huffman Prairie just eight miles outside their home town of Dayton, Ohio. In November 1904 Wilbur flew more than three miles during a flight of over five minutes, a feat matched by Orville on 1 December. By 1905 they were confident that they were in possession of the world's first practical aircraft, for which they had been granted a British patent during 1904.[7] As a result they took the extraordinary decision not to make another public flight until May 1908, but to use their time approaching interested parties in the hope of obtaining the financial rewards from their achievements which they felt were their due.

In the first instance, they approached the American and British authorities and in the case of Britain immediately thought of making their approach through their friend John Capper. On 10 January 1905 they wrote to him at Aldershot enquiring whether his government would be interested in purchasing their aeroplane, together with its scientific knowledge and tuition in piloting it. Nine days later they wrote in similar fashion to another personal contact, Robert M. Nevin, their congressman for the Dayton district of Ohio. This letter was swiftly forwarded to the American Board of Ordnance and Fortification and within a week they received a reply that showed its recipient had clearly got the wrong end of the stick, probably as a result of the Board's earlier disaster with Professor Langley. It informed them that before considering any allotment from the American Government for the development of mechanical flight 'the device must have been brought to the stage of practical operation without expense to the United States'.[8]

Wilbur thereupon wrote angrily to their friend and mentor Octave Chanute.

It is no pleasant thought to us that any foreign country should take from America a share of the glory of having conquered the flying problem, but we feel that we have done our full share toward making this an American invention, and if it is sent abroad for further development the responsibility does not rest upon us.[9]

The obtuseness of the American Board of Ordnance and Fortification appeared to give Britain a better chance of acquiring the Wrights' plane, but the British authorities were not so quick to react. Capper's response to his letter from the Wrights was utterly correct, if considered rather than enthusiastic. He sent it to his superior officer confirming the brothers' probity, and requesting that he be allowed to tell them that their offer would receive consideration from His Majesty's Government. In the event, the War Office wrote directly to the Wrights asking them for a definite offer. Even so, Capper kept open his own channel of communication with the Wrights by apologising for his delay in replying while at the same time congratulating them on their achievement, and confirming that any negotiations were in his Government's hands.

On 1 March 1905 the Wrights responded positively by proposing to send a single aeroplane capable of carrying two men and supplies for a flight of not less than fifty miles, for a price calculated at the rate of £500 for each mile covered.

This amounted to a figure of £25,000, which was a considerable but by no means outrageous figure for such advanced technology. In 1903, for instance, Samuel Cody had asked twice this figure from the Royal Navy for his kiting patent, which was far less significant from both a strategic and engineering point of view.

Their proposal was passed on to the Royal Engineer Committee at the War Office responsible for new inventions. Predictably, the price was considered much too high, although millions of pounds were being allocated for dreadnought battleships and being spent by the White Star Line on luxury liners like the *Olympic* and *Titanic*. Nevertheless it recommended that the Wrights be asked to carry out flying trials in the presence of the British Military Attaché in Washington. The Attaché at that time was Colonel Hubert Foster who was away in Mexico on a visit but, in spite of this, the War Office made no attempt to hurry things along and five months elapsed before the Wrights received any further communication. In the meantime they had conducted a number of private flying tests at Huffman Prairie and after experiencing major difficulties, they significantly improved their plane's performance. Eventually tiring of the disappointing responses, they dispatched a second group of letters, one to their own Secretary of War, another to Captain Ferdinand Ferber of the French army and a third to the British War Office.

Their approach to the American authorities was again unsuccessful. In France Captain Ferber offered far less than the Wrights had proposed and when the British Attaché, Colonel Foster, finally replied he asked to be shown a flight as soon as possible. Wilbur responded immediately by offering signed statements by witnesses who could confirm their most recent flights at Huffman Prairie; he refused, however, to show Foster their machine until they were assured that the terms of the sale would be satisfactory.

In a subsequent exchange of letters neither Colonel Foster nor the Wrights appeared prepared to give way. The Wrights believed that by this time any public flight was bound to attract publicity and would inevitably result in a most detailed observation of their machine, while Colonel Foster, in his letter to them of 7 December, seemed strangely content to accept 'that there is thus a deadlock'.[10] Foster's impending retirement might have influenced him, for he also appeared unprepared to visit Dayton to talk directly with the Wrights, contenting himself with a written report to the War Office on 28 November 1905.

Elsewhere in Britain there was far greater enthusiasm for the Wrights' achievements and their plane. On 17 November Orville sent one of his regular letters to Patrick Alexander setting out the extent of their 1905 flights, and at a subsequent meeting of the Aeronautical Society Alexander read out Orville's letter, which included his claim that the plane remained in flight for more than half an hour. Orville's claim, together with Major Baden-Powell's heartfelt congratulations upon it, appeared in the Aeronautical Journal of January 1906.

In contrast, a full year after the Wrights first wrote to Colonel Capper, the British War Office decided to refer the whole question back to the Royal Engineers Invention Committee. In its turn the Committee referred it to Colonel Capper, their expert in aerial navigation. The advice he gave them was remarkable: although he showed he was in no doubt the Wrights had done what they claimed, he still queried their aeroplane.

I cannot think that a machine so limited in capacity can have good practical value except as leading to the building of better ones and therefore the purchase of a single one without power to construct more on similar lines, would be of no great assistance to us.[11]

Although he did not actually reject a fixed-price contract for a single aircraft, he prejudged the result by concluding that 'I am inclined to think that the sum asked will be too great for acceptance'. This was followed by his conviction 'that we must do our utmost to build successful machines ourselves and learn their use'.[12] The only place in Britain where such machines could be built at this time was at Farnborough's Balloon Factory

Since the time of the Wrights' first letter in January 1905 Capper's attitude to taking their plane had undoubtedly become more negative. During the intervening period Cody had produced his glider and was working on his powered kite,[13] while Capper had been aware of John Dunne for some time before he was able to recruit him – clandestinely at first – and then in an official capacity on 7 June 1906. Capper's advice, together with the Wrights' refusal to arrange a demonstration flight, enabled the War Office to reject the Wrights' offer on the grounds of only providing 'hearsay evidence'. The Master General of the Ordnance, Sir James Wolfe Murray, Capper's ultimate superior, spelt out the decision. 'We should inform Messrs Wright that their terms do not recommend themselves to us and we should pursue our own investigations.'[14] On 8 February 1906 a letter was despatched to them to this effect.

The Wrights were not to be deterred. While they were understandably disappointed, they remained convinced that they possessed a weapon of such military potential that other governments would be bound to deal with them, whereupon the British would conceivably change their minds. Following further unsuccessful negotiations with the French during April 1906, they requested a formal interview with President Theodore Roosevelt and sent yet another letter to the British War Office.

By May Capper had the dual responsibilities as Superintendent of the Balloon Factory and Commandant of the Balloon School: not only had he to be consulted about the new application, but he was also expected to take part in any negotiations relating to it. Capper's response was similar to his earlier one, namely to recommend asking the Wrights for their price (which he considered too high) and their plane's date of delivery. Britain's War Department was notoriously cautious in financial matters, and this was bound to cause problems. He also pointed out that the Balloon Factory would shortly be able to produce a plane superior to that designed by the Wrights.

As before, it was the British Military Attaché in Washington who contacted them. The newly appointed Attaché was Colonel Albert Edward Wilfred Gleichen, godson of Edward VII and a confident soldier of a different stamp from Colonel Foster. Gleichen wasted no time and he approached the Wrights in

July 1906, who informed him they could supply an aircraft capable of flying for 100 miles by May 1907, at a cost of £20,000. Following his subsequent meeting with the Wrights at Dayton during early August Colonel Gleichen's report reached the War Office on 18 September 1906 and was firmly in their favour. He said they were asking the sum of $100,000 for the flyer, training a British operator and granting full rights to manufacture under patents. Listing their plane's military capabilities, he made two most favourable points, namely that the Wrights were five years ahead of anyone else and that (contrary to the general belief otherwise) after a few trials anyone would be able to pilot their plane.[15] He concluded that the aeroplane was, in his opinion, a device 'of almost incalculable military importance'.

A copy of Gleichen's report was immediately sent to Colonel Capper asking him for any remarks he might wish to add before it was submitted for a decision. Capper stood by his first minute which questioned whether it was worth paying so much for the plane's advantages, and again urged his superiors to reject the Wrights' proposals so that he could concentrate on Dunne's aerial experiments. On 25 October Capper's superior, Colonel Ruck, discussed things further with him and, as a result, wrote to the Master General of the Ordnance recommending no further action at this stage on the Wrights' latest proposal. He raised the prospect of purchasing the 'plane package' at a much reduced price before long, and mentioned that in the meantime 'we are making experiments at the Balloon Factory which seem likely to lead us in the same direction as Messrs Wrights' developments as far as we know them'.[16] As instructed, on 31 December 1906 Colonel Gleichen wrote officially to the Wrights telling them that the Army Council had decided that 'especially in view of the great cost it would not be advisable to purchase your inventions'.[17]

Even now the Wrights, who had previously shown such perseverance with their aeroplane researches, were far from giving up: if Governments were unwilling to buy their planes they would sell them to interested buyers from across the world. To this end they had entered into negotiations with a wealthy New York businessman, Charles Ranlett Flint, to sell their aeroplane and all its secrets and also made representations to Germany, France and certain Latin American countries. Approaches were also made to two eminent politicians in Britain, Richard Haldane, Secretary of State for War, and Lord Tweedmouth, First Lord of the Admiralty. Flint's representative in Britain was Lady Jane Taylor with impressive connections – her brothers were the Marquis of Tweedale and Sir John Haig, and her other relations included the Duke of Wellington, Sir Robert Peel and the Earl of Dalhousie.

Nevertheless Lady Jane found Haldane a hard bargainer who requested plans and specifications both for himself and officers of the Aeronautical Society, together with a demonstration of the plane in a public competition. Lady Jane had higher hopes from Lord Tweedmouth, who promised to bring up the question before the Board of Admiralty during March 1907. However, by 7 March 1907 she was compelled to tell Flint that both Haldane and Tweedmouth – who were friends – had refused to entertain his proposition. Meanwhile, unbeknown to Lady Jane, within the Balloon Factory John Dunne was engaged in constructing a full-size glider capable of carrying a man, which was due for a secret trial at Blair Atholl in the Scottish Highlands. Since Haldane had a deep interest in this project it was no wonder that Lady Jane's proposals did not impress him favourably.

In the event, the attempts made to fly at Blair Atholl from July to October 1907 proved notably unsuccessful and certainly did not equal the feats of the Wright brothers. The Dunne glider – piloted by Capper himself – travelled along tracks down a hill until it drifted sideways into a dry-stone wall: it was extensively damaged and Capper suffered a facial injury. Among the spectators was a highly critical Richard Haldane.

The failure to buy the Wrights' aeroplane, together with the subsequent failure of the Dunne plane, undoubtedly delayed Britain's progress towards manned flight and led to the country being overtaken by France, where Europe's first aero engines were also being built. In 1906, Alberto Santos-Dumont (b. 1877), a Brazilian living in Paris, had succeeded in flying a short distance, while on 13 January 1908 the Anglo-French air pioneer Henry Farman would make the first circular aeroplane flight in Europe – even if it still lacked the Wrights' manoeuvrability.

Britain however was not without some success, limited as it was. During 1907 the Balloon Factory under Capper (with invaluable help from Samuel Cody) launched the first British airship, proudly called *Nulli Secundus*. It was unquestionably small compared with the German Zeppelins, but nevertheless it succeeded in flying from Farnborough to London – although it was badly damaged there and never flew again. Plans were made to launch a second airship during 1908 and to conduct further aeroplane trials at Blair Atholl with Dunne's plane.

Alberto Santos-Dumont, who in 1906 was the first to fly in Europe. (*Author's Collection*)

Henry Farman, who made the first circular flight outside America. (*Author's Collection*)

The airship *Nulli Secundus* which delayed Cody's work on his aeroplane. (*Jean Roberts*)

Restricted funding caused the aeroplane being constructed at Farnborough by Samuel Cody to be delayed: although largely finished it awaited an engine.

Capper, however, still harboured hopes for a British breakthrough, in particular with Dunne's revolutionary plane, and this was the reason he helped deflect the Wrights' final attempt to sell their plane to the British government. A letter from Orville to the British War Office, dated 10 April 1908, offered to undertake the manufacture in Britain of one or more of the Wrights' latest machines, under contract or on payment of suitable royalties. Capper appeared determined to delay such a step until after the Dunne aircraft had been tested again at Blair Atholl. While he recommended the Wrights should be asked to fix a price for an aircraft and to instruct two officers in flying it, he made this conditional upon an additional specification that he had thought up, namely a requirement that the aeroplane would not deteriorate after remaining out in the open in all ordinary weather for a calendar month. He later added flight tests (covering six pages of foolscap) including the need for the machine to rise from the ground under its own power, when it was generally known that the Wrights routinely used a catapult device to thrust their machine into the air.

When the letter from the War Office arrived at Dayton specifying the tests required, the brothers were away but their father, Bishop Milton Wright, having read it had no doubt about their arduous nature. He passed it for Wilbur to see, remarking that 'they only ask that an applicant should jump over the moon! Through a hoop!! Six times!!!'[18] As a result Britain was denied the Wrights' aeroplane when in France, for instance, in contrast to John Dunne's stuttering attempts and Cody's lack of an engine, significant advances were occurring, including the first circular flight.

The main British hopes still rested on the second attempt by Dunne's aircraft to fly at Blair Atholl during trials lasting from 2 September to 11 December 1908. These proved far different from the Wrights' earlier ones at Kitty Hawk. The time allocated would possibly have been sufficient if the gliding tests had already been completed but to attempt both gliding and powered tests proved decidedly optimistic, exacerbated still further by the damaged condition in which the aircraft arrived in the north. In addition its ENV engine which, unlike the Wrights' power unit, had not been specifically designed for the plane, was always underpowered. Neither did Dunne prove a good leader: while undoubtedly understanding the principles of heavier-than-air flight, he was mechanically clumsy, entirely lacking a sense of humour, afflicted with frail health and, according to Farnborough author Percy Walker, experienced trouble distinguishing between west and east.

To Dunne's advantage, one of his two glider pilots, Lieutenant Lancelot Gibbs, proved outstanding – he was a natural pilot 'who should have been born with wings'[19] and who later became an international test pilot. Dunne also received powerful support from Capper's second-in-command, Captain Alan Carden, who accepted responsibility for the engine and propeller systems and also took over the onerous task of writing a detailed daily account of their progress, upon which Colonel Capper insisted.

The site selected for the trials added to the difficulties. While away from prying eyes, unlike Kitty Hawk, Blair Atholl had a restricted plain with ground covered with heather and punctuated by rabbit holes. In addition it was also known for its uneven winds, frequent rain and early winters. The end result was that, despite the team's best efforts, after being sent down a slope Gibbs' longest run with the unpowered glider was 143 yards, while the powered aeroplane achieved just three small 'hops', the last of which was 40 yards, before everything had to be suspended as a result of the deteriorating weather.

Ironically, the Balloon Factory's greatest success was achieved by its comparatively unsung second designer, Samuel Cody. Having installed its French Antoinette engine six weeks after receiving it, in mid-October 1908, at Farnborough he became the first man to fly in Britain, making two level flights, the first of 75 yards and the main one of 440 yards. It ended with him crashing and breaking a wing to avoid a copse of trees positioned along his flight path.

Samuel Cody's historic first flight. (*The Aldershot Military Museum*)

Here Capper's influence once more became evident, if in a negative sense. Although his factory had succeeded in its goal of manned flight, he was most disappointed that it was Cody and not Dunne, his favoured designer, who had achieved it. Capper gently broke the news to Dunne, explaining that Cody's machine had flown nicely 'but he tried to turn too sharply and too close to the ground, with the usual result, wing dipped, touched the ground and the whole concern turned round and fell on its end'.[20] More seriously, his sparing report to his superior officer of Cody's achievement made it difficult to understand that he had, in fact, flown at all, although he did go so far as to say that 'I do not propose to abandon trials with this machine. It appears that it is probably somewhat better than the Farman-Delagrange type'.[21]

Capper's responsibility for Britain's disappointing progress in aviation during 1903–8 is unquestionable. His personal ambition and xenophobic pride made him determined not to buy the Wrights' technology. In fairness, his attitude was not limited to Britain, even if the country arguably had most to lose by falling behind. But Capper compounded matters by being unduly influenced by John Dunne's high-ranking father into seriously over-estimating his son's capability while underrating and misjudging the flamboyant American outsider Samuel Cody, whose natural genius and drive well deserved supporting.

In this Capper was a man of his age who exhibited some of the attitudes prevalent in Edwardian Britain. While undoubtedly brave and with a rooted sense of national superiority, he was not fully at ease with the accelerating technological changes, nor willing to acknowledge the extent of the progress being made by other countries, particularly America and the new German Empire.

Dunne's safety biplane circa 1911. (*Author's Collection*)

His neutral reporting of Cody's amazing first flight to his superior, Colonel R.M. Ruck, proved a dangerous ploy. After ensuring the Wrights' plane was rejected, the failure of the factory's aircraft trials at Blair Atholl exposed him to powerful criticism from Richard Haldane and others about Britain's limited achievements compared with other countries. The Government's concerns about this led to a request from Prime Minister Herbert Asquith for the convening on 23 October 1908 of a powerful sub-committee of the Committee of Imperial Defence under Lord Esher, to examine the whole future of British military aviation and the disappointing progress made so far.

Whether this would reach the decisions needed to regain the ground already lost remained to be seen.

Chapter 7

Thumbs Down for the Aeroplane

Apart from Samuel Cody's achievement in Britain on 16 October, undoubtedly the most momentous event for European aviation during 1908 was the decision by the Wright brothers to resume their public flight trials. Orville undertook to demonstrate their plane (now with two upright seats) during the autumn before a panel of American army officers at Fort Myer, Virginia, while Wilbur was to give a flying display at Auvours, near Paris, during August. In both cases the results were remarkable. Air historian Charles Gibbs-Smith has described Wilbur's performance at Auvours between 8–13 August in rapturous fashion. 'It was not just the achievement of duration and height records that made such an impression; it was the flying of an aeroplane as it should be flown, smoothly, expertly and with complete mastery of manoeuvre; climbing, banking, turning – with rapid and graceful circuits and figures of eight – and even glides with the engine off, displayed both an aircraft and a flying technique undreamt of in Europe.'[1]

On 3 September Orville began his first flight at Fort Myer. He, too, astounded those watching, breaking all previous records by staying in the air for more than an hour, flying at over 40mph and coming to earth as lightly as a feather.[2] His tragic crash on 17 September, when something in the aircraft broke, causing him to be badly injured and his passenger, Lieutenant Selfridge, killed, underlined the dangers of early flight, but in no way diminished the Wrights' achievements. It did, however, delay acceptance of the US Army's first aeroplane until August 1909.

Wilbur and Orville's startling performances confirmed the Wrights' technology was essential for further progress. From 1905 both France and Britain had already baulked at the cost of buying a Wright aircraft, although the true reason was the conviction that they could quickly equal and even surpass the Wrights' achievements. This seemed reasonable enough in the case of France where remarkable progress had already been made, particularly in engine technology. Engineer Leon Levasseur, for instance, had built an eight-cylinder Antoinette engine developing 24hp then 50hp for its 110lbs weight, compared with the Wrights' four-cylinder engine producing 12hp then 30hp for 80lbs weight. The outstanding need for French aviation was to learn the secrets about the controls the Wrights used, some of which were bound to have become apparent during the 1908 public trials in the following year Santos-Dumont (the first to fly in 1906) had constructed a successful small monoplane which he called 'Demoiselle'.

In contrast, Britain was yet to produce a successful aero engine while at the end of Samuel Cody's first flight, which at one bound promised to catch up with aircraft construction, he had crashed his plane – with its many Wright features – requiring it to undergo prolonged repairs and significant modifications. In spite of demonstrating levels of manoeuvrability not yet possessed by the French planes, Cody had far to go before he could raise his plane's performance up to that achieved by the Wrights. Nor, because of Colonel Capper, had the flight been fully appreciated.

With Cody's ill-publicised success and the failure of Dunne's aircraft trials at Blair Atholl, it was only to be expected that Cody and Dunne, together with their chief, Colonel Capper, should come under the scrutiny of the sub-committee of the Imperial Defence Committee whose brief was to examine the significance of aerial navigation for the nation's defences. Its findings, however, were to prove far less predictable, although due to the dynamic nature of the aerial developments elsewhere, its appointed members included leading politicians and senior officers from the two services.

Under the chairmanship of elder statesman Lord Esher, David Lloyd George, the Chancellor of the Exchequer, Richard Haldane, the current Secretary of State for War, and Reginald McKenna, the recently appointed First Lord of the Admiralty, made up its civilian members, while from the services there was General Sir William Nicolson, the Chief of the Imperial General Staff, with two other generals, General Sir Charles Hadden, Master-General of the Ordnance and General Ewart, the Director of Military Operations, representing the army, while the Navy's appointee was Captain Reginald Bacon acting on behalf of Admiral Sir John Fisher, the powerful First Sea Lord. (Another sailor, Rear-Admiral Sir Charles Ottley, was secretary, with a Royal Marine Officer, Captain Maurice Hankey, as assistant secretary.) With such powerful and confident individuals, positive recommendations were to be expected – and clashes of personality likely.

The Committee's appointed task was to report on the following:

(1) The dangers to which Britain would be exposed on sea or on land by any developments in aerial navigation that were reasonably probable in the near future.
(2) The naval or military advantages that Britain might expect to derive from the use of airships or aeroplanes.
(3) The amount that should be allotted to expenditure on aerial experiments and the department to which it should be allocated.

Four meetings were held: on the first day the committee discussed matters among themselves; throughout the second they interviewed two aviation experts, the Hon. C.S. Rolls and Major Baden-Powell; the third was spent questioning Colonel Capper, whose interview was followed by a lengthy discussion, and during the fourth, Sir Hiram Maxim, the ageing and unorthodox aviation authority, was interviewed both by the Chairman, Lord Esher, and Richard Haldane. Following this the Committee decided upon their final report, the general outline of which had already been drafted.

The rambling nature of the Committee's discussions are apparent from the length of its report, amounting to around 80,000 words. Both its meetings and recommendations have been examined in detail by two leading aviation historians, Farnborough authority Percy Walker and American historian Alfred Gollin. Neither approved of its findings and recommendations, although Walker was understandably the more angry about the decisions affecting his beloved Farnborough. Walker stated roundly that the report of the sub-committee was 'open to much adverse criticism',[3] and Alfred Gollin was even more condemnatory, referring to 'the failure of this sub-committee'. Gollin concluded that this was largely due to the fact that only two of its members 'knew exactly what they wanted to obtain as a result of its deliberations and conclusions'.[4] To Gollin these were Sir William Nicholson, the Chief of the Imperial General Staff, and Admiral Sir John Fisher, the First Sea Lord (who did not attend).

While it was fully understandable that the senior service chiefs should predominate, this became all the more serious when neither of these highly distinguished and powerful men had any belief in the aeroplane. Sir William Nicolson appeared to be against all forms of aeronautical vehicles, whether kites, observation balloons, dirigible airships or aeroplanes. His arguments were consistently negative, if not fatuous, but this did not stop him pursuing them with undiminished vigour. Nicolson believed, for instance, that while travelling in the air at 40mph one would be unable to see anything clearly. Although the committee's first expert witness, Charles Rolls, who had flown in different aerial vehicles at such a speed, utterly disagreed with him, this seemed to have such little effect that after giving his evidence to the Committee, Rolls felt compelled to write to its Chairman 'to emphasise the ability to recognise features on the ground when travelling by balloon at 50 miles an hour'.[5]

The Hon. Charles Rolls at the controls of his Wright aircraft circa 1910. (*Author's Collection*)

Nicolson's disdain for flight induced him to adopt a rough stance when questioning the Committee's expert witnesses and to dismiss the majority of their arguments. In fact, he failed to browbeat Rolls, who emphasised that the aeroplane would be the master of the airship and in the future 'England will cease to be an island for it makes not the slightest difference to these machines whether it happens to be water underneath or land underneath'.[6]

The second expert witness called on 8 December 1908 was Major B.P.S. Baden-Powell, President of the Aeronautical Society, who also came down firmly in favour of the future utility of the aeroplane compared with the airship. He believed the aeroplane to have far more scope for improvement and if, for instance, a plane could rise to a height of 10,000 feet 'I should say myself that it was infinitely preferable in every way to a dirigible balloon'.[7]

If witnesses like Charles Rolls, with his broad experience of aviation, and Baden-Powell, also with considerable experience and speaking from his position as Chairman of the Aeronautical Society, had the utmost difficulty in countering the bombastic – and amazingly ignorant – General Nicolson, it was bound to be far more difficult for Colonel John Capper. As a career officer whose prospects for future promotion were certain to be affected by his achievements at the Balloon Factory, he was more vulnerable to hostile questioning from his Chief of the General Staff. In fact, under such verbal assault he showed himself well below his best, blaming the French Antoinette engine for the failure of the Balloon Factory's second airship although it had many other serious faults. When questioned about Dunne's aeroplane, Capper talked of its stability – 'it is one which is very difficult to upset' – before placing the blame for its disappointing trials on French Buchet engines which gave insufficient power to get off the ground.

With Cody, however, he showed himself manifestly unfair, even when under the more emollient questioning of Lord Esher rather than General Nicolson.

Esher: What is the exact position of Cody?
Capper: Cody is Chief Kite Instructor to the British Army; but he is also, under his contract, bound to assist in every possible way to get success in flight, and when he is not engaged in instructing or making kites he is working on an aeroplane.[8]

Capper's response made no mention of Cody's first sustained flight in Britain. As a result the Committee had scant appreciation of the Balloon Factory's most creditable achievements (despite its strictly limited funding) and – criminally – no knowledge of Cody's triumphant first flight.

The Committee's official conclusions about Farnborough made this all too apparent.

The two dirigibles built hitherto have been of small dimensions and low power, and are only useful for instructional and experimental purposes. Two aeroplanes have been constructed, one at Aldershot under the superintendence of Mr Cody and the other in Scotland by Lieutenant [J.W.] Dunne

RE; for the latter great stability is claimed, and in this respect it is stated that an improvement over the machines constructed on the continent has been effected. At present the machine has no practical value.[9]

That the arch-sceptic General Nicolson was to prove so influential with the committee was due not only to his exalted rank and powerful personality, but also because other members were willing to step aside for him.

Such was the case with the two army members. Although General Sir Charles Hadden was considered the recognised authority on activities at Farnborough, he soon revealed his ignorance in this regard and as a result generally came to echo General Nicolson in opposing aerial activity. As Director of Military Operations, General John Spencer Ewart was professionally directly responsible to General Nicolson and although he did not enthusiastically support Nicolson's views, he was understandably careful not to reveal any disagreement between them.

For different reasons other members of the Committee also failed to oppose General Nicolson. David Lloyd George was absent from many of its deliberations and was therefore in no position to do so, while Lord Esher always prided himself on his detachment, and in this instance set himself to obtain the uninhibited views of the army and navy representatives, however absurd they might be.

Significantly, Richard Haldane, the country's outstanding Secretary of State for War, had other pressing interests. He had already decided to replace the Balloon Factory's practical empiricists with a truly scientific body modelled on the government-funded Institute of Physics in Berlin, and to bring it under the control of an engineer and scientist rather than a serving officer. His other aim was to create an Advisory Committee for Aeronautics, composed of eminent scientists and representatives from the two services, which would initially consider the principles of flight: for only when these were properly understood he believed could the needs of the army and navy for flying machines be met. Haldane was therefore content to allow Nicolson full rein to criticise the Balloon Factory's work since he had a better replacement in view which Nicolson could make it easier for him to achieve.

The other member of the Committee with a precise agenda was naval Captain Reginald Bacon, who faithfully acted as Admiral 'Jackie' Fisher's mouthpiece in seeking approval for the large dirigible that his chief believed the navy required. Captain Bacon also took pains not to offend General Nicolson, possibly to prevent an inter-service dispute. Despite the intervention of Winston Churchill (already a devotee of airpower) that led to a last-minute decision to hear Hiram Maxim, the Committee did not change its recommendations. Maxim was an outrageous egotist and by this time he was unquestionably an old man, yet, as Churchill well knew, Maxim firmly believed in the future of aeroplanes and predicted that they would fly at least a mile above the earth where the air, if thinner, was more static.

However, to most of the committee's members Maxim's views appeared so extreme that, notwithstanding his whole-hearted support for aeroplanes the negative views of General Nicolson continued to hold sway. For these reasons the conclusions reached by the Committee turned out to be a reflection of General Nicolson's negative views on airpower, acknowledging only the needs of the navy.

Airships and aeroplanes were considered separately. Although its members were confident that the former did not present a serious danger at this time, they decided that an airship would be important to the navy for scouting and possibly for destructive purposes, while other dirigibles would be useful from a military point of view. The Committee therefore recommended a paltry sum of £35,000 to be included in the naval estimates for a rigid airship and £10,000 to be included in the army estimates for navigable balloons of a non-rigid type and for the purchase of airships. (How many they expected to obtain with such a sum was not recorded.)

In the case of aeroplanes, the Committee recommended that the experiments carried out with them at the military ballooning establishment should be discontinued, although advantage should be taken of private enterprise, i.e. a token Wright aeroplane which Charles Rolls intended to purchase, the details of which he undertook to pass on to the government.

That the Committee's eminent members could reach such a decision at this time beggars belief, but the continuing naiveté shown towards airpower in Britain was revealed by the support given to its decisions at the highest levels. The sub-committee's report was duly confirmed by the Committee on Imperial Defence, with the Prime Minister remarking 'that the report of the Sub-Committee discouraged military experiments with aeroplanes, and he considered that the recommendation that they be discontinued was a good one'.[10]

Quite apart from its obscurantist attitude to aeroplanes the Imperial Defence Committee's decision to allocate just £45,000 towards aerial vehicles for the two forces was totally unrealistic when the French were not only producing leading aviators such as Santos-Dumont, Leon Delagrange, Louis Blériot, Henry Farman and Louis Paulhan but also developing a range of excellent aircraft engines, including their famed rotaries, and when the German army was subsidising a civilian airship line.

The Committee's unjustifiable animosity towards aeroplanes was soon exposed as unjustified when Louis Blériot flew across the Channel on Sunday, 25 July 1909, while other French aircraft regularly established new distance and height records. Nonetheless, during 1909 the British defence debates were still dominated by heated exchanges in Parliament over the requirement for eight more dreadnought battleships to help maintain Britain's naval supremacy in the face of German warship production. In comparison, the development of airpower (and even submarines) represented an unwelcome strategic and financial liability.

Such an attitude was demonstrated by the British General Staff in their memorandum of 11 July 1910 upon an International Conference on Aerial Navigation held in Paris earlier in the year. This proposed that peaceful aerial navigation above foreign countries should in principle be declared free. However, the British General Staff rightly 'argued that as an absolute minimum we should insist upon

The French flyer Louis Paulhan in a Voisin aircraft circa 1908. (*Author's Collection*)

our right in the interests of national defence, to forbid aerial navigation by foreign airships over certain zones of reasonable extent ...'.[11] They went on,

> It may no doubt be argued that we cannot arrest or retard the perhaps unwelcome progress of aerial navigation by standing out of an agreement which may commend itself to a majority of other European Powers and which, if the smaller States of Northern Europe are parties to it, must in any case operate to our disadvantage ... It must be borne in mind that the distinction made between military and private airships and aeroplanes is a distinction without a difference ... German writers made no secret of the hope that the command of the air which they are striving to obtain will also give them the command of the sea.[12]

However sound this caution towards unrestricted use of airspace, the General Staff did not say how Britain could oppose hostile airships, with the navy expected to have just one of its own by the autumn of 1911, and with no aeroplanes as yet and no sense of urgency in obtaining them.

Subsequently, the 1908–9 sub-committee's chairman, Lord Esher, was to show much courage in recognising its mistaken conclusions. In his note to the Committee of Imperial Defence in 1910 he suggested that 'thirty or forty of these machines (aeroplanes) should be purchased without delay for the use of the Army, both regular and territorial, in Great Britain and for the Army overseas', he also concluded that the aeroplane was superior to rigid and non-rigid airships.[13] Regrettably, he lacked support. Richard Haldane, for instance, was far less convinced about the immediate need for aircraft. His proposed Advisory Committee for Aeronautics, which contained the highest scientific talent, was never intended to be responsible for commissioning or constructing aerial vehicles. Its role was to analyse the scientific and technical problems being encountered, which would be passed over to a new department of the National Physical Laboratory committed to carrying out scientific tests and aeronautical experiments. As late as 1911 he was still telling the Parliamentary Aerial Defence Committee that (with aerial science relating to aeroplanes) it was desirable to move cautiously and not commit themselves to an idea that might be obsolete in a few months.[14]

Haldane's other major initiative towards air, which he carried out with notable speed, was to re-organise the army's Balloon Factory by removing Dunne and Cody and in 1909 replacing Colonel Capper with Mervyn O'Gorman, a successful consulting engineer recommended by the distinguished scientist Lord Raleigh. O'Gorman, who was to report directly to the War Office, also enjoyed the support of Haldane's Advisory Committee on Aeronautics. To his credit O'Gorman moved swiftly to redress the sub-committee's bias against aircraft, for amongst his first initiatives was the recruitment of the promising engineer F.M. Green and the young pioneering aviator Geoffrey de Havilland, who had already designed and built an aeroplane which, on his appointment, the factory agreed to purchase. A decision was also taken to purchase the Short-built Wright aeroplane, the property of Charles Rolls. O'Gorman specifically warned de Havilland that the War Office officials were strongly in favour of airships,

Mervyn O'Gorman, Brigadier General Sir David Henderson and E.T. Busk with King George V and Queen Mary at the Royal Aircraft Factory Farnborough, inspecting RE1. (*Royal Aeronautical Society [National Aerospace Library]*)

but in taking on both him and his co-designer, Frank Hearle, O'Gorman had decisively moved the Factory into aeroplanes.[15]

Haldane agreed to it being renamed 'The Royal Aircraft Factory' where new aircraft could be designed by the Government, although for the most part it was expected that the Factory would improve existing prototypes submitted to it that could subsequently be farmed out for construction by private manufacturers.

Because of Haldane's studiously unhurried approach and the heavy financial demands of the naval building programme, together with Lloyd George's social reforms, including old age pensions and compulsory health insurance, money for aerial projects continued to be heavily restricted. Many officials in the War Office still wished 'air power would go away so that wars could be fought as they always had been',[16] and it was little wonder that both France and Germany were vastly outspending His Majesty's Government.

Much therefore would depend on committed individuals who were unwilling to countenance their country being placed at a serious disadvantage with more air-minded opponents in a future war, and who were determined to raise the national awareness towards aeroplanes, and to demand support for British military aviation and the country's embryonic aircraft industry. They would come from the Press, including journalists in aerial publications, from enthusiasts who took part in or attended the air races and air shows, from specific pressure groups and dedicated MPs, from engineers and designers who became aspiring aeroplane and aero engine builders, from entrepreneurs committed to the new industry, from military flyers whose passion was 'not sport but patriotism', from other servicemen whose military careers came to depend on the new arm of warfare and from young men, both civilians and members of the armed forces, who were eager to compete with would-be rivals in disputing the untrammelled vastness of the skies.

It would take remarkable efforts from them to help persuade a sceptical populace and a generally reluctant and complacent political establishment into accepting the financial and manpower commitments required to create air forces, without which the outcome of the First World War would have been so different.

Chapter 8

Challenging the Doubters

With the advent of popular journalism at the beginning of the twentieth century, the British Press took an increasingly keen interest in the startling developments of manned flight, in marked contrast with the apparent disinterest of the British government. The Press's most prominent representative at this time was Alfred Harmsworth, First Baron and Viscount Northcliffe who, in 1910, was forty-five years of age and at the height of his mental powers. Never unduly modest, it was rumoured that he liked to use the initial N to indicate his position as the Napoleon of Fleet Street but, whatever the validity of such comparisons with the great Corsican, Northcliffe had unquestionably come a long way since, at nineteen, he edited the magazine *Youth* for £2 a week and at the age of twenty-five, after saving £1,000, he launched the pictorial magazine *Comic Cuts*, aimed at adults unaccustomed to reading.

Together with his brother Harold, Northcliffe built up the Amalgamated Press Company until, six years after starting *Comic Cuts* he was able to launch *The Daily Mail*, his paper for 'busy men in a hurry'. Aimed at the lower-middle classes, the first issue sold an amazing 397,213 copies with its daily sales peaking in 1890 at 989,255 and never falling below 713,000 before the Great War, thus providing him with a massive popular platform from which to express his opinions. In 1903 he added a women's paper called *The Daily Mirror*, created by female staff which, after an initial failure, following a re-launch in 1904 recovered its sales, and thus broadened his readership. In 1905, Northcliffe went on to realise his greatest ambition by buying *The Times*, Britain's traditional mouthpiece, for £320,000 which he promised to keep independent; this did not prove difficult since its then editor, Geoffrey Dawson, agreed with his chief on most major issues.

Leaving financial matters to his brother Harold, Alfred not only took advantage of current technological advances to foster the production and distribution of his papers, but remained a hands-on journalist who believed he could get inside 'both the mind of the common man and the English Middle classes'.[1] Northcliffe's luxuriously appointed office at Carmelite House with its deep carpeting, family photographs, book-lined walls and extravagant vases of flowers, provided the setting for his famed editorial conferences, during which the day's leading news feature was identified and the group approach decided. If he did not like what had been written he would rewrite it himself, for Northcliffe firmly believed he could see further ahead than most, including leading politicians, an ability strongly supported by his private secretary and sometime mistress, Louise Owen. She believed he was an unashamed patriot with 'his love of the British Empire marking the great passion of his life which almost became an obsession',[2] and when he wrote the leading articles for *The Daily Mail* she was certain it was them that gave the paper its dynamic force, that independence and total disregard for the 'feelings of politicians and other prominent people'.[3] Additionally, Northcliffe always believed that Germany was the enemy of the British Empire and subsequently claimed that *The Daily Mail* foretold the war.

Northcliffe's strong interest in air matters had developed from his boyhood passion for bicycles, through automobiles to aerial vehicles, particularly planes with all their exciting possibilities. In February 1909 Northcliffe went to Pau in France (taking with him Arthur Balfour, the leader of the Conservative Party) to watch Wilbur Wright's masterly flying and was excited by what he saw. He was convinced the Wright brothers had a device that would alter the nature of warfare, particularly when improvements in aircraft were developed, and decided to encourage such advances in Britain (notably through his *Daily Mail*) by offering massive prizes in air competitions to help bring the British nation to a state of air-mindedness. In the meantime his other newspapers would help persuade the British War Office to purchase a Wright aeroplane. *The Times*, for instance, argued that 'at this stage of the business we can do nothing useful without well-equipped aeroplanes which will fly with reasonable security and speed. Until we are in possession of the best that has been done we are not in a position to do anything better'.[4]

Northcliffe always believed in contacting the people at the top and not pulling his punches. From Pau he wrote straightaway to the Secretary of State for War,

Lord Northcliffe with Orville Wright. (*Royal Aeronautical Society* [*National Aerospace Library*])

Richard Haldane, drawing attention to the backward nature of the aeroplane that Samuel Cody was in the process of presently restoring at Aldershot,[5] and sent another letter to Lord Esher complaining about the War Office's negligent attitude towards air power. *The Times* of Wednesday, 24 February, took up Northcliffe's attack on Farnborough, exposing the work on aeroplanes and balloons carried on in the 'same broken down establishment and by the same inadequate staff which in addition has to supply ordinary non-dirigible balloons. In such conditions anything that can be called progress is obviously impossible . . . It says much for the zeal with which the work is directed under these distressing conditions that an aeroplane has at last been got to make a few short flights'.

Such letters and leaders were supplemented by a series of articles which appeared in *The Daily Mail* during early March 1909, emphasising the importance of purchasing one of the Wrights' planes and on 6 April *The Times*' leading article ended with a strident cry for action. 'Probably we shall again be told that the Government policy is one of masterly inactivity combined with economy, and that, when we have seen the best that other nations can do we shall be better able to do something for ourselves – it is a beautiful policy for dreamers.'[6]

By May, although *The Daily Mail* approved of Haldane's Advisory Committee for Aeronautics, it was clear that what Northcliffe most wanted was 'for Britain to acquire successful aircraft . . . and so build up at once a military aeronautical organisation based on them'.[7] The country's new found vulnerability was much in Northcliffe's mind. Following Wilbur Wright's earlier demonstrations in France during 1908, Northcliffe suggested he make a cross-Channel flight to help shake the British out of their complacency. When Wilbur hesitated on account of the dangers involved, *The Daily Mail* offered £500 for the first plane to succeed, a figure subsequently raised to £1,000.

By 20 July 1909 this brought three would-be competitors: Hubert Latham, a young French flyer of English descent, the Comte de Lambert, a pupil of Wilbur Wright, and French aeroplane designer, builder and flyer, Louis Blériot. When Blériot succeeded on 25 July 1909 Northcliffe rewarded him with lunch at The Savoy, where he presented him with his cheque for £1,000. The next day Blériot's flight featured in both *The Times*' and *The Daily Mail*'s leading articles. In the latter paper a note was struck expressing Northcliffe's own fears, namely that 'We have to reckon with the fact that a small and inexpensive machine which can readily be multiplied by the hundred has bridged the channel . . . British insularity has vanished.' Thirty-five years later, Harry Harper, *The Daily Mail*'s former air correspondent, still believed Blériot's flight had given the British public a big mental jolt and he still felt 'it was a thousand pities our authorities did not profit sufficiently from the warning'.[8]

In late August 1909 Northcliffe attended the world's first great international flying meeting near Rheims, where he met the British competitor, George Cockburn, who complained that there were not enough flying grounds in England where pilots could learn to fly. Northcliffe wrote to Haldane on the subject, only to receive an urbane answer from one of Haldane's private secretaries to the effect that 'responsible aviators had permission – subject to certain

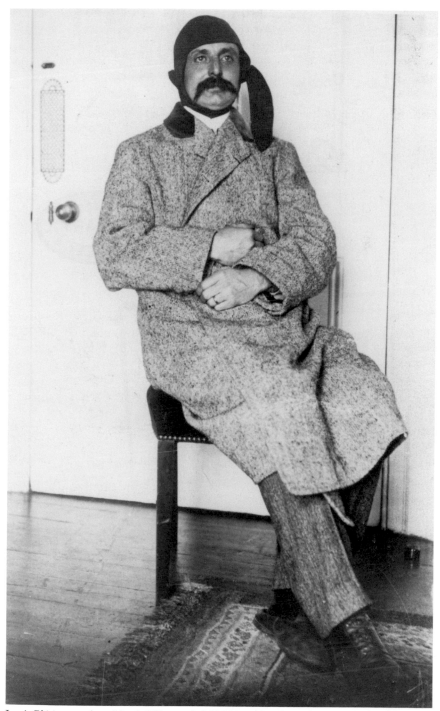

Louis Blériot, to whom Northcliffe awarded £1,000 and lunch at The Savoy for being the first to fly across the English Channel. (*Royal Aeronautical Society* [*National Aerospace Library*])

conditions – to erect sheds and carry out trials in some military commands'.[9] By that autumn Samuel Cody's rebuilt aeroplane was flying satisfactorily, although *The Times* of 30 August rightly reminded its readers that 'we have a good deal of leeway to make up before we can regard ourselves as on an equality with friends or rivals'.[10]

In April of the following year the Englishman Claude Grahame-White and the French flyer Louis Paulhan competed for the £10,000 prize offered earlier by *The Daily Mail* to the first person to fly the 186 miles from London to Manchester and taking no more than two stops for refuelling. As Northcliffe intended, the race became 'a nationwide sensation' but to his huge disappointment it was won by Louis Paulhan, although the second-placed Claude Grahame-White was given a consolation award of a 100-guinea cup. Both flyers used French Farman aircraft in the absence of any British equivalents.

In September 1910 *The Daily Mail* printed a letter from the British aircraft pioneer, George Holt-Thomas, emphasising the importance of aeroplanes to land warfare and three days later he pointed out that at the coming British military manoeuvres there would be just one small dirigible and two borrowed aeroplanes for the purposes of reconnaissance. Public opinion had induced the French War Office 'to purchase a large number of machines ... (and in Britain)

Louis Paulhan, who won the £10,000 prize offered by Northcliffe for being the first to fly from London to Manchester in 1911. (*Author's Collection*)

the nation has waited long enough'. Holt-Thomas also described the performance of the volunteer flyers during these manoeuvres and criticised senior officers for neglecting to give them adequate instructions.

Northcliffe's next prize of £10,000 in what came to be called the Circuit of Great Britain Race was designed to demonstrate the rapidly improving performances of aircraft and help stimulate British constructors. This was scheduled to take place in July 1911 over a circuit of 1,010 miles from Hendon to Edinburgh and back, which had to be covered in a maximum flying time of twenty-four hours. Although, as intended, it attracted a number of British constructors, with the exception of Samuel Cody their planes either failed to start or crashed during the race. Cody came fourth overall in a technically obsolete aeroplane powered by a cumbersome British Green engine. The race was won by the French flyer Lieutenant J. Conneau (Beaumont) who, together with his compatriot Vedrinnes, had the finish to themselves, both flying French monoplanes powered by French Gnome rotary engines. In spite of the poor performance of the home-built machines, the British public's growing enthusiasm for aircraft was shown by the 30,000 spectators at Brooklands, and the similar numbers at intermediate airfields along the route. Northcliffe duly handed over the prize, and he treated the winner and runner up to lunch at *The Savoy* where he once more took the opportunity to call for Britain to take up the opportunities offered by aviation.

In spite of all Northcliffe's and his papers' efforts so far Haldane, the British Secretary of State for War, continued with his strictly measured policy. Apart from setting up an Advisory Committee for Aeronautics and dismissing Colonel Capper and the Farnborough aeroplane designers, no decision was reached on what aircraft should be purchased and no orders were placed. *The Daily Mail* continued to emphasise the need for aeroplanes and personnel for what would conceivably become a national air force, but although an air battalion of the Royal Engineers came into existence on 1 April 1911 it was very small, and from 1 March just four Royal Naval officers were selected for pilot training out of a large number of applicants. Such limited opportunities were quite inadequate for the large number of officers wishing to fly and, writing after the First World War, the official historian Sir Walter Raleigh acknowledged a deliberate dragging of feet here.

> Up to the end of the year 1911 the policy of the Government with regard to all branches of aerial navigation was based on a desire to keep in touch with the movement rather than hasten its development. It was felt that we stood to gain nothing by forcing a means of warfare which tended to reduce the value of our insular position and the protection of our sea-power.[11]

This was something Northcliffe felt must change. In early 1911 Major Bannerman incurred the anger of *The Daily Mail* with his public ignorance of aeroplanes and on 13 February the paper blamed Haldane himself for the lack of necessary action in their development. Haldane responded in a memorandum (published in *The Morning Post* of 25 February 1911) in which he said a sum of £85,000 was included in the estimates for acquiring both aeroplanes and dirigibles, and after impending trials, particular types of aeroplane would be chosen for further development. In reality, the trials were not scheduled to commence until 1 August 1912, which meant that any major order for military aircraft could not be placed until the autumn of that year.

In spite of Haldane's attempts to calm the situation, Northcliffe did his utmost to keep aeroplanes and their growing capabilities in the public eye. In July 1911, prior to his nationwide organisation of the Round Great Britain Air Race, he vigorously supported an offer by Claude Grahame-White to give the first public demonstration of a plane's bombing capability, which was attended by the Prime Minister and other people of influence, and Grahame-White succeeded in dropping 100lb sandbags from a height of 2,000ft on the outline of a battleship whitewashed in the grass, a feat he repeated many times. Predictably *The Daily Mail* declared it a great day for airmanship – the greatest in the history of flying in this country.

Its immediate result was to provoke a deputation to Haldane by sixty members of Parliament concerned about Britain lagging behind other countries in aeronautical developments. On 18 July Colonel Seely, who had become Secretary of State for War, responded with a major policy statement in the House of Commons declaring that during the coming military trials prizes would be given by the War Office for the winning aircraft designs and that from eighty to one hundred officers would be trained as pilots. *The Daily Mail*, however, was not impressed and on the following day its leader dismissed Seely's statement as inadequate as well as reflecting on the timidity of recent War Office policy.

Whatever Northcliffe's attempts, it was the presence of the German gunboat *Panther* during the autumn of 1911 at the port of Agadir in Morocco that finally brought about a powerful response to Britain's deficiencies in airpower. This came with the Prime Minister's request for the aerial sub-committee (of the Committee of Imperial Defence) 'to carry out a wide-ranging enquiry into Aerial Navigation for the country to obtain an efficient Aerial Service'. As a result it was decided to create a separate Flying Corps consisting of a Naval Flying Wing, a Military Wing and a Central Flying School for the training of pilots. The Flying Corps would work as closely as possible with both Haldane's Advisory Committee for Aeronautics and with the Royal Aircraft Factory. This time action was swift and the new service (that was granted the title Royal) became effective through a Royal Warrant of 13 April 1912 with the former Air Battalion of the Royal Engineers also being absorbed into the new organisation.

On 28 February 1912, in a leading article entitled 'A Real Air Service at Last', *The Daily Mail* gave its approval and highlighted its own contributions (which, of course, were predominantly those of its master, Lord Northcliffe).

Thus after several years of effort on its part the importance of the new arm has been recognised by the British military authorities. The great competitions which we have organised have produced their effect ... have opened the eyes of the nation to the promise and potency of the flying machine. The first steps have now been taken; it only remains for the Navy and Army to go firmly forward in the path which Lord Haldane has traced.

Northcliffe's crusading newspaper was right to emphasise its genuine contribution to the creation of the RFC, although in 1911 the navy decided to keep its separate air service and it was not until 1918 that its elements were incorporated into the Royal Air Force (RAF). Problems over supplying the required aircraft also increased when the military trials of 1912 did not produce the results anticipated. Despite the success of an inspired Samuel Cody, flying an obsolete airframe assembled in three weeks from the debris of planes that had crashed earlier (into which he inserted a magnificent Austro-Daimler engine) the best English plane was undoubtedly Geoffrey de Havilland's BE2 which was barred from the competition because it had been constructed with the help of funds voted to the Royal Aircraft Factory. By the time very considerable numbers of BE2s reached the RFC, however, their deficiencies in speed and manoeuvrability were already becoming apparent

Despite Northcliffe's undoubted influence and his vigorous lobbying for air, including his offers of massive prizes to encourage British aircraft manufacturers, there were limits to what he could achieve in the face of deliberate governmental obstruction. At the beginning of the war therefore official preparations for the RFC still lagged far behind those made for the air forces of France and Germany. This was particularly the case with aero-engines. Yet without Northcliffe the position could have been far worse. As a patriot and vigorous air enthusiast, he was fully aware of the country's belated preparations for which he held Haldane chiefly responsible, and although he subsequently gained his revenge by helping to drive Haldane out of office in 1916, by then Northcliffe's own dynamo was slowing down through ill health.

*   *   *

While much the loudest, Northcliffe's was by no means the only voice raised in the Press against the lack of support for aviation. During the three years before the war another journalist, Charles G. Grey, ceaselessly attacked the British War Office for its complacency and neglect of developments in the air. Unlike Northcliffe and his mass newspapers, Grey was editor of *The Aeroplane*, a weekly publication whose core readers worked within Britain's air industry and whose primary aims were to help British aeroplane manufacturers not only survive but expand.

Grey operated from an office in Piccadilly from where, seated behind a high-stacked desk, with his hair carefully brushed back and his characteristic monocle in place, he held court. Visitors were genuinely welcome and those interested in the air industry, whether in junior or high positions, were accustomed to drop in on him 'where you were sure of a glass of sherry from Jacksons in the morning or a cup of tea and slice of cake from Fortnums in the afternoon'.[12]

Although Grey had no special gifts in the way of scientific ability or technical achievement, his trenchant writing caused him to become of great concern to

Charles G. Grey, editor of *The Aeroplane*. (*Royal Aeronautical Society [National Aerospace Library]*)

civil servants and industrialists alike. After talking to visitors for much of the day his articles were mostly written after normal working hours, when he also wrote personal letters to a large number of contacts, many of whom acted as his unpaid news correspondents (and) to whom he customarily penned his replies until ten o'clock at night.[13] Grey's chief weapon was the paper's leader, which he subsequently boasted he had written each week throughout his twenty-eight years of editorship, although his reputation rests largely on the period 1911–14.

In the paper's inaugural edition of 8 June 1911, Grey fearlessly set out his stall.

There really is room today for a thoroughly independent weekly paper dealing with aviation in all its phases, a paper which is unconnected with any club or society and so can give vent freely to criticism of the doings of anybody and everybody ... devoted solely to aviation ... of such importance to every man, woman and child in this country.[14]

He went on to point out that the country did not possess a single aeroplane capable of competing with the best machines of other countries and that to have any hope in the future everything had to be done to encourage British constructors with Government contracts. His customary practice of favouring heavy irony, combined with unashamedly strong prejudices, was already becoming evident.

In *The Aeroplane*'s second edition, Grey wrote that it was hardly fair to accuse the War Office (his favourite Aunt Sally) of apathy for 'they have had a phenomenal burst of energy lately. They have set down another machine and got themselves another pilot'.[15] By now his regular subjects for prejudicial treatment included French rotary engines, the Army Aircraft Factory and the Royal Engineers. Grey was convinced that French rotary engines needed far more maintenance than orthodox ones which should, of course, be made in Britain, while he considered the Aircraft Factory, by buying and copying foreign aircraft, used its privileged position unfairly against English manufacturers. He singled out Royal Engineer officers as being 'apt to become self-centred ... and only too often narrow and old fashioned as they get to middle age'.[16] To Grey, of course, their unforgivable crime was to try to prevent the air force from becoming independent of their corps.

In his perceived role as a constructive critic, he was quite prepared to move from expressions of general dissatisfaction at the slow pace of developments to personal allusions. By November 1911[17] he reckoned that the Air Battalion needed at least 300 first-class aeroplanes and officer aviators to fly them, at which time he compared Germany's vote for aerial equipment, that amounted to the equivalent of £1,500,000, with the total resources devoted to the aerial forces of the British Empire of one monoplane and one biplane. Moving to the personal approach he took Defence Secretary Richard Haldane to task for saying that Britain needed an air service for its small army when its air service had to protect 'an extremely rich, an extremely helpless and an extremely thickly populated country'.[18]

In February 1912 Grey appeared relatively satisfied with the sum of £880,000 allocated for a 'compact air force', but he was soon showing displeasure with the clique at the War Office 'for purchasing a few machines to stifle further opinion and [instead of using private manufacturers] trusting to the Aircraft Factory for the bulk of the output'.[19] In April Grey's frustration turned against the British electorate for its relative disinterest. 'The present programme gives the British Empire about one fifth of the aerial force it needs and twice as much as it deserves

– considering the hopeless apathy of the people of this country as a whole where aviation is concerned.'[20]

For Grey, while there might have been explanations for ordinary people not to understand the position, the politicians had no such excuse. 'Viscount Haldane not only does not realise the progress that aviation is making but cares considerably less.'[21] Later in the year Grey acknowledged the new enthusiasm for air demonstrated by the thousands of people who turned out at Hendon and other airports at weekends – whose awakening he attributed in part to his writings in *The Aeroplane* in contrast with Haldane's whole approach, which appeared completely wrong.

> In our aeroplane-making there is too much theory and not enough practice, too much talk and not enough do, too much scientific experiments and not enough aeroplane building, too much of Eiffel and not enough of Cody or rule of thumb school. We have got the capital, the businessmen, the designers, the workmen, the material and the pilots in this country but no one seems to have combined a portion of all six under one roof.[22]

As in the previous year, during December 1912 Grey summarised what he believed was required. More than anything else each firm needed a sufficiency of orders to ensure aeroplane building would be a business proposition and this had to be combined with the necessary spending on infrastructure, 'for along with quantities of aeroplanes new landing grounds and sheds were needed together with some dirigibles'.[23]

As the war clouds gathered, Grey's anger at the continuing slowness of progress in Britain increased.

> We are not the peers of the Great Powers, France, Germany, Austria, Italy and Russia and are somewhat inferior to the Balkan States, Bulgaria and Greece ... the total effective strength of the fighting squadrons after twelve months of strenuous endeavour is thirteen aeroplanes ... Now the country wants planes in a hurry it cannot have them.[24]

By this time the much increased figure of £430,000 which had been allocated for aeronautics in the budget no longer satisfied him and he called for at least a million pounds to provide the 500 planes needed for the Military Wing and 200 or more for the naval stations round the coast.

The new Secretary of State for War, Colonel John Seely, soon became the target for his dissatisfaction and Grey's personal comments grew ever stronger and more virulent. He commenced with the comparatively mild criticism that 'the unfortunate Minister's trouble seems to be that he now covets unqualified praise for his failure to accomplish the task he set himself'[25] but then referred to his massive culpability concerning 'the equipment of the RFC (which) has been so grossly mismanaged by Colonel Seely and his parasites at the Royal Aircraft Factory',[26] until finally Grey could see no redeeming features whatever. 'Discredited as a politician and dishonoured as a gentleman Colonel Seely is now stripped of every shred of respect anyone may ever have had or him.'[27] Grey repeatedly stressed the need to order aeroplanes – and subsequently engines – from British firms where competition for such orders would be beneficial in every way.

When in December 1913 Grey produced his by now traditional summary of the past year it was to be the last occasion before the war. In it he congratulated himself on the extent of his contributions and concluded that, 'Most people will, I think, agree that outspoken unbiased criticism in the Press carried more weight than most other influence. I venture to hope it has helped to shape the course of aviation in this country to some degree.'[28] His semi-judicial tone, however partial he was at reaching it, was rather spoilt in his next issue by personal whimsy. 'There are certain products of nature whose reason for existence is hard to explain, such for instance as wasps, worms, technical journals and government officials.'[29]

Whatever his pet animosities, Grey was always the patriot and before the year was over he came to approve of the BE2 aeroplane built at the Royal Aircraft Factory, while unsurprisingly an aircraft produced privately by Sopwith was greeted with great enthusiasm.

At the opening of 1914 Grey relished what had actually been achieved, namely that 'we are not so far behind as we were and in one or two matters we are ahead of our rivals'.[30] In March he proudly referred to the allocation of £1 million to aviation for which he had long campaigned, and in April Grey congratulated his own newspaper for bringing about the resignation of Seely, who had unquestionably deserved its criticism. 'He prevaricated inconsistently but very regularly as to the state of the RFC. It became necessary to destroy him.'[31] He departs 'unwept, unhonoured and unsung'. The strong implication was that without *The Aeroplane* and its acute editor Seely would still have been pulling the wool over most peoples' eyes.

In August, with war imminent, Grey became more sombre, believing that 'our position should be a good deal better and it is to be hoped that when the war is over someone in authority will have sufficient strength of character to lay the blame where it is deserved', although he could not resist pointing out that 'practically every recommendation made in this paper for the allocation of the Royal Aircraft Factory's designs has been carried out'.[32]

With his pungent, sometimes excessive, language, his special sense of impartiality, strong self-belief and willingness to conduct personal attacks, Charles Grey's was a clearly recognisable voice. However, he could only write so freely because he was the editor of a newspaper (with a small circulation) devoted to the British air industry, even though he claimed to be speaking not just for the industry but for the interests of the nation. Whatever Grey's claims, it was the more powerful lobbying of the Northcliffe Press and the growing likelihood of war that provided the major reasons for greater political support and much increased funding for air power.

In the years immediately before the Great War the aeronautical industry was served by another weekly newspaper, *Flight*, the official organ of the Royal Aero Club (RAC), which, under its editor Stanley Spooner, was notably less aggressive and more supportive of the Establishment. It fully appreciated that in the case of Colonel Seely, he had to act within the limitations of the funds allocated to his department[33] and, while highly supportive of a private aircraft industry, it did not believe that the Royal Aircraft Factory was interested in competing with private enterprise beyond the scientific and experimental sides of flight.[34] During 1914 after re-examining the charges of privileged conditions for the Royal Aircraft Factory against private constructors, it declared itself satisfied that all future tenders for aircraft would be sent out from the factory to private constructors as well.[35] In contradiction to *The Aeroplane*, *Flight* maintained that the competition which embarrassed the industry was not between the Factory and private firms but between the large and small firms. But however different from Charles Grey's explosive prose, *Flight*'s leaders joined with him in emphasising the need for greater funding towards the development of the country's air arm.

* * *

Whatever the contributions of individual newspapers – whether through Northcliffe's proselytising dailies, papers such as *The Morning Post* and *The Manchester Guardian* or the aircraft industry's own publications – there is little doubt that collectively they materially influenced public opinion and were a significant contributory cause towards persuading a reluctant political administration to meet its responsibilities for airpower in the years leading up to the Great War. If further proof of the Press's influence was needed, it was surely demonstrated by the draconian censorship soon to be imposed upon the newspapers by Prime Minister David Lloyd George at the commencement of the war.

However much the Press endeavoured to champion the aircraft industry, their difficulties were insignificant compared to those of the early pilots in struggling to keep their frail aircraft in the sky, or the constructors and entrepreneurs who staked both capital and reputation in attempting to design and produce aircraft which were equal or superior to their country's opponents.

THE ACHIEVERS

Chapter 9

Early Flyers – Flying for the Hell of It

During the pioneering days of flight in Britain relatively little attention was paid to the particular skills needed to keep their vehicles in the air. George Cayley had used his coachman and his grandson to fly his gliders and Hiram Maxim's great aeroplane, running along its rails, required a pilot with no more ability than an average train driver. Manipulative skills became more important with Percy Pilcher's hang glider and although the American Wright brothers still flew in business suits and stiff collars, by now such outfits belied their expertise.

In the modern era genuine recognition of a pilot's skills came with the first aeroplane flights in Europe, commencing with Santos-Dumont and Henry Farman in 1906, followed by accomplished airman Louis Paulhan, the so-called 'wonderful little Frenchman' who took part in the first air meeting at Rheims and later won the £10,000 prize offered by *The Daily Mail* for flying from London to Manchester. Above all there was the highly-skilled Louis Blériot who, while still recovering from extensive burns suffered in an earlier crash, successfully shepherded his frail aircraft across the English Channel. British pilots also began to demonstrate the full capacities – and deficiencies – of the planes they had acquired.

Louis Bleriot's monoplane XI 'Militaire'. (*Author's Collection*)

One of the best known at this time was the automobile driver and balloonist John Moore-Brabazon who, on 30 October 1909, gained prominence as the first Englishman to fly a circular mile at a height of between 8 and 10ft in an aircraft made by the Short Brothers. He was the first to be awarded a Royal Aero Club pilot's certificate and the first to win the British Empire Michelin Cup for the longest flight in an all-British machine, which he did covering eighteen miles in thirty-one minutes on 31 March 1910. He graphically described the instability of such early flying as 'feeling like sitting on a blancmange in a strong draught', but Moore-Brabazon's appetite for flying was much affected by the shock of a fatal accident later in the year to his fellow pilot and great friend, Charles Rolls.

Although Brabazon joined the RFC in the First World War his principal role came in the development of aerial photography. The honourable Charles Rolls – considered elsewhere in this book – who founded C.S. Rolls and Co., Automobile Engineers and Concessionaires for Continental Cars (later Rolls-Royce Ltd), was a better-known racing driver than Brabazon and flew longer distances, including a double cross-Channel flight in a French Wright aeroplane before his death at the Bournemouth Aviation Meeting in July 1910.

Whatever the extent of Brabazon's and Rolls' flying skills, together with those of aeroplane constructor Alliott Vernon Roe, the outstanding pilot in Britain from 1908 to 1913 was unquestionably the one-time American cowboy, Samuel Franklin Cody (b. 1867). As showman, playwright, kitist and aircraft constructor Cody was an extraordinary figure. He was the first in Britain to fly a powered aeroplane of his own construction and throughout his life promoted the aeroplane's future roles both in peace and war. Cody merits consideration as a publicist, constructor and pilot, although with his lack of technical knowledge (his formal schooling ended before he was ten) other constructors such as Sopwith

John Moore-Brabazon and plane. (*Author's Collection*)

John Moore-Brabazon makes the first official 'air freight' flight in 1909. The pig was secured in a waste paper basket which was attached to the fuselage of a Short biplane. (*Royal Aeronautical Society [National Aerospace Library]*)

and Roe came to build more advanced aeroplanes and Claude Grahame-White, with his regular air shows at Croydon, acquainted more people (undoubtedly more Londoners) with aircraft than Cody. As a pilot, however, Cody was outstanding. Like all notable pilots, he was passionate to get into the air, which became evident with his flights in man-carrying kites followed by others in the British army's first airship *Nulli Secundus* and in his unpowered glider, and then his first aircraft.

Cody's opportunity for genuine manned flight came at Farnborough where he was employed as the army's chief kiting instructor and airship technician, and where he was also permitted to build an aircraft. On 16 October 1908, after putting his large biplane through a series of taxiing tests, he attempted to fly it although it was still largely undeveloped. It had been built to highly demanding specifications required by the British army, one of which was an ability to carry two passengers at an average combined weight of 340lbs – with their equipment and a Maxim gun – together with enough fuel for four hours' flying time. Such requirements, and the limitations of the engine allocated to him, gave his plane a far less favourable power to weight ratio than the Wright's flyer of 1903.

Among the major problems facing Cody was that (having never flown) he had little idea about how to handle his front elevator (to lift him up and down), a

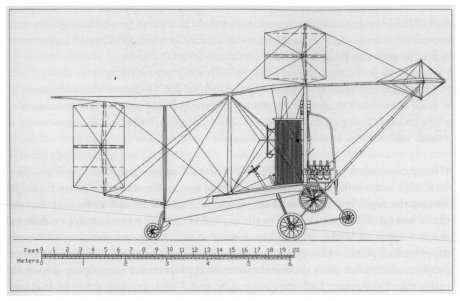

Side view of the BAAI (British Army Aircraft No. 1). (*Drawing by John Roberts*)

control that gave the Wrights so much trouble during their initial flights. Cody's difficulties at Farnborough went far beyond such mechanical guesswork for the site, with its limited area for take-off and landing, and encumbered by small copses of trees and a horse trough, complete with railings, was notably ill-suited for manned flight. Buoyed by an initial flight of just seventy-five yards, Cody quickly went on to a second. Although he again took off successfully, after reaching a height of 30–40ft he was caught by the wind and projected towards a group of trees. By inspired use of his front elevator he succeeded in narrowly clearing them, although in so doing he met with severe air turbulence which caused his plane to roll and its left wing to strike the ground. In spite of sustaining some damage, he brought it back to level flight, but then encountered another copse of trees which were too close to be overflown. After using his rudder sharply, his banking wing hit the ground and he crashed. This eventful journey of twenty-seven seconds across hazardous terrain demanded a range of flying skills never required by the Wrights in their level flights across sandy flats. Typically, Cody escaped with cuts and bruises, although his plane was badly damaged.

Despite his achievement (which was not properly acknowledged by his chief, Colonel Capper) one week later it was decided that the army's experimental work with aeroplanes should be discontinued. Notwithstanding, Cody was allowed to continue work on his aeroplane (which was presented to him in April 1909) from a shed measuring 150ft × 150ft which he erected on Farnborough Common.

From this base during early 1909 Cody acted as Britain's first test pilot by reputedly trialling and modifying his plane until it flew well enough to take up a passenger. Its performance needed improving for, following his dismissal from

Farnborough, to survive he needed to win prizes at the current air competitions both against the improved Wrights' aircraft currently being built on licence in Britain and the prevailing French biplanes and monoplanes. At first opportunities were lacking: during the autumn of 1909 any chance of showing his skills at the Doncaster Air Show (for which he received £2,000 appearance money) was foiled by bad weather, although he used the opportunity to take out naturalisation papers for British citizenship which made him eligible for all races held in Britain.

Cody's first major flying success came at the end of 1910 when he competed against Tommy Sopwith and Alex Ogilvie for a Michelin Trophy, bringing a cash award of £500 and a handsome bronze trophy of Pegasus to the pilot who by the end of the year flew the longest distance round a set circuit. Like many of his other triumphs, it came against the odds. Ogilvie had already covered 139.75 miles and Sopwith 150 miles before, at 8.30am on a frosty New Year's Eve, Cody set off on the two and a half mile circuit at Farnborough. Through constant manipulation of the rudder and other controls he coaxed his heavy aircraft around the circular course, and completed the first forty-nine laps, totalling some 120 miles, flying at between 150 and 250ft, but with the wind increasing he was forced to descend to within 30ft of the ground before he began experiencing decreased engine speed caused by thick ice building up around the inlet pipes. Notwithstanding, Cody continued until 1.14pm, by which time he had covered 185.46 miles in 4 hours 47 minutes, exceeding Sopwith's total by thirty-five miles. Throughout the flight, made in sub-zero temperatures, Cody was completely unprotected and he landed with his beard, moustache and clothing

Cody and his first passenger – Colonel John Capper. (*Jean Roberts*)

Cody with his Michelin Trophy. (*Jean Roberts*)

covered in ice. In a rare demonstration of skill and endurance, he set a new all-British record for both duration and distance.

Cody's next major competition came with the Circuit of Great Britain Race in July 1911. This offered a massive £10,000 prize to the first pilot who completed a circuit from Brooklands to Edinburgh and back (with compulsory stops on the way) within a flying time of twenty-four hours. It was open to all-comers and nineteen competitors set off, the clear favourites being two highly experienced pilots in French monoplanes that enjoyed a higher speed and a far better power-to-weight ratio than Cody's massive biplane. Although they duly came first and second, he flew an incredible race, coming fourth overall and ahead of any other British aeroplane.

His race was full of incidents: at Tinsley Wood in Yorkshire he came down with a burst water pipe in his radiator, which was repaired, but before landing at Harrogate he was compelled to fly the last seven miles with one hand steadying a split fuel tank. Landing again at Brandon Hill Colliery near Durham to check his direction, he damaged his plane by hitting a wall. Setting off again he stopped at Newcastle, before moving on to Edinburgh. South of Edinburgh he described the weather as 'the worst I have ever had in my life', during which he was blown out to sea before approaching the Scottish capital in thick fog. On his return he made stops at Stirling, Paisley, Lanark and Carlisle, where by now his engine was running very badly. To raise money for the engine to be de-coked, he gave an impromptu presentation at Carlisle's Theatre Royal after its normal performance. Off again into strong headwinds he made stops at Workington, Moresby, Manchester, Bristol and Weston-super-Mare. At Weston he landed on the sands and at its Pavilion Theatre gave another account of his journey so far, before returning to Brooklands via Salisbury and Brighton. Although the organisers extended the race time by ten days to allow him to finish, his rare flying skills and exceptional endurance enabled his home-built plane to succeed against those of all other British manufacturers.

By now Cody's place in popular regard seemed unmatchable, but his greatest feat of flying was still to come. After winning the Michelin Trophy again in October 1911, his next objective was the military trials due to be held at Larkhill during the summer of 1912 to select the most suitable aeroplane for use by the RFC. In this competition he was competing against nineteen other entrants, representing the great names from European aviation as well as the major British aircraft constructors. Prior to the race Cody met with amazingly bad luck when both his entries crashed and were virtually destroyed, but with just three weeks to go he built a new plane from the debris of those that had been written off. In such circumstances he had to play safe with one of his semi-obsolete biplanes, although he discovered and installed a powerful 120hp Austro-Daimler engine from an Ettrick monoplane which had crashed during the Round Britain Race.

During the trials, which lasted three weeks and involved a range of flight tests – including one requiring the plane to be dismantled and reassembled – Cody failed to win one outright, although his bamboo and wood biplane, with its powerful

Austro-Daimler engine and magnificent pilot, scored most points overall against more technologically advanced competitors.[1] Although it prevailed in his strong but sensitive hands, Cody's plane offered the RFC not the slightest development potential. His achievement at Larkhill has been likened to that of a 500–1 outsider winning the Grand National, and was one which he capped by going on to win his last Michelin Trophy.

Cody's success at the Trials earned him £5,000 and, although he was in the process of setting up his own aeronautical company, he determined to keep on flying, despite being older than the other constructors. For a Coastal Circuit of Great Britain Race he built his largest aeroplane so far, and while practising he adopted the habit of taking up passengers for short flights over Aldershot heath. On 7 August 1913, with leading cricketer W.H. Evans on board, he was preparing for a descent over Laffan's Plain, Aldershot, when his plane appeared to double up in the middle. Whatever his flying skills he had no chance of regaining control and his plane plummeted into a group of oak trees, instantly killing both himself and his passenger.

If, like Tommy Sopwith and Grahame-White, Cody had concentrated on construction or, like Moore-Brabazon, had virtually ceased flying, he might have lived a long life. This, however, was not his way. Flying was everything to him and he had already taken steps to build a plane to cross the Atlantic, in which he would surely have been its chief pilot. For Cody, riding the air in his open plane with both hands on the steering wheel went beyond any other sensation – even straddling a spirited horse – which he valued so much. His inexhaustible courage and his performances with distinctly crude aircraft captured the imagination of Britain's soldiers and public alike: 100,000 people attended his funeral and

Cody's funeral procession at Aldershot in 1913. (*Author's Collection*)

subsequent interment in Aldershot Military Cemetery, the first civilian to be given such a privilege.

* * *

The colourful and voluble Samuel Cody was markedly different from another outstanding British pilot, Bentfield 'Benny' Charles Hucks, born on 25 October 1884 in Essex at the small village of Bentfield (from where he acquired his first name) whose greatest exploits were in the last two years before the war.

As the son of a consulting engineer he was expected to follow his father's career but, like other young men who loved speed and who witnessed the rapid development of the internal-combustion engine, he not altogether surprisingly had other ideas. At the age of twenty, he persuaded his father to let him take an apprenticeship in the infant motor car industry where he worked assiduously and, with his father subsidising his meagre wages of eight shillings a week, fulfilled his dreams of buying a second-hand car. His mechanical skills enabled his car to perform outstandingly but this, together with the draconian speed restrictions of the time, made it virtually inevitable that (like Charles Rolls) he should catch the attention of the authorities. After being fined on several occasions, in 1907 he received a three-year driving ban.

For such an enthusiast, if he could not drive the alternative was to fly, but this only seemed possible for far wealthier men. Hucks did the next best thing – he found employment as a mechanic with someone who flew, in this case the virtuoso aviator and air publicist Claude Grahame-White who, on 23 April 1910, made his second attempt to win the £10,000 prize offered for flying the 185 miles from London to Manchester in under twenty-four hours. Although White lost to

Benny Hucks. (*Royal Aeronautical Society* [*National Aerospace Library*])

the French flyer Louis Paulhan who set off before White learned of it, Hucks had become so valuable to him as a mechanic that on 1 September 1910 he accompanied White on the liner *Cymric* to Boston, Massachusetts, where White achieved many competitive successes, including winning the main international air race. Hucks could not fail to notice how Graham-White was lionized for his piloting skills and how he crowned his stay with a visit to the American president in Washington DC and landing on Executive Avenue, near the White House. Why should he not achieve similar success?

In late November 1910 the two men returned to Britain on the SS *Mauritania*, and by now Hucks had succeeded in persuading White to let him make a number of short flights. Hucks' promise must already have been apparent – and known to others – for early in 1911 Robert Blackburn, the Yorkshire aeroplane designer and builder, engaged him at £3 a week as pilot and mechanic for his second prototype monoplane which was due for flight testing on the sands at Marske, near Filey. Blackburn's monoplane was powered by a temperamental Isaacson radial engine that Hucks had running satisfactorily, but when, on 8 March 1911, Hucks began the flight tests his inexperience brought major problems: while in the process of executing a turn 'he lost flying speed, stalled and side-slipped on to the beach'.[2] The plane suffered serious damage, although Hucks escaped unscathed. Blackburn soon repaired the plane and Hucks went on to make many successful flights.

In fact, so proficient did he become that, although he had not yet qualified for the Aero Club's Flying Certificate, Robert Blackburn made him Chief Instructor for the flying school he established at Saltburn. On 30 May 1911, flying the Blackburn monoplane, Hucks was duly awarded the Aero Club's Certificate No. 91. Two weeks earlier he had climbed to 1,200ft, a record height for the north of England, and on 18 May he had already satisfied the Aero Club's examiners, although he had not yet been awarded his certificate due to a technicality. The hazards of such early flying were demonstrated when, while repeating his test manoeuvres, his engine seized and sheared off the propeller shaft. Hucks was injured in the resultant crash but not before he successfully qualified.

The Blackburn Company set its sights on winning *The Daily Mail* Circuit of Great Britain Race on 22 July 1911, for which they entered two Mercury monoplanes powered by 50hp Gnome rotary engines. Although Hucks flight tested both of them, he had little luck in the race, when his engine cut out near Luton and on landing he hit a wire fence that tore off his undercarriage. The company's second pilot, Conway Jenkins, did even worse, overturning his plane on take-off. Blackburn's Mercury subsequently attracted much attention and Hucks made a number of exhibition flights in front of would-be purchasers during an extensive and successful tour of the West Country. By the end of 1911 Hucks had become an accomplished and stylish flyer who had completed more than fifty flights, covering a thousand miles in all, including flying across the Bristol Channel three times.[3] In his hands the Blackburn Mercury II became highly regarded, both for its durability and general reliability.

Hucks also piloted a Blackburn two-seater aircraft powered by an 80hp Gnome engine to win the Trophy for the 'Wars of the Roses Race', instituted by the *Yorkshire Evening News*, competing against P. Raynham and A.V. Roe flying an AVRO 504 biplane. His skilled flying had already impressed the onlookers and his old boss Claude Grahame-White, who by now had established weekly aviation meetings at Hendon, offered him a six-month contract to fly a 50hp Blériot X1 monoplane for both exhibition flying and racing. Hucks accepted and arrived in time for Grahame-White's wedding at Widford Parish Church near Chelmsford, where the guests included aviators Tommy Sopwith, Gustav Hamel and Robert Loraine, all of whom arrived by aeroplane. When the couple left the church Hucks (who had been circling overhead) began his exhibition flying for Grahame-White by accurately swooping down to shower the bride and groom and their guests with confetti.

During July and August 1912 Hucks formed part of White's flying circus that aimed to 'wake England up' to the dangers that aircraft could pose in time of war, and also gave flying exhibitions at Birmingham, Loughborough and Long Eaton. At this time he received an offer from wealthy sportsman Harold Barlow to accompany him to Australia and New Zealand, to give exhibition flights in a new 70hp two-seat Blériot which Barlow proposed to purchase. So keen was Barlow to have Hucks that he offered Grahame-White £1,000 to release him, but following the sudden illness and subsequent death of Barlow, the tour was cancelled. Hucks however purchased the Blériot (which he called 'The Firefly') from the executors and formed his own company with an office at 166 Piccadilly, from where his promotions manager Colonel Jack Savage offered exhibition flights. As a result Hucks attended flying displays at widely different locations, in the process becoming accustomed to making cross-country flights in all weathers.

Benny Hucks in his Blériot aircraft. (*Author's Collection*)

By now, the quietly spoken but supremely confident Hucks was unquestionably one of the country's leading aviators and on 20 September 1912 he won the Shell Trophy for the Aerial Derby Sealed Handicap. At this time he heard about the ability of the French aviator Adolphe Pegoud to loop the loop and even fly upside down – when as a rule pilots were very nervous about attaining any unusual attitude in the air, and it was generally considered that 'if an aeroplane was turned vertically on its side, or inverted, it would inevitably become uncontrollable and crash'.[4] Pegoud was Louis Blériot's star pilot and Blériot approved of the manoeuvre because it demonstrated that if, for any cause whatever, his monoplane turned upside down the pilot need not panic, but by skilled use of his controls could regain the normal position of flight. Hucks went to France to watch Pegoud, and while there he ordered a specially strengthened Blériot XI aircraft for himself. On returning to Hendon, he practised by strapping himself into a purpose-built inverted seat, increasing his time in it until he could apparently 'read a newspaper for 15 minutes without ill effects'.[5] As a result when Pegoud demonstrated his skills at Brooklands on 1 November 1913 before 30,000 spectators, Benny Hucks was able to repeat the manoeuvres in a faultless display to become the first British airman both to loop the loop and fly inverted.

Two months before, on 30 August 1913, he took part in a notable race against another outstanding British airman, Gustav Hamel. Hucks' manager challenged Hamel, for a stake of £500 a side, to race round a circuit near Birmingham using Blériot XI monoplanes. Unfortunately, Hamel could not obtain a Blériot and borrowed a more powerful Morane Saulnier monoplane so the bet was withdrawn, although the race went on with Hamel agreeing to carry his mechanic by way of a handicap, while Hucks flew alone.

During the race – before 30,000 people – the planes flew neck and neck and what Hamel gained in superior speed Hucks made up for by better course keeping, benefiting from his knowledge of the area. In a contest of fluctuating fortunes, Hucks went two minutes ahead, then fell fifty-five seconds behind, reducing it to just nine seconds before Hamel eventually won by twenty and two-fifths seconds – after one of the most thrilling races ever flown.[6]

Following Cody's death Hucks continued his competitive flying and aerobatic displays into 1914. On New Year's Day he gave a magnificent display at Manchester, and two weeks later Grahame-White and the Hendon aviators made him their guest of honour when at the Royal Automobile Club they held an 'Upside Down' dinner. It began with an announcement by megaphone that coffee was served, whereupon the company drank the loyal toast in liqueurs. The waiters, dressed in mechanics' overalls, then served the savoury, followed by the sweets, until the tortured palates of the guests had grappled with various joints and entrees and arrived, via lobster and soup, at the hors d'oeuvres.[7] It was said to have been an occasion that few present were likely to forget and showed the high regard in which Hucks was held.

During March Hamel joined him in a combined demonstration at Hendon which included upside down flying, and in April Hucks flew across the Channel at 400ft above the Royal Yacht while his cameraman from the Warwick Bioscope

Chronicle Film Company filmed King George and Queen Mary with a hand-cranked camera. With the coming war threatening an end to such antics, Hucks flew like a man possessed; and teaming up in the early summer of 1914 with Marcus Manton, then still in his teens, he carried out the first synchronised

The flamboyant French flyer Adolphe Pegoud, from whom Hucks got the idea of flying upside down. (*Author's Collection*)

Silver cup awarded to Hucks for coming second in a competition with Gustav Hamel.
(*Barbara Reese*)

aerobatics display. 'They took off together, looped in unison and then finished off their show with a skilfully-timed spell of inverted formation flying.'[8] Earlier Hucks had been in Lincolnshire taking part in a barnstorming tour where he flew his Blériot monoplane between the towers of Lincoln Cathedral and looped the loop; a watching reporter from *The Lincolnshire Leader* declared, 'if you want to shout with the very joy of living, just take to the air with Hucks'.[9]

At the outbreak of the war Hucks was the best all-round pilot in England, if not the world. Although he never made any spectacular long-distance flights, or broke any major height or distance records, he was a cross-country pilot of great ability and unequalled in aerobatic flight, giving heart-stopping exhibitions of looping, bunting (flying upside down) and half-rolls. He invented the delayed loop in which he flew upside down for several seconds before pulling back the joystick at the last possible moment. Such flying needed peerless judgement and nerve; air commentator Dallas Brett acknowledged that 'Hucks's handling of a Blériot was a joy to behold and his stunt flying was fluid and effortless'.

Harry Harper, *The Daily Mail*'s and Britain's first air correspondent, gave an admiring account of Hucks' acrobatics at this time.

Hucks mounted his DH4 biplane and climbed several thousand feet. Then as I watched him through my glasses, his biplane appeared suddenly to go completely out of control. It fluttered in mid-air; then, one wing down, it came slipping swiftly sideways. The next instant it came to a pause, swinging back for a moment on an even keel, only to fall back tail-first directly afterwards. Next came a succession of dives, side-slips and momentary pauses – the whole impression being that the plane was simply fluttering down, uncontrollable, like 'a falling leaf' of the title given to this trick. Hucks let his plane come down like this to within a few hundred feet of the ground. Then with a swift and masterly movement, he regained control and made one of his dextrous landings. I have seen others do this trick but none of them with quite the artistry which Benny managed to impart to it.[10]

Through his skills, Hucks gave a practical demonstration of how far aircraft had progressed since the first European flight less than eight years before, how effective they had become and, by co-ordinating his manoeuvres with another pilot, showed how pilots could multiply any likely effects through formation flying.

At the outbreak of war Benny Hucks offered himself and his plane to the RFC. However, it was too early for his skills to be used in aerial fighting and the strain of his peerless stunt flying had taken a toll on his health. Following a severe attack of pleurisy he was invalided out of the service before, in the war's final stages, he joined the long list of deaths from influenza. Nothing, however, could diminish the supremacy Hucks had possessed in early 1914.

While the slimly-built Hucks was physically very different from the massive Cody, both were the fiercest of competitors whose control and panache carried piloting skills into a new dimension, tempting the brave and adventurous to join them. In their day they were unsurpassed.

Chapter 10

First Flyers – Pushing the Margins

In the years leading up to the war, two pilots distinguished themselves by going beyond the bravura of the great showmen and seeking to extend their aircrafts' utmost capabilities, at times putting themselves in hazardous situations over which they had limited knowledge and control.

The first was Gustav Hamel (b. 1889), the son of a naturalised German surgeon, who took up aviation from an early age. Following his studies at Westminster School and Cambridge University he went to the Blériot School of Flying at Pau where, flying a French Morane monoplane, he qualified for his brevet flying certificate on 6 February 1911, and obtained his British certification a few days later. To John Ledeboer, the editor of *Aeronautics*, Hamel was truly a hero, the finest pilot who ever flew an aeroplane. 'His touch was ever that of a master: for sureness, for sheer brilliancy it has never been equalled let alone excelled. He was a born pilot; no need for him to climb the laborious steps of achievement.'[1]

However quickly and well Hamel mastered the skills of flying, as a relatively affluent young bachelor he had other clear advantages. Unlike Cody, he had no pressing need to support a wife and family and to work for men who underestimated him, nor like Hucks did he have to undergo a demanding apprenticeship and make himself indispensable as a mechanic before being given an opportunity to fly. To his credit, Hamel carried such privileges lightly, even if he used his youth to full advantage, with his quiet speaking voice, spare – almost frail – figure, clean-cut looks, crisp curly hair and teddy bear mascot. This tended to conceal his remarkable ambition and determination but what Hamel intended was not only to fly as often as he could but prove it could be done whatever the conditions and over very considerable distances.

From the time Hamel first appeared at Pau he positively embraced the new element of the air, and so rapidly did he develop as an accomplished flyer that within a month of taking his pilot's licence at Hendon he won the inaugural race between the Hendon and Brooklands authorities. He also temporarily took over from Pierre Prier as Chief Instructor of the Blériot School at Hendon. His talent and good connections guaranteed that he would represent Great Britain in the Blue Riband of speed races, inaugurated by the American James Gordon Bennett and due to be held at Eastchurch on the Isle of Sheppey during early July 1911.

Hamel was chosen to pilot a Blériot Type XXIII aeroplane equipped with a 100hp Gnome engine. Its power compared favourably with others such as Alex Ogilvie's Wright biplane, equipped with a 50hp engine and Graham Gilmour's Bristol monoplane, with its 80hp Gnome engine (which, in fact, did not prove

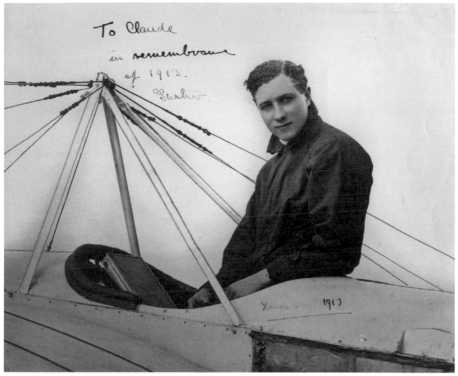

To Claude
in remembrance
of 1913.

Xmas 1913

Gustav Hamel in his plane, Christmas 1913. (*Royal Aeronautical Society* [*National Aerospace Library*])

ready for the race). However, on the morning of the race, to achieve extra speed, Blériot reduced the plane's wingspan by clipping 18in from both wings, thus vastly reducing the plane's controllability. As the race opened Hamel was the first pilot to get away and he flew off low and fast but, on reaching the first pylon marking the three and three-quarter mile course, turned at too sharp an angle for his modified wings, side-slipped and crashed. Miraculously he was thrown clear, rolling over and over 'like a shot rabbit', and escaped with slight concussion.[2] (The race was won by Charles T. Weymann of the United States in a French Nieuport.)

Hamel's next competitive challenge was the Round Britain Air Race due to be held on 22 July and, although not fully recovered physically, he was determined to take part. After reaching Newcastle, Hamel was closely following the eventual winner when his engine failed and, although he succeeded in making a remarkable forced landing just north of Dumfries, it was two days before he was joined by his mechanics – and by then any chance of success had gone.

Hamel appeared to be quite unaffected by such mishaps and he set himself different – and more difficult – challenges. As Harry Harper, the air correspondent of *The Daily Mail*, pointed out, more than anyone else he set out to master the difficulties of bad weather flying. 'That's the notion. I am making it my business to knock the bottom out of . . . this idea that one can't fly regularly in bad weather. One <u>can</u> provided one goes about it the right way.'[3]

To this end, on 9 September 1911 Hamel was one of the first to volunteer to act as the pilot for a pioneer mail plane carrying a 23lb mailbag from Hendon to Windsor. He was engaged with two other pilots, Cresswell and Hubert, who during the first day of delivery considered the wind so dangerous they refused to start. Undeterred, Hamel set out and Harry Harper concluded that only his superb handling of his machine saved him from a crash in the critical seconds immediately after take-off. It was a notable performance at the time and it astonished the officials who saw the tiny windswept plane approaching them at something like 105mph in the strong tail wind. Harper believed this flight of Hamel's, which amazed the public and astonished the postal officials, was one of the most significant in the history of early British aeronautics. 'Thenceforward it was no use for critics to go about saying that the aeroplane was a mere fine-weather machine. Hamel demolished the argument once and for all.'[4]

In just over three years Hamel made a remarkable number of different flights; he crossed the Channel several times, flew from Cologne to Dover non-stop and competed in the first aerial derby in which he was second, before winning it at his second attempt. He took part in the Hendon–Brighton–Hendon race, made innumerable cross-country flights and performed at air shows all across Britain. An account of his skills during the Naval and Military Meeting at Croydon on 28/29 September 1912 appeared in *The Times* the next day. It explained that after displaying his skills in a strong wind he was followed by Lieutenant Spencer in a Deperdussin plane, who was compelled to land within a few minutes.

> Almost immediately Mr Hamel rose from the ground once more . . . shooting up in a wide circle, he steadily rose to a height of some 2000 feet and here he encountered the full force of the wind: for minute after minute the monoplane scarcely advanced suspended almost motionless; at last with a swift turn it headed about and shot away before the wind with amazing speed . . . Then in two sharp spirals, left and right-handed, the aeroplane shot down, finishing up with a steep glide before the wind just over the enclosure and within a few feet of the heads of the crowd – a fine performance, it is true, <u>but one not devoid of the element of danger.</u>[5]

Such accomplishments can be better appreciated when the still limited speed of most aeroplanes at this time is taken into account as revealed by the notes written about Hamel and his plane for a Floral Carnival and Air Show held at Whitchurch on 11 September 1912.

> Mr Gustav Hamel is one of the foremost of these (experts); he is an Englishman, 23 years of age; the machine he pilots is a Blériot monoplane fitted with a Gnome engine 50hp by which he attains great speed, normally 65 miles per hour, with the propeller swishing around at 1400 revolutions per minute.[6]

Hamel also proved that when he wanted to he could hold his own against the aerial acrobats when he wanted to and joined Benny Hucks at Hendon in March

1914 to match his manoeuvres by looping the loop and performing side overturns and tail slides. However, Hamel felt it more important to demonstrate his aircraft's long-range ability in varied weather conditions and on 23 May 1914 he set out from Paris to London in a new Morane-Saulnier monoplane on what would have been his eighteenth Channel crossing – far more than any other flyer of his generation. The weather was very changeable and – like another early airman, Cecil Grace – he just vanished. It was most likely that some form of mechanical trouble overtook him, although during this period of war fever tall rumours circulated that because of his name he was really a German spy and had gone to Germany. However, these became less credible when two fishermen found a body floating in mid-Channel. As they used a boat hook in an attempt to bring it aboard, the rough seas tore the body away, but they were able to snatch 'a pair of goggles from the face of the dead man which were positively identified as Hamel's'.[7]

From 1911 to 1914 Hamel excelled as a precise, stylish and above all intrepid master of his craft. He broke no world records for which he held little regard and, unlike others, he did not need to hunt for prize money. He was far from merely being a playboy, and he never went to extremes like Graham Gilmour, who buzzed the Henley Regatta, for Hamel was keener on helping to stage flying exhibitions that would demonstrate to the Parliamentary Aerial Defence Committee what good pilots and improving aircraft could achieve.

On the other hand, Hamel never doubted his popularity, especially with women, and he was the first to take a female passenger across the Channel from London to Paris. There were numerous accounts of such journeys: Hamel routinely advised his passengers to wear warm clothing and one of his female passengers interpreted this by wearing two pairs of silk combinations under her flying suit while over it she had a long woollen coat, an American raincoat and a

Gustav Hamel with Mrs Trehawke Davies as his passenger. (*Author's Collection*)

large sealskin stole to go over her shoulders. Notwithstanding, Hamel reputedly remained so concerned for her welfare that he personally tied a hot water bottle round her waist.[8]

But in spite of the clowning, Hamel never forgot the high risks involved and aimed to move aviation forward by flying in conditions hitherto considered impossible. In addition, towards the end of his short career he gave evidence of considering the future of flight more broadly in a book of over 300 pages, which he wrote in collaboration with Charles Turner, about his own practical experiences. As a compendium of his notes, it varied in its depth of approach. His views on what made good pilots were unsurprising. He believed they should be men, as he did not consider women made good pilots, they should be young – but not too young – and should sleep for some eight hours a night.[9] However, he went on to cite aspects of flying not previously considered, including the effects of wind eddies and disturbances, the use of wireless in aircraft (citing notes made by Guglielmo Marconi) and the increased facilities necessary for civilian flying.

In a chapter about the aeroplane in war, including seaplanes, Hamel sagaciously concluded that the conquest of the air needed a new type of soldier, 'not one whit less courageous than the dashing cavalryman of the wars of fifty years ago, but scientific, cool, calculating and self-sacrificing'.[10] Such a profile could well have applied to the coming fighter aces of the RFC such as Mannock, Bishop and McCudden – and Hamel as well had he lived to join their ranks.

*   *   *

The qualities which Hamel specified for future 'air soldiers' were apparent in Edward Teshmaker Busk (b. 1886). Unlike other outstanding early flyers, Ted Busk was never a lone player demonstrating his skills in air races or other public competitions, although like Charles Rolls his flying career was quite short, stretching from 12 June 1912 to 5 November 1914. During this time he flew planes provided for him by the Royal Aircraft Factory at Farnborough, where he carried out a series of experiments using in-flight instruments or modified control systems. The inherent dangers were made all the greater by virtue of the fact that the tests were conducted to the limits of known technology.

Busk's intellectual capacity and aptitude for such work would prove outstanding, although this had been far from obvious during his boyhood. He was the eldest of four children, whose father died when he was eight, although not before he had encouraged Ted's early interest in anything mechanical. The family was comfortable financially but his mother did not consider his intellect very highly, believing him to be deliberate and slow although capable of flashes of brilliance. Even so, at preparatory school such practical inclinations were encouraged by his headmaster allowing Ted to set up a model railway in his garden. At Harrow, however, it was decided he should not specialise in science at a young age, although by eighteen he had shown enough scientific ability to be accepted as a scholar at King's College, Cambridge, to read for the Tripos in mechanical sciences.

Edward Teshmaker Busk in REI. (*Royal Aeronautical Society* [*National Aerospace Library*])

Whatever his mother's early doubts, at Cambridge the diffident boy was transformed; 'eagerly taking up work that he loved in surroundings that greatly appealed to his sense of beauty'.[11] As she put it, 'he rapidly shook off the chrysalis wrappers and expanded into freedom',[12] which included owning a rackety motor cycle and rowing for his college. The emergence was so great that he showed himself to be the most promising engineer of his generation, gaining a First Class Honours degree and the opportunity to research for a further year, during which he was given a room in an old building to work on an engine, for which he designed a self-regulating paraffin carburettor.

At Cambridge, Busk became an established yachtsman and climber, spending time both in the Alps and the Lake District. With so many of his friends wanting to join his climbing expeditions in the Lakes he formed them into a club called 'The Broad Teeth', made up mostly of scientists or mathematicians, where conversation often turned to their individual ambitions. What path Ted would take in engineering was not yet clear, although (like others) he had been inspired from boyhood by the work of the Wright brothers, and he not only wanted to fly but become 'involved in machines for that purpose'. Busk approached Walter Wilson, the one-time business partner of pioneering aviator Percy Pilcher, on whose advice he joined Messrs Halls' General Engineering Works at Dartford where he distinguished himself during a stay of some two years.[13]

After leaving Halls he went back to the family home in Sussex in order to set himself up in an old barn and 'start a series of experiments on flying machine designs and proposed to learn to fly',[14] where he was already especially interested in researching the nature and causes of wind gusts, and where he built several curious devices and instruments to test the wind.

Busk began taking flying lessons at Hendon where, despite many curtailments due to bad weather, he made rapid progress. So highly was he considered elsewhere that in June 1912 – without his knowledge – Professor Hopkinson of Cambridge had awarded him the Winbolt Essay Prize and recommended him to Mervyn O'Gorman, the Superintendent of the Royal Aircraft Factory at Farnborough, for the post of Assistant Engineer Physicist.

Both Professor Hopkinson and Dr Glazebrook of the National Physical Laboratory at Teddington wrote to Busk informing him about the post at Farnborough and saying they hoped he would take it up. Unsurprisingly he accepted, joining the Royal Aircraft Factory on 10 June 1912, where he rapidly perfected his flying skills under the expert tuition of Geoffrey de Havilland, who was already there as designer and test pilot.

Busk set his branch to develop and produce new in-flight instruments which were still limited in number. In May and June 1913 some of these were exhibited at the Royal Society, including his 'ripograph', an early form of black box, which recorded 'on one photographic strip, the pilot's movements in warping and in steering vertically and right and left, together with the speed, inclination, and roll of the machine and the time'.[15]

However, Busk's main responsibility was connected with the mathematics and dynamics of stable flight. At the time this was considered most important because the military authorities saw the purpose of flight largely in terms of battlefield reconnaissance, together with the taking of accurate photographs. Both functions were performed more effectively from a stable aircraft, the possession of which was likely to give its country clear battlefield advantages.

Over an eighteen-month period Busk carried out intensive researches to this end, flying in all weathers, both against the wind and in storms. Additionally he learned to fly de Havilland's aircraft, the BE2, to a great height, lower the nose straight down and release the controls. Fortunately he found she righted, as he had expected. Never one to exaggerate, some idea of the risks he was taking can he gathered from a letter he wrote to his mother in February 1914, in which he said 'it is a pity that everything that is the most interesting is also the most dangerous'.[16] The detailed nature of his work at this time was illustrated in the Reports and Memoranda made by both O'Gorman, as project leader, and Busk, who performed the experiments.

To determine longitudinal stability they carried out a number of calculations on the influence of both airscrew slipstream on the plane's body and on the speed of the air passing the tailplane. This was achieved by taking readings from pressure tubes fitted on the forward wing struts, for which engine revolutions had to be kept constant and repeated glides were required.[17] Some of the tests required adding different types of wing flaps and modifying the wings' dihedral angles, while others discarded the flaps altogether and kept the rudder straight. Despite the matter-of-fact language in the reports, iron nerve and high piloting skills were needed, as demonstrated in the following test, when 'the rudder (was) adjusted for straight flight and then held fast by the feet, friction of the heels against the floor making absence of movement certain'.[18]

Busk's third report contained more hair-raising details of his tests. On 18 November, for instance, he flew in gusts of wind reaching 45mph when he was forced to release the plane's elevator in case it lost such speed that it would tend to 'pancaking'. At one point the plane was found to be quite unstable and the centre of gravity had to be brought forward 'by placing lead on the front skids, while during a subsequent experiment the landing chassis was replaced, causing the plane's centre of gravity to move backwards and render the machine unstable, even with the elevator fixed. In this case it was found that the dives or rearings did not tend to check themselves even when the elevator was held in a fixed position'.[19]

With war expected, the utmost priority was placed on completing such experiments upon which so many hopes rested, and when it eventually came Busk's mother was convinced he was already very tired and greatly in need of a holiday. However, by then 'he had worked out the problem of inherent stability to a degree never before undertaken',[20] and was therefore able to take up VIPs and give them an opportunity to experience the plane's performance. On 14 May 1914 he took up Colonel Seely and on 16 May when the King and Queen visited the Factory, Busk conducted them through its departments and afterwards took up Colonel Clive Wigram, the King's secretary, when the balancing controls and elevator were not used and the plane was subject to the rudder alone. However deserved, Busk was not allowed to enjoy a hard-earned holiday, for with war expected like other staff he was confined to Farnborough. There his mother and sister often visited him, as they did on 31 October which proved to be the last time they would see him alive. On Thursday, 5 November, he went out flying as the sun was setting: at 1,000ft petrol from the fuel tank fell on the exhaust and the aeroplane burst into flames, killing the pilot. It drifted aimlessly for a few minutes and then glided downwards to Laffan's Plain where it hit the ground. Busk was buried with full military honours within the Aldershot Military cemetery, in a plot close to the graves of Farnborough's other outstanding pilots, Samuel Cody and Reginald Cammell.

Mervyn O'Gorman rated Busk very highly and talked afterwards about his custom of landing after his experiments and, with his hair still awry, excitedly reporting on his latest findings. On 5 November he wrote in the following terms to Busk's mother.

He did the most magnificent things without announcing any intention and without applauding audience . . . He knew it was interesting, he forgot that it was brilliant, or it did not occur to him. He worked out a result, knew it was right, but simply had his results checked, and then proved them in his own person, over and over again. He was a genius. That we know and you knew. He knew what he was about when he relinquished his voluntary regimental duty for the risks of this service.[21]

Mrs Busk also received letters of condolence from the King, Lord Rayleigh, Sir Richard Glazebrook and Lieutenant Colonel Sir W. Sefton Brancker, then Assistant Director of Military Aeronautics. The Aeronautical Society posthumously awarded him their gold medal.

Busk's grave in Aldershot Military Cemetery. (*Paul Vickers*)

Farnborough Memorial for Test Pilots. (*Farnborough Air Sciences Trust*)

Like Hamel, Busk committed himself to the unforgiving skies in a conscious effort to extend the knowledge of flight. His particular contribution was to be the brilliant first in a proud line of technical test pilots who applied scientific principles to the investigation of their aeroplanes' flying qualities and control systems, work which in Busk's case was considered critical in giving his country an advantage in the forthcoming war.

*   *   *

In such ways the outstanding early pilots, whether great showmen or those committed to extending the boundaries of flight, captured the wonder and admiration of kings and ordinary citizens alike in the performance of aeroplanes, thereby furthering their cause. So, too, would those in Britain who designed and constructed the first aircraft without which the pilots were powerless.

Chapter 11

The Constructors 1908–1914:
Going it Alone

Private aircraft constructors depended heavily on the orders they were able to place with the military authorities and on the British government's negative attitude towards airpower. This resulted in the RFC being formed less than two and a half years before the Great War and meant that they had to design and produce the craft for what had become a strategic industry within a remarkably short period.

The situation was aggravated further by Samuel Cody winning the military trials with his outdated biplane, which led the War Office to adopt the Royal Aircraft Factory's BE2 aircraft (developed by Geoffrey de Havilland) and for this to be used exclusively until 1913 by the National Physical Laboratory for its work with wind tunnels and flight tests. Although firms like Vickers and Handley Page benefited by taking on contracts to manufacture the BE2, and the breakaway Royal Naval Air Service (RNAS) was already ordering a range of new aircraft from other constructors, the future of British air power (especially after de Havilland moved to the private sector) depended largely on the ability of private manufacturers to come up with new aircraft equal or superior to those of other countries.

To what extent this could be achieved depended on the calibre and nature of the men who became the pace-setters for aircraft construction at this time whose achievements are shown through brief life studies of selected individuals, five of whom, the Short brothers, Alliott Vernon Roe and Geoffrey de Havilland appear in this chapter with Sir Thomas Sopwith and Sir George White in the next. While any selection is arbitrary, preference has been given to these over other constructors such as Claude Grahame-White, Frederick Handley Page, Richard Fairey, George Holt Thomas, Captain Herbert Wood (of Vickers) and Robert Blackburn, who would subsequently play major roles but whose aircraft had not made a major contribution at the commencement of the war.

The three Short brothers, Horace (b. 1872), Eustace (b. 1875) and Oswald (b. 1883) were unquestionably in the forefront of early aircraft construction. They came from a family with strong engineering traditions since their father, Samuel Short (whose own father had been a miller at Berwick-on-Tweed), owned a ship-repairing yard on the Tyne and was one of six brothers, all of whom had been apprentices at Robert Stephenson's locomotive works at Newcastle-on-Tyne.

Horace, the eldest, was outstanding. Although he had suffered a head injury in childhood that caused meningitis and led him to develop an abnormally-sized head, it had no deleterious effects on his remarkable intellectual and physical

The Short Brothers at Mussel Manor, Shellbeach, 4 May 1909. Back row (left to right):
T.D.F. Andrews, Oswald Short, Horace Short, Eustace Short, Francis McLean, Griffith Brewer,
Frank Butler, Dr W.J.S. Lockyer, Warwick Wright. Front row (left to right): J.T.C. Moore-
Brabazon, Wilbur Wright, Orville Wright, Hon. C.S. Rolls. (*Royal Aeronautical Society* [*National
Aerospace Library*])

powers. After being employed up to the age of eighteen in the Stanton ironworks,
Horace travelled to the Far East where he enjoyed a number of astonishing
adventures (including falling among cannibals in Samoa) before, at twenty-one,
he moved on to run a silver mine in Mexico.

Meanwhile, following their father's death from consumption in 1891, the other
two brothers were experiencing severe financial problems, which led to twenty-
year-old Eustace going to Mexico to seek help from Horace. After travelling
steerage from Liverpool he travelled by mule for over 200 miles along mountain
tracks before he found his brother, who responded by giving him the considerable sum of £500. After returning to Britain Eustace and Oswald bought a
coal merchant's business in London. This proved relatively successful and more
importantly it enabled them to follow their enthusiasm for ballooning.

In 1897 they bought a second-hand balloon for £30[1] which they inflated with
coal gas. Both made a number of ascents and on one of these Oswald was accompanied by two future champions of powered flight, Griffith Brewer and John
Moore-Brabazon. In the same year Horace returned home, proudly carrying a
trumpet-like device that he called an Auxetophone which amplified sounds to a
remarkable degree and which, by developing it further, he had high hopes of

making his fortune. As yet, he did not show the same enthusiasm for air matters as his two younger brothers and when, in 1898, Eustace persuaded Horace to join him in a balloon ascent from Teddington it had apparently proved highly adventurous, following which Horace labelled him balloon-mad and pronounced balloons 'nasty, useless and dangerous contraptions'. He continued to promote his auxeto-gramophone and in 1900 he installed it in the Eiffel Tower during the Paris Exhibition from where he broadcast arias recorded by the stars of the Paris Opera that could be heard all over the city.

In 1903, however, he went to Newcastle-on-Tyne where he sold his Auxeto-phone patents to the Hon. Charles Parsons and contracted to become his personal engineer on steam turbine development for a term of five years.[2] In his absence the younger brothers endeavoured to extend their engineering skills: by 1901 they had built their first balloon and had received several orders for others. They were helped by a visit from Colonel James Templer (Superintendent of the Army Balloon Factory) when he purchased balloons for the Indian army and, after praising their workmanship, introduced them to Charles Rolls who proceeded to order four more, two for himself and two for the Aero Club.[3] On the strength of such orders the two Shorts had become the country's leading balloon manufacturers and in 1906 they moved to premises under the railway arches at Battersea Park.[4]

Such work brought them into contact with other aerial pioneers and enabled Eustace to watch Wilbur Wright flying at Le Mans. During a second visit on 5 December 1908, he was taken up in a plane and became an aeroplane enthusiast (although he did not learn to fly until much later). From 1907 Eustace and Oswald extended their activities by attempting to build aeroplanes from designs given them by Aero Club members but these were not successful and, realising their limitations, they decided to approach their brilliant elder brother over the possibility of constructing aeroplanes together.

Oswald went to Newcastle thinking Horace might be reluctant to join them, but to his surprise Horace replied, 'Yes, but you'd better be quick; I'll be with you in three days and if you aren't ready by then I'll start without you'.[5] In November 1908 (the month following Samuel Cody's first flight in Britain) the firm of Short Brothers was registered at Battersea, each brother subscribing £200 towards its accumulated capital of just £600. The younger brothers had already built a glider for Moore-Brabazon, but although he installed an engine it failed to leave the ground. Horace's positive contributions soon became evident when the three produced the glider on which Charles Rolls learned to fly. In the process they proved themselves fast and accurate workers for, after ordering it in May 1909, Rolls was using it from July of the same year.

Within weeks of setting up at Battersea, the Shorts began building their own fixed-wing aircraft, a biplane with front elevators and rear rudders. Horace apparently drew up the designs for it in his mother's flat at Battersea, where he used her living room as a drawing office. Wealthy air enthusiast Frank McClean was quick to place an order and its uncovered frame featured at the 1909 Olympia Aero Exhibition, although its 40hp Nordenfelt car engine proved too heavy for it to take off. However, the aeroframe appeared sound enough and during the same year the Shorts commenced building a second aeroplane for Moore-Brabazon.

By now the railway arches were proving too restrictive and the brothers moved to Leysdown on the Isle of Sheppey, which had been discovered by Griffith Brewer and where Frank McClean had constructed a crude airfield which he made available for use by both the Aero Club and the Shorts. Brewer now recommended the Shorts as responsible craftsmen to the Wright brothers, who assigned them the right to build their planes under licence and authorised them to build six replicas for members of the Aero Club. On the strength of this order the Shorts erected a factory at Leysdown which proved to be the first purpose-built aeroplane factory in Britain, if not in the world.

Completed before the end of the 1909 Aerial Exhibition at Olympia, it was a simple pre-fabricated structure consisting of two buildings with wooden frames and galvanized iron roofs. The main one of 120ft × 45ft was large enough to hold all their machinery and still have sufficient room to build aeroplanes, while the other could house another plane. In March 1909 Wilbur Wright sent them a formal request to build six 'Model A' flyers and soon the Shorts had eighty men working for them. Both Horace and Oswald lived at Leysdown in a small farmhouse owned by the Aero club with the impressive name of Mussel Manor, where other pioneers such as Frank McClean, Cecil Grace, Charles Rolls, Maurice Egerton and John Moore-Brabazon would occasionally join them for lunch parties where the confident, forthright Horace usually acted as president.

By mid-summer 1909 the Short's second aeroplane was ready. This was powered by an engine designed by Gustavus Green and it unquestionably flew for, on 30 October Moore-Brabazon won the *Daily Mail* prize of £1,000 for the first British pilot, aircraft and engine to fly a mile round a closed circuit.

The Wrights made two visits to Leysdown, to see how the construction work was progressing, where they met the Shorts and other notable members of the Aero Club. During their visit in late November 1909 Orville made a point of praising the Shorts' workmanship and in response Horace presented the Wrights with a tracing he had made at Pau showing the plan, side view and elevation of their aeroplane, which they said was the first complete drawing of the machine they had ever had.[6] The Wrights subsequently went on to appoint the Shorts as their financial agents to handle all transactions between them and their customers in the UK.

Whatever its other benefits, the Wrights' contract did not make the Shorts a fortune, for the six Shorts/Wright aeroplanes were priced at £1,000 each, out of which the manufacturers received just £200 to cover their labour, materials and profits. Their customers, however, were all notable early pioneers whose good will was valuable: No. 1 on 1 October 1909 went to Charles Rolls; No. 2 on 1 October 1909 to Alex Ogilvie; No. 3 on 16 October 1909 to Frank McClean; No. 4 on 26 November 1909 to Maurice Egerton; No. 5 on 11 January 1910 to Cecil Grace; and No. 6 on 23 March 1910 again to Charles Rolls. Rolls needed this second plane because he had sold his first to the War Office for the full £1,000, despite having made extensive use of it. After completing this contract for the Wrights' planes, the Shorts were offered the opportunity to build further machines which Horace declined in favour of developing their own aircraft.

As yet there were no orders from the army and some idea about the precarious nature of their early activities and the major role played by Horace in the Shorts' fortunes can be gathered from Oswald's statement that 'the reason we survived our first few years at Leysdown (and Eastchurch) was due to the fact that Frank McClean bought any machines that Horace would design for him. He bought our first aeroplane and our first seaplanes and the first multi-engined aeroplanes, the first in the world.'[7]

By 1910 the Royal Aero Club considered the site at Leysdown, with its hazardous dykes, too small and transferred its activities to Eastchurch on the western edge of Canvey Island. The Shorts followed and erected a larger factory on a site they bought from Frank McClean for £25 and it was at Eastchurch they constructed what were probably the world's first successful multi-engined aeroplanes.[8]

At Eastchurch, while George Cockburn taught the first four naval officers to fly on two Short biplanes purchased by Frank McClean, Horace lectured on the technical aspects of the aircraft. From now on the Shorts began to flourish. From their factory on Canvey Island they had a unique opportunity to respond to the requirements of the RNAS prior to the commencement of the war. Inspired by the energy and design skills of Horace, they received an increasing stream of orders for aircraft which were notable not only for their strength and reliability but also for their capacity to carry out tasks required by the Royal Navy. Their first seaplane with floats flew in April 1912 and it was ready for the Fleet Review that was held at Weymouth in May of the same year. Horace also devised the first naval aircraft to have a wing-folding mechanism that thus made it possible for seaplanes of large dimensions to be carried aboard Royal Navy ships. A Short biplane, flown by Lieutenant Charles Samson, was the first to take off from a moving ship, and yet another was the first to launch a torpedo.

Early in 1914 the Shorts had produced a small number of folding-wing sea-planes for the RNAS and by the next year with their Type 184 they were able to meet the navy's need for an aircraft capable of carrying out the triple tasks of torpedoing, bombing and patrolling. So successful was this that it continued in production throughout the war, enabling the Shorts to establish a seaplane factory at Rochester in 1913–14 and, after their tender for two rigid airships was accepted, to establish a separate airship works at Cardington, Bedfordshire.

Inspired by the determination, energy and brilliance of Horace, after building the Wrights' Flyer, the Shorts went on to produce notable planes for the RNAS. Like the following two constructors, such successes followed years of uncertainty and financial difficulties that would have deterred lesser men.

* * *

Born in 1877, the son of a Manchester doctor, Alliott Vernon-Roe's early school life was undistinguished with him preferring sport to anything else. However, when he went to St Paul's School in London he developed an interest in engineering and technical drawing and soon displayed an early talent for inventiveness.[9] By the time he was fifteen Roe was keen to leave school and in 1883, after an adventurous year in British Columbia, he took on a five-year apprenticeship with the Lancashire and Yorkshire Railway Works. Following this and with no civilian occupation in mind, he decided to join the navy and enrolled at King's College, London, to study marine engineering. In his naval examinations he scored well in the engineering subjects but failed in general knowledge and was therefore forced to join the merchant service as an Engineer 5th class.

It was on board ship voyaging to South Africa that his lifelong enthusiasm for flight began, aroused as he said by 'the Albatross gliding majestically on motionless wings'. The energetic Roe soon built a number of aerial models, ranging from monoplanes to multi-wings, and after leaving the sea he took employment as a draughtsman with the Sheffield Simplex Motor Car Company before, in 1906, deciding 'to devote his time entirely to aviation'.[10] His ambitions were evident from a letter of his in *The Times Engineering Supplement* for 24 January 1906, which gave details of his success with 3ft models fitted with vertical and lateral rudders and, more importantly, his intention to enter a competition for a prize offered by Sir David Salomons for the first successful full-size Wright-type aircraft to be built in Britain. Roe demonstrated his confidence by adding that 'if immediate steps are taken I see no reason why a motor driven aeroplane should not be gliding over England by the middle of the summer'.[11]

In fact the first European flight actually took place in 1906, but not until the autumn with the French-based Brazilian aviator Santos-Dumont, and *The Times* could not be said to have encouraged Roe's enthusiasm. It published his letter, together with the rider

> that whilst giving that encouragement to new enterprise denoted by the admission of what is patently a free advertisement to our literary columns it is not to be supposed that we in any way adopt the writer's estimate of his undertaking, being of the opinion, indeed, that all attempts at artificial aviation on the basis he describes are not only dangerous to human life, but foredoomed to failure from an engineering standpoint.[12]

Like other constructors, Roe's heroes were the Wright brothers and in February 1906 he boldly wrote to them offering to sell some of their motor driven aeroplanes.

> I thought perhaps we could come to some terms as I would be pleased to act as your agent or representative in this country in this important subject ...
> I might add that I am 29 years old, athletic and have had over 12 years engineering experience in locomotive, cycle [and] marine, drawing offices and the last three years in the motor industry so I am well suited to represent this new mode of locomotion.[13]

Unsurprisingly the Wrights wrote back with a refusal, if a friendly one.

During the same year, Roe continued to seek advancement by applying for the post of Secretary of the Aero Club. Rather surprisingly, for someone so inexperienced, he was accepted, but after a few weeks he left to work as a draughtsman for an over-ambitious helicopter project in America. His work there soon ended and after resolving a dispute over non-payment of his salary, he wrote next to Major Baden-Powell, President of the Aeronautical Society of Great Britain, suggesting they united in constructing a motor-driven plane. Like the Wrights, Baden-Powell responded in a friendly way but no such partnership resulted.

Although Roe had yet to find a wealthy collaborator for his ambitious plans, he continued building his model aircraft and, despite financial problems, started constructing a full-size biplane glider similar to those built by the Wright brothers. Evidence of Roe's undoubted constructional ability came when five of his models were displayed at the International Motor Car Exhibition from 6–13 April 1907, for which *The Daily Mail* offered prizes of £250. There were 200 competitors but only Roe's model and one submitted by a Mr Howard achieved credible flight and Roe's, with a 9ft 6in wingspan and rear steering, outperformed the rest, achieving one flight of 85ft. Disappointingly, the judges offered Roe the second prize of £75 as they ruled that none of the models deserved the £150 first prize. He consoled himself by concluding that the judges were balloon aeronauts who did not seem to be in full sympathy with aeroplanes.[14]

While Roe continued his work on a full-size biplane, he discovered that the Brooklands' management welcomed aspiring constructors and were offering a prize of £2,500 to the first aviator to fly round their track by the end of the year. He obtained permission to erect a shed there for his aeroplane but soon fell foul of the circuit's bullying track manager, Mr Rodakowski, who only allowed him to test his aircraft between nine and ten in the morning. Roe however succeeded in carrying out a series of clandestine flight trials during the early hours of the morning along the finishing straight of the racetrack, resulting in hops off the ground. His first engine was an underpowered 9hp JAP, which by the spring of 1908 had been replaced with a 24hp Antoinette engine which had been loaned to him.

On 16 July 1908 Roe again contacted Major Baden-Powell, this time with the offer of a directorship in a proposed aircraft company. In his letter he told Baden-Powell that he would have to leave Brooklands by 25 July although, after working day and night since receiving his larger engine, 'I have made several towing flights rising six feet or so, towed by motor cars and have nearly left the ground with present engine and next time out should see something interesting'.[15]

He continued working on his own but, although Roe had learned much, his biplane still had serious limitations. In the April 1912 issue of *The Aero* Roe had written that his failure to fly was due more 'to poorness of engine efficiency than to anything else', but his biographer Philip Jarrett concluded that it went far further than this for 'it had very inefficient lifting surfaces, it had a very inefficient propeller that was turning at high revolutions and it had an inadequate control system'.[16]

Roe refused to be deflected by his ban from Brooklands, and his brother gave him permission to use a coach house in Putney where he began constructing a small triplane which he planned to power with his 9hp JAP motor-cycle engine. He badly needed more room but he was refused permission to emulate Samuel Cody and carry out trials on Laffan's Plain at Aldershot. Success finally came when he succeeded in renting two railway arches at Lea Marshes, with a small area of half a mile in each direction for flying, although they were far from ideal as they were bordered by the River Lea. Howard Flanders recalled that, after a trial and the inevitable crash, Roe and his helpers would work for days in the very damp and dark railway arches to prepare for the next crash. Roe's average pro-gramme was two week's work, a fifty-yard hop, crash, then work again.[17] Roe's triplane was almost certainly inspired by one built for Ambroise Goupy in the summer of 1908 by the Voisin Company, although he reportedly used his own designs.

His protracted attempts finally succeeded when in a second biplane (rather than a triplane) he made a hop of about 100ft at Lea Marshes on 13 July 1909. This he claimed was the first British flight of an aeroplane with a British engine in England. (Samuel Cody's flight in the previous October had used a French Antoinette engine.) He followed this with others and, while Howard-Flanders did not believe the 9hp engine produced 9hp and vibrated in the most appalling way,[18] by September Roe was making short flights to confirm his position as a leading British constructor/pilot. However, on 30 October he was thwarted in his plans to win *The Daily Mail's* prize of £1,000 for a one-mile circular flight by John Brabazon flying a Short biplane Roe still had much distance to make up on overseas flyers, since Louis Blériot had crossed the English Channel on 25 July and the Wrights had made a number of flights of up to forty miles during the previous year, but towards the end of 1909, after suffering a number of frustra-tions over likely backers, he was given his best chance yet. His brother H.V. Roe, head of an engineering firm in Manchester, agreed to enter into partnership with him and A.V. Roe and Company was founded on 1 January 1910 with A.V. responsible for development and his brother for finance and management.

With his brother's capital Roe was at last able to buy better engines and enjoy better flying grounds. He used Wembley Park for a short time, but after the appointment of a new Clerk of the Course at Brooklands, under whose super-vision a large area was levelled inside the track, he returned there. By 1 June 1910 Roe made his first circular flight and on 20 July he qualified as a pilot with the Royal Aero Club, gaining their Certificate Number 18. It was a just reward for someone who had worked virtually unaided against such recurring physical and financial difficulties.

Things were still far from being plain sailing however, for when Roe attempted to sell his Roe II triplane complete with its Green engine for £550, together with a guarantee of a five-mile flight before payment was required, it attracted just one order – from Walter Windham (later Sir Walter Windham MP) – and no interest from official circles.

Like other flyers, Roe found that poor weather posed his greatest hazard and he undoubtedly enjoyed good luck to survive a frequent number of low-level crashes. Luck seemed to have deserted him, if temporarily, when in August 1910 he entered two aircraft for the Lancashire Aero Club's Flying Carnival at Blackpool, only to have both destroyed on the train journey by sparks coming from the engine. Working day and night he got another triplane ready and flew three circuits of the course, although he considered it the worst plane he had ever made.

From now onwards, Roe discounted triplanes and near the end of the year he built a tractor biplane with a 25hp engine. Despite previous work by the Shorts, when it was fitted with floats it became the first seaplane to rise off water at Barrow in Furness.

The breakthrough, which he had sought for so long, came with the building of his remarkable Type 504 biplane. This neat and responsive aircraft could carry a passenger plus three hours fuel and when tested at Farnborough during November 1913 reached a speed of 80mph, with a stalling speed of 43mph. Reports on it were most favourable and in 1914 the War Office ordered twelve and the Admiralty one. The navy subsequently ordered another four, three of which took part in the bombing of the Zeppelin sheds at Friedrichshafen. The AVRO 504 was a revolutionary aircraft that came to be used tactically with the RFC and then formed the foundation of modern pilot training with the RFC and RAF, in which role it continued for a quarter of a century. In all 8,340 504s were produced.

With the AVRO 504 Roe's place among constructors favoured by the RFC was assured. Unlike the others, he had seemed content to work largely alone,

A.V. Roe alongside his Triplane at the 1910 Blackpool Air Meeting. (*Royal Aeronautical Society [National Aerospace Library]*)

AVRO 504. (*Author's Collection*)

although for years his limited finances had prevented him from hiring much additional help. Like the others he was influenced by the omnipresent Wrights, and he also adopted the designs of the triplane designer Ambroise Goupy to his own thinking, although, as Philip Jarrett observed, they 'did not always meet with a great deal of success'.[19] The time and energy Roe devoted to triplanes undoubtedly lengthened his development cycle compared with, for instance, Tommy Sopwith, whose first aircraft soon succeeded. It must also be acknowledged that Roe experienced a remarkable number of design failures and crashes[20] – which he faced indomitably. It was when Roe finally joined up with his brother that he progressed dramatically, first with his 504 aircraft and later in the war with his elegant AVRO 533, The Manchester, which compared well with the Handley Page 0/100 and de Havilland DH10 bombers.[21]

* * *

With a clergyman for a father, Geoffrey de Havilland (b. 1882) did not come from a recognised engineering background although, like his older brother Ivon, Geoffrey was always fascinated by anything mechanical, an enthusiasm which was reflected in the pattern of his education. In 1900, when he was eighteen, following spells at Nuneaton Grammar School and St Edward's School, Oxford, to the dismay of his family he opted to attend a three-year course in mechanical engineering at the Crystal Palace Engineering School. There in addition to his main studies he drew up plans for a petrol-driven engine that he built and installed in a modified bicycle. This apparently went well.

Over the next five years de Havilland was to gain extensive experience in the design offices of motor and turbine engineering companies before, in the spring of 1908 while working at Walthamstow on bus designs for the Motor Omnibus Construction company, he took the massive step of deciding to go it alone. His father had no spare capital and he therefore turned to his grandfather (an Oxford businessman) as a possible benefactor. After receiving the remarkable news that, as well as his overwhelming desire to fly, Geoffrey was confident he could construct his own aeroplane, the old man offered a thousand pounds in two instalments that he had intended to give him after his death.

In a remarkable show of self-confidence – for it was not until the autumn of the same year that Samuel Cody made his first flight in Britain – de Havilland resigned his position, took on a small flat in Kensington and rented an additional room near Bedford Square where he worked on drawing up plans for his aeroplane's engine. He had in mind a four-cylinder engine developing 40–45 brake

Geoffrey de Havilland. (*Royal Aeronautical Society [National Aerospace Library]*)

horsepower at 1,500 revolutions a minute and weighing an overall 250lbs. After four months his design work was nearing completion and it was his good fortune that the IRIS Motor Company, where (before his untimely death from influenza) his brother Ivon had been chief designer, agreed to build the engine for a most reasonable figure of £250.

De Havilland did not believe he could succeed alone and to his great relief his friend, Frank Hearle, a mechanic who in 1914 would marry de Havilland's sister Ione, agreed to join him for a paltry wage of thirty-five shillings a week. De Havilland's next step was to find premises in which he could build his air-frame. After some searching in Fulham, he discovered off an alley a large upstairs room which he rented, setting to work with Hearle. They spent long days toiling there, and in addition another major event occurred in de Havilland's personal life with his engagement and marriage to Louise Thomas, former governess to his two sisters. Following their marriage in May 1909, she joined him in his Kensington flat and with her hand sewing machine was soon involved in sewing together the fabric coverings for the plane.

Once the plane was complete it needed somewhere for flight testing and with this in view de Havilland approached the pioneer flyer, Moore-Brabazon, who agreed to sell him two sheds which he had erected at Long Barrow on the Hampshire Downs just five miles from his father's church at Crux Easton. De Havilland bought them for a bargain £150, including ample grassland to their front where his plane could taxi and take off – if it had the capability. The main requirements needed by de Havilland were now in place, but writing some fifty years later he acknowledged both his own and Hearle's 'wonderful faith and optimism'[22] in undertaking such a project when neither had even seen an aero-plane fly, let alone examined it. De Havilland's experience was restricted to pictures of planes in magazines where he was most influenced by the Wrights' Flyer and the French Farman aircraft.

By the time de Havilland commenced his own halting attempts to fly he had seen just one aircraft in flight, that of Grahame-White who, on 27 April 1910, flew from Wormwood Scrubs on his attempt to reach Manchester, and it was highly doubtful whether de Havilland could have gained much from this. As a result, when he began his airframe it was from his own rough sketches, where he followed the highly optimistic principle that 'the quickest progress would be made by building an aeroplane upon a rough idea of centre of gravity, weight and lift; however wrong it was one would learn from it'.[23] His design was for a biplane with a fixed tailplane and a front elevator (like the Wrights') driven by two propellers with aluminium blades.

In May 1909, having constructed the airframe it had to be transported to Long Barrow for flight-testing. For this de Havilland hired a lorry from Commer Cars, whose crew gently manhandled the fuselage down the narrow steps of the Fulham workshop before delivering it safely to Long Barrow. Apart from the materials needed for the final assembly, the cost of Hearle's wages and the accommodation at Long Barrow, the other main call on de Havilland's fast diminishing capital was a well-worn open top Panhard car, bought for £45. From now onwards the two constructors based themselves at the Carnarvon Arms three miles from Seven Barrows, where they worked daily on the plane, using the Panhard for journeys to the de Havilland family at Crux Easton or to his wife in London.

Summer turned to autumn, as the assembly took far longer than expected with both the engine and transmission giving unexpected problems. Finally, on a cold calm day in December, de Havilland was taxiing downhill into the wind when he found he was actually off the ground. The shock of this and the novelty of using his controls when airborne led him to put his nose up too sharply, with the result that the plane crashed down causing struts to part, its upper wings to fold and for de Havilland to be sitting amid a pile of wreckage, with one propeller revolving slowly above his head. His discomfort was complete when he waved to Hearle to indicate he was all right and the propeller struck his wrist a painful blow. Even so, neither had any intention of giving up. Before it was dark they had moved all the debris into the shed, including the engine which appeared undamaged, and had decided their only course of action was to build a simpler and stronger aeroplane.

Taking the wreckage back to Fulham they again set to work. While they struggled on, de Havilland's wife went back to Crux Easton where their son Geoffrey Raoul was born, following which she returned to Kensington. This time they used stronger wood and modified the airframe to resemble more closely those of other aircraft at the time; they also simplified the controls and strengthened the undercarriage. The work went more smoothly, by the summer of 1910 the Commer lorry was carrying the revised airframe back to Long Barrows where they substituted a single wooden propeller for the previous two, and upon starting up de Havilland reported that the plane felt very different. After taxiing, he asked Hearle to lie on the ground to confirm that the wheels had risen off it; hops followed, and the first flight of about a quarter of a mile took place on 10 September 1910.

After further modifications, de Havilland completed a circuit and then carried out figures of eight. As the flying tests continued and de Havilland's confidence grew, his first passenger was Frank Hearle, followed quite closely by his wife holding their baby son, Geoffrey. This could have marked his greatest moment of success, for he had no money to enter competitions and, even if he borrowed more money, little chance of winning them in his home-built plane. As chance had it, during November he was at the Olympia Motor Show when he met Major Frederick Green (whom he knew already) the senior engineer to Mervyn O'Gorman at the Aircraft Factory at Farnborough.

When de Havilland told him that he and Hearle would probably have to give up flying because of their lack of money and return to the motor industry, Green recommended that he write to O'Gorman offering him his aeroplane. This he did and, after weeks of delay, just after Christmas 1910 he and Hearle were taken on in the Factory's drawing office (for de Havilland had made employing Hearle a condition of his own engagement). At O'Gorman's request the War Office also gave permission for the Factory to buy his aeroplane for £400. One condition specified by Farnborough was that de Havilland should give an observed test flight of an hour's duration, which he exceeded by ten minutes, and then took up Major Green. On selling his plane, he duly wrote to his grandfather offering him the balance of £1,000, but was told he could keep it.

Unlike the earlier time when his chief restriction was lack of capital, at the Factory he found that he had to pursue his work in a clandestine way. The private aircraft manufacturers had succeeded in preventing the Factory from designing new aircraft, but as de Havilland put it, 'There was nothing to stop us repairing or reconstructing damaged ones, and we quietly got round this ruling by making use of odd pieces of crashed machines and reconstructing them – adding our own ideas here and there – into entirely new 'planes'.[24]

De Havilland's own biplane was taken on strength as FE1 (Farman Experimental 1) and he produced an improved version using a 50hp Gnome rotary engine, which gave better protection for the pilot, and in which he practised and qualified for the Royal Auto Club's special certificate involving a cross-country round-trip of 100 miles. He was also involved in reconstructing a Blériot with a pusher ENV engine, although his modifications were not complete when Lieutenant T.J. Ridge crashed it and was killed.

De Havilland moved on to design a tractor-engined biplane, the BE1, officially 'reconstructed' from the wreckage of a Voisin. This and its successor, the BE2, were orthodox biplanes chiefly made of wood with welded steel for the tailplane, elevators and rudder on the lines of the originals. He was helped by a gifted young draughtsman, H.P. Folland, and in 1912 by Edward Busk worked with the experimental RE1 plane to change the BE2 from an unstable aeroplane needing constant pilot adjustments into the BE2c, a plane with a high degree of stability which could be flown 'hands and feet off'. In August 1912 de Havilland flew his BE2 at the Larkhill Military Aeroplane competition, where it put up the best all-round performance. Although not allowed to compete officially it became the official choice for the RFC.

BE2a. (*Author's Collection*)

In spite of the Factory's restrictions, de Havilland continued with his designing that included the BS1, a single-seater scout with a 100hp radial engine. After it was built, he realised its rudder was too small and ordered a larger one but, before it was delivered, he nevertheless took it on a first flight on which it developed a spin and crashed, breaking de Havilland's jaw, tearing his lip, knocking out some teeth and causing a deep wound to his ankle. Following his recovery he flew the modified BS, the development of which led to the successful SE5 aircraft.

Prior to the commencement of the First World War de Havilland had established his place among leading British aircraft designers. His orthodox BE2 tractor biplane (in improved form) was in extensive use during the earlier part of the war and it became the most familiar aircraft of the conflict, while his SE5 was later to gain an enormous reputation in the war as a fighting machine.[25] In de Havilland's case, this only marked the beginning for he was to excel with his designs both during the war and over the next half-century. By June 1914 de Havilland, who had been pressured at Farnborough to become an inspector of aircraft, had left to join Holt Thomas's Aircraft Manufacturing Company (AIRCO). There he designed aircraft with the prefix DH, including his combat machine the DH2, which fought at the battle of the Somme, and his even more successful all-purpose DH4. Production at AIRCO reached nearly 300 aircraft a month and de Havilland's designs went on to make up a significant number of the total allied air strength.

Outside our timescale de Havilland's design and managerial skills would continue for more than half a century. His company went on to produce such renowned aeroplanes as the Gypsy Moth, the Mosquito, the Vampire jet and the Comet airliner. Yet when his friend and long-time director C.C. Walker was asked to consider the reasons for de Havilland's remarkable achievements, he said he was sure they owed most to his early struggles. 'It need only be said that to design and build one's own aeroplane and engine and then teach oneself to fly is a good introduction to an aviation career.'[26] De Havilland himself maintained that 'a successful designer should have much of the creative artist in him backed up by a lot of practical engineering experience'. In its obituary *The Times* also acknowledged that 'his early struggles against the odds led him to acquire the skills to produce aircraft that set the lead and the priceless capacity for getting on with an enterprise'.[27]

The Shorts, A.V. Roe and de Havilland finally succeeded in producing aircraft that had major roles to play in the First World War, after protracted struggles that would surely have defeated men who, however talented, had not possessed their commitment, amazing self-confidence and unremitting work ethic.

The following chapter features two other early British constructors who, as natural business leaders, took the different route of establishing flying schools and bringing together rudimentary design teams to produce outstanding aircraft.

Chapter 12

The Constructors 1908–1914: Born Winners

As the son and grandson of leading engineers from Northumberland, Thomas 'Tommy' Sopwith (b. 1888) seemed destined for some form of engineering career. Born in London, he was the eighth child and only son of a family that was financially comfortable, despite his father being killed in a shooting accident when Tommy was ten years old. The Sopwiths were accustomed to spend their summer holidays in Scotland and Tommy's great enthusiasm for sport and sailing, which he enjoyed as a boy, stayed with him all his life. He was educated at Cottesmore boarding school at Cove, Hampshire, until the age of thirteen, when he entered the Seafield Park engineering college at Lee on Solent near Portsmouth: there the essentially practical rather than academic training was much more to Tommy's liking.

Together with his inherited capacity for engineering, Sopwith was strongly attracted by the speed and danger offered by the twentieth century's new technology. While still a teenager he set up as a consultant to the motor trade, and together with a boyhood friend, Phil Paddon, opened a showroom at 1 Albemarle Street to sell Rolls Royce cars. While Rolls raced his vehicles to help his sales, Sopwith was good at selling such proven cars and he raced for fun. In 1904, when only sixteen, he had purchased his first motorcycle and in November of that year won the Hatfield 100-mile Reliability Trial for three-wheeled cars. Two years later he competed as the youngest driver in the Isle of Man Tourist Trophy race. At eighteen he sought new adventures which he found both on the sea and in the air. He joined with his friend V.W. (Bill) Eyre to buy a dilapidated 166-ton schooner, *Neva*, and made balloon ascents with other aeronauts, including Charles Rolls, where his eldest sister May acted as his constant companion and supporter. Even at this early stage he had already demonstrated his knack for picking remarkable colleagues with the engagement at just £2.14s.0d a week of the highly-talented Fred Sigrist who, although poorly educated and with no formal engineering training, did excellent work in helping to refurbish the schooner.

In 1910 Sopwith's interest in aviation received a powerful boost; when coming into Dover harbour aboard the *Neva*, he learned that an American, Johnnie Moisant, had just flown across the Channel carrying with him his French mechanic, Albert Filieux, and a kitten called Mademoiselle Paree. Although during the previous year Sopwith had already watched the French flyers, it was Filieux's flight across the Channel that helped to arose his particular interest in aeroplanes. Sopwith went to Brooklands where he paid £5 for being given two circuits over the racetrack, after which he rapidly bought an Avis monoplane with a 40hp ENV engine from Howard T. Wright for £630. On 22 October 1910, without any previous instruction, Sopwith flew his Avis at Brooklands where, after taxiing around, he took off only to come down sideways and damage a wing. Following this, he bought a biplane with a larger 60hp engine with which, on 21 November, he 'practised rolling along the ground during the morning, made straight hops before lunch and complete circuits in the afternoon, all in time to be tested by Harold Perrin of the Aero Club, who issued him with Aviator's Certificate no. 31'.[1] That evening he took up his first passenger.

From then on Sopwith took to the air whenever possible, and on 18 December 1910, with just ten hours flying to his credit, he started from Eastchurch in a plane prepared by Sigrist, and flew eastwards across the Channel to the Continent before landing at Beaumont in Belgium, having covered 169 miles. This earned him £4,000 in prize money. By now Sopwith was becoming so well known as a pilot that in the following year King George V asked him to fly to Windsor where he landed on the East Lawn, to be met by the king and his sons, the Princes Henry, George and John.

Sopwith bought two further aircraft, both monoplanes, a Martin-Handasyde with a 50hp Gnome engine and a 70hp Blériot from France. In April 1911 he went by ship to America accompanied by a powerful support team consisting of

A 21-year-old Thomas Sopwith in his Avis biplane at Brooklands in December 1910.
(*Royal Aeronautical Society* [*National Aerospace Library*])

Fred Sigrist, Harry England and Jack Pollard, where he flew outstandingly well. At Chicago Sopwith won $14,000 in prize money and at Boston, together with Claude Grahame-White, he took most of the prizes on offer. In front of large appreciative audiences, Sopwith competed against some of the finest pilots in the world and, despite being younger, won on many occasions. By October he was back in England flying anything available and using his skills in the role of a test pilot.

By now the Sopwith entrepreneurial instincts were surfacing and by February 1912, like Grahame-White, he invested his competition winnings in aviation by setting up the Sopwith School of Flying at Brooklands. One of his pupils was the 39-year-old Hugh Trenchard, future commander of the Royal Air Force, who arrived in July with the object of getting his aviator's certificate during the fortnight remaining before his fortieth birthday. After one hour and four minutes flying, dual and solo, he gained Royal Aero Club Certificate No. 270 – although Sopwith later concluded that however outstanding as a leader of men, Trenchard would never have made a good pilot.

Far more important for Sopwith was the arrival of a young Australian, Harry George Hawker, and his friend and fellow engineer, Harry Kauper. Within a year they were both working for Tommy Sopwith's newly founded Aviation Company. On one occasion, at Hawker's request Sigrist asked Sopwith whether he would teach Hawker to fly with a figure of £50 being suggested rather than the normal £75. 'At first [Sopwith] was not very keen and, at that point, Hawker rolled up his trousers and took a wad of £5 notes (to the value of £50) out of his socks.' Years later Sopwith said he produced the money '... like some old tart from the top of her stocking'.[2] After gaining Aviator's Certificate No. 297 on 17 September 1912, Hawker was to show that, in conjunction with his rare

Harry Hawker, Sopwith's brilliant Australian designer and pilot. (*Author's Collection*)

engineering and design talents, he would prove a remarkable test pilot and another member of what would soon prove to be an outstanding management team, which Sopwith had recruited.

By 1912 Sopwith had decided to stop giving flying instruction or entering air competitions in order to concentrate on establishing himself in an industry which he believed would, apart from its sporting aspects, have a major role to play in travel, commerce and warfare. Sopwith had been encouraged in such an aim during the year when he had flown two aircraft built by Coventry Ordnance and Company that were intended for the military trials shortly to be held at Larkhill to decide on suitable aircraft for the RFC. They were so unsuccessful – one engine would not run at all – that he became convinced he could do better himself.

On Sopwith's return from Larkhill (where they were soon joined by Hawker) he discussed things with Sigrist, which led him to remark that 'if I take the engine out of the Blériot and the wings of a Burgess Wright biplane and add a fuselage [I] will make it a better aircraft than either of them'.[3] They chalked plans on the floor of Sopwith's Brooklands shed for an aeroplane which they appropriately named the Hybrid and which, in later years, Sopwith would say 'was an exercise in one-upmanship on the Wright brothers'.[4] Hawker damaged it during one of its early flights but the rebuilt model, while slow, proved a good weight lifter and – to Sopwith's delight – on 21 October 1912 the Admiralty agreed to purchase it, following which they gave an order for three more.

The shed at Brooklands soon proved too small for aircraft construction on any scale and for a few hundred pounds Sopwith bought a roller-skating rink at nearby Kingston-upon-Thames. During the autumn of 1912 the triumvirate enjoyed another break, with an attempt by Hawker on the British Michelin Trophy involving a duration race round the Brooklands circuit. Hawker used Sopwith's Burgess Wright biplane, which Sigrist had meticulously prepared, to complete a magnificent flight of eight hours and twenty-three minutes. It was pitch dark when he landed and flares were put out to guide him in. This not only represented another success for Sopwith, but also established Hawker as one of Britain's leading pilots.

Sopwith's firm had started with about six people whom he called 'The Gang'. Apart from Sopwith himself, Sigrist and Hawker, they were joined by R.J. Ashfield, a teacher from nearby Tiffins School, who became its first draughtsman, together with Reggie Carey, who kept a record of their finances in his pocket book, and finally Jack Whitehorn, the tea boy from Kingston's roller rink days. While Sopwith led the process of persistent questioning and analysis – a technique that was to prove so important for their aircraft construction – Sigrist and Hawker were fearless and intense participants with their chief's humour ready to bring them back to earth. In such a climate new ideas were not only likely to surface but be swiftly adopted and, on 7 February 1914, a three-seater aircraft of Sopwith design made its first flight before featuring at Olympia later in the month. Almost immediately it 'began to win competitions and establish records'[5] and on 31 May Hawker used it to register a new British altitude record of

11,450ft. It was ordered by both the RFC and the RNAS and by now the Sopwith Aviation Company, with a share capital of £26,000 and a payroll of twenty-one people (with a fast-growing design office), was breaking other new ground by designing the first British Flying Boat for the RNAS, which they called the 'Bat Boat', a larger version of which had a 200hp engine. (Later in the war would come the Cuckoo, a torpedo-bomber.)

The year before, a number of circumstances led to the design of an aeroplane which anticipated the Sopwith fighters. Hawker was anxious to visit his parents in Australia so they decided he should carry out a sales tour in that country by taking with him a small two-seater aircraft that could be carried on board ship. Although the project was instigated by Hawker, Sopwith and Sigrist made significant contributions and this resulted in a small biplane, dubbed the Tabloid, which was years ahead of its time, with both a high top speed and an astounding rate of climb. While Hawker was in Australia, a seaplane version was entered for the second Schneider Trophy race on 20 April 1914. During the race, where in Hawker's absence it was piloted by Howard Pixton, it completed five laps for every four being flown by the opposition and won easily. In Australia Harry Hawker's performances proved so remarkable that the Australian authorities decided the Tabloid was too advanced for their pilots and no orders were placed.

By the beginning of the war 130 Tabloids had been ordered – although the plane's significance lay in the class of aircraft developed from it, which in 1917 culminated in the Sopwith Camel, the RFC's most successful fighter, 5,700 of which were built. With the Tabloid at the opening of the war and its 'follow on' aircraft such as the 1½ Strutter and, most of all, the Camel, Tommy Sopwith and his Aircraft Company made the largest contribution of any private constructors towards the different types of aeroplanes that helped to make the Royal Air Force the world's leading air arm.

Sopwith Tabloid. (*Author's Collection*)

That Sopwith succeeded as he did owed much to his outstanding personal qualities, which his friend Peter Masefield famously summed up as 'A merry head, a steady hand, a determined will, a kindly presence and one of the best brains in the business'.[6] In the latter regard, Sopwith was quite happy to take over lesser firms that were long on technical skill but short on the business side. Although undoubtedly shrewd and skilled with money, it was his capacity to recognise outstanding talents like those of Sigrist and Hawker and his willingness to give them a loose rein to contribute their ideas which, together with his own, resulted in many original features and truly outstanding British planes. However ambitious and, in Sigrist's case, ruthless (he had an arrangement to receive £50 for every machine manufactured by Sopwith during the war which amounted to £800,000 by the end),[7] Sopwith's originals, like de Havilland's later management team, would remain with him for the rest of their working lives. Such loyalty seemed the right of a man with an easy confidence, combined with a swift understanding bequeathed by his engineering ancestors, whose instincts always proved sound, enabling him to remain one of the most influential men in British aviation for well over fifty years of his long life.

*   *   *

Sir George White (b. 1854) was quite different from Sopwith or the others in that he never flew nor became directly involved with aircraft. A self-made businessman, he was much older and, as the second son of painter and decorator Henry White and his wife Eliza, a former domestic servant, came from a far more modest background. At the age of fifteen, White joined a Bristol law firm as a junior clerk where, by the time he was twenty, his industry and ability led him to be appointed Secretary of the Bristol Tramways Company. After setting up his own stock broking and accountancy firm he began investing in transport companies, where he specialised in taking over ailing concerns and rejuvenating them. In the process, he became very wealthy and was a legendary figure in Bristol with his characteristic vigorous speech, brisk gait, formal frock coat and favoured curly-brimmed, grey Homburg hat.

George White's connection with flying started in 1909. While on one of his frequent visits to south-west France for his health, he was at Pau to witness Wilbur Wright's remarkable flights and to share in the French spectators' enthusiasm for aviation. At Pau flying not only captured his imagination but alerted his entrepreneurial instincts towards building an aeroplane industry. As Harry Harper, aviation correspondent for *The Daily Mail*, recalled:

> Sir George had reduced the problem to a factual basis as was his habit. Land and sea transport, he reminded me, was already near the limit of economic speed. But speed in the air promised to be another proposition altogether; the possibilities it offered made the future of flying almost illimitable, as far as he could see. And there was the immense and more immediate scope in military and naval operations.[8]

Sir George White. (*Royal Aeronautical Society* [*National Aerospace Library*])

On 16 February 1910 White told startled shareholders of the Bristol Tramways and Carriage Company, of which he was chairman, that while aviation was hardly ripe for practical undertaking by such a company as theirs, his brother and himself had determined 'to take the risks and expense of the endeavour to develop the science both from the spectacular and commercial or manufacturing point of view'.[9] He went on to unfold his ambitious plans, telling them 'that they already had several planes of the best design on order with the intention of developing a British Industry and making Bristol its headquarters (which would secure for the Tramways Company a very important source of new traffic)'.[10]

On 19 February 1910 White set up the British and Colonial Aeroplane Company with a capital of £25,000 subscribed by himself, his brother Samuel and his son G. Stanley Wright. He restricted it to the family because he was fully aware that other members of the Bristol Stock Exchange would have considered it far too risky an adventure – and in such a case he would have had to share the rewards of the success he confidently expected. It was agreed that the company should operate from two iron sheds leased from the Bristol Tramways Omnibus Depot at Filton, some four miles from Bristol's city centre. With White in charge, events could be expected to move quickly. He appointed George Challenger, son of the Tramways Company's general manager, as his Chief Engineer and transferred a group of their skilled wood- and metal-workers to Filton. Representatives of the White family were immediately sent to the Zodiac Factory in France, where they were briefed upon the manufacturing skills required for aircraft production. Arrangements were also agreed for a Zodiac aeroplane to be sent over and shown on the Bristol and Colonial stand at the 1910 Aviation Exhibition at Olympia.

In addition to obtaining the required aeroplanes, Sir George next considered how they could be publicised and how potential pilots could be found for them. To this end he told a *Daily Mail* reporter that accommodation at Bristol would be provided on Durdham Down for up to 100,000 spectators 'where during the summer of 1910 we shall give occasional demonstrations of flight with the machines on trial',[11] and also established a Bristol Flying School at Brooklands which opened in September of the same year. The Company's Minute Book for May 1910 revealed that it was his intention to enter two biplanes for the proposed Aviation Meeting at Lanark during August.

Sir George's high ambitions seemed likely to be frustrated by an unexpected lack of aeroplanes, for after the Zodiac had featured at Olympia it was sent to Brooklands but there it failed to fly, although after prolonged negotiations lasting until May 1912 it was agreed that the Bristol and Colonial Aeroplane Company would receive 15,000 francs in compensation for the plane failing its warranty. Undeterred, Sir George sought other opportunities, such as the agency for the French 50hp Gnome engine which Captain Bertram Dickson, Britain's leading pilot of the widely praised Farman biplane (whom Sir George had appointed as a consultant), recommended installing in an updated version of the Farman. Sir George agreed and, after his works manager, George Challenger, had completed a set of working drawings for the proposed aeroplane, it was decided that twenty should be built immediately.

Sir George made less progress with the British War Office when, in May, speaking as both businessman and patriot, he offered to place the Company's resources 'solely at the disposal of the British War Department and to abstain from all business with foreign powers'. Richard Haldane, Secretary of State for War, was unwilling to be committed, stating that he would prefer 'the Company should endeavour to develop business relations in the fullest way with all foreign countries without restriction'.[12] However, in June 1910 the company was granted rights to lease a site at Larkhill on Salisbury Plain with permission to fly over

2,284 acres of army ground. This seemed an ideal place on which to establish another flying school whose flights were likely to attract the attention of army officers at nearby Bulford Camp.

The school's hangers were erected in June 1910, with White readily agreeing to place them where they would not obscure the rising sun on Midsummer's Day for the annual festival at Stonehenge. Soon afterwards, on 29 July 1910, the seventh of the modified Farman aeroplanes built at Filton and equipped with the 50hp Gnome engine was flown at Larkhill by the French pilot Maurice Edmond. Although the plane had not yet been named, it was soon to be referred to as the Bristol Boxkite and as such would provide a reliable platform for many service-men learning to fly. When, for instance, Captain Bertram Dickson and three other service pilots were invited to take part in the 1910 autumn army man-oeuvres on Salisbury Plain, he chose to fly a Bristol Boxkite and by November Boxkites were being produced at Filton at the rate of two a week. On the fifteenth of the month, a sale was agreed for eight to be built for the Russian government, with the company also undertaking a sales tour of India and Australia.

By the end of 1910 seven pupils had passed their flying tests at the Bristol schools, and sixteen biplanes had been built. Although the first two planes ordered by the War Office were French, on 14 March 1911 the first four aircraft intended for the Army Air Battalion were Bristol Boxkites. Plans were made at this time for

A Bristol Boxkite, flown by Maurice Tetard at Larkhill in 1911. (*Royal Aeronautical Society* [*National Aerospace Library*])

a third Bristol Flying School to be established at Eastchurch, but the Admiralty gave preference to an offer from George Cockburn to give instruction there on biplanes built by the Short brothers. Even so, with Filton now employing eighty men and five planes being laid down at a time, on 18 January 1911 White felt confident enough to increase the British and Colonial's capital to £50,000.

The Farman Boxkites were quickly becoming outdated and new designs of aeroplane were needed for the ambitious and expanding company. Under George Challenger, a monoplane and biplane were built for the 1911 Exhibition at Olympia, where the British and Colonial had the largest stand. However, new plane construction remained somewhat limited until, during the spring of 1911, White invited Pierre Prier, an outstanding pilot and engineer, to Filton where he designed a fast monoplane for entry in the international Gordon Bennett Cup Race held in America. There followed a family of two-seater aircraft which sold both at home and abroad and which joined the Boxkites for more advanced flying instruction at the company's schools. As a sign of further progress, on 30 December 1911 the company's capital was doubled to £100,000.

In October the directors of the Bristol and Colonial wrote to the War Office and the Admiralty offering flying tuition for 250 army officers and equal numbers for the Royal Navy at advantageous rates. The offer was declined, although the War Office decided to grant £75 to officers who decided to qualify at commercial schools for the Royal Aero Club Certificates. In April, despite the RFC's Central Flying School (CFS) at Upavon on Salisbury Plain, tuition by the Bristol company continued to expand and in February 1912 flying schools were formed simultaneously at Madrid, Halberstadt in Germany, and at Malpensa and Mirafiore in Italy, where Bristol aircraft were flown and demonstrated their qualities.

Meanwhile White, who had become convinced that above all gifted new designers were needed to propel the company's growth forward, was impressed by the work of a Romanian designer, Henri Coanda, with a jet engine using a ducted fan rather than an airscrew. He recruited him to improve the Prier monoplanes further and, not content with this, White also took on a marine designer Frank Barnwell and his assistant, Clifford Tinson, whom he installed in a 'secret' design office where they were to collaborate with Lieutenant Charles Burney RN in the development of seagoing naval aircraft.

After a succession of accidents the War Office placed a temporary ban on monoplanes, which stopped the sales of Bristol's Coanda monoplanes, and to fill the vacant production space the company accepted a contract to build Farnborough's BE2a biplanes. Despite frustration with the disappointingly small batches ordered and the number of minor modifications required by the Royal Aircraft Factory, this led to another increase in the company's capital, which, in February 1913, rose to £250,000. In spite of the temporary ban on monoplanes, there was no question of design work not continuing at Bristol, including converting Coanda monoplanes into biplanes, although the most exciting breakthrough came when Frank Barnwell, now released from his flying boat work, sketched out a baby biplane that became the first of the Bristol Scouts. The high appreciation of this aircraft led to official orders, the War Office ordered twelve in November 1914 and the Admiralty twenty-four in December, and over the next two years the plane became the major product for a new works at Brislington.

While during the early stages of the war Filton's main production facilities were given over to BE2 production, in early 1916, following German ascendancy with the Fokker monoplane, Frank Barnwell, by then a captain in the RFC, returned to Filton 'on indefinite leave without pay' to resume his former work as Chief Designer. The result was the adaptation of the Scout into the single-engined, two-seater F2B that became known as the Bristol Fighter and which, from 1916, came to be ordered in large numbers.

In founding and then expertly guiding the Bristol and Colonial Aviation Company from 1910 onwards, George White made a fundamental contribution to British aviation. Bringing in Frank Barnwell was no random act. As a brilliant and fearless businessman, White had the imagination to realise that outstanding planes were the essential requirement for success, for which gifted designers were required.

During the industry's early days White also understood that, hand-in-hand with the planes, his company needed to create facilities for pilot training and that these flying schools would act as most effective shop windows for his company's aircraft. Although the Admiralty and War Office declined his ambitious offer to train 500 service pilots at very competitive rates, by the commencement of the war 308 of the UK's certificated pilots had been trained by British and Colonial, and 80 per cent of the country's qualified pilots had qualified on Bristol aircraft.[13]

Sir George White died in 1916 and so did not live long enough to see the full results of his work, although by then his foresight and enthusiasm, high standards

Bristol Scout. (*Author's Collection*)

and inspired business sense had brought about the founding of an aircraft company that made an increasingly significant contribution during the First World War, survived the turmoil at its close and was to continue throughout the Second World War and beyond.

*   *   *

In Britain private constructors who entered the field shortly before the First World War had found themselves in a most difficult environment where they lacked the commercial sponsorship offered on the Continent and had to compete with the Royal Aircraft Factory. They also needed to produce technologically advanced aircraft on a scale they could never have imagined. This might easily have led to disastrous consequences, but with such determined individuals it so tempered their competitive instincts that they produced a plethora of designs (more than any other country) to seek the approval of the naval or army authorities. Sopwith, for instance, was accused of 'hectic gambling in the hope that one design would be a winner'.[14] But some of the planes turned out by him and others proved to be very good indeed.

It was as well that, as a group, they had the optimism, vision and energy of young men. At the outbreak of the war Sopwith was just twenty-six, Handley Page and Robert Blackburn twenty-nine, Horace Short an advanced forty-five – although his brother Oswald was thirty-one – with Fairey twenty-seven and Roe thirty-seven. Predictably, such frenetic activity was bound to take a toll: after Sir George White's death in 1916 Horace Short suddenly collapsed and died in 1917, having worked extraordinary hours all his life, and A.V. Roe lost much of his earlier dedication to the aeroplane business.

In such a headlong environment it was remarkable that they seemed able to retain the capacity to recognise their planes' frail beauty or continue to wonder at their accelerating performances. As if the inexorable demands for more planes were not enough, the British government that had treated them with such scant regard prior to the war found further ways of making life very difficult both during and after it. The worst stroke came in the form of its Excess Profits tax on profits 'in excess of a stipulated peacetime standard' which in 1917 was levied at a punitive rate of 80 per cent. This hit the aircraft industry especially hard for without commercial sponsorship its pre-war profits were miniscule and, during the war, the firms regularly put the majority of their profits into their expanding undertakings while at its end, when tax demands (requiring immediate payment) were still coming in, the requirement for aircraft abruptly ceased.

Chapter 13

Air Publicists – Practical Visionaries

Whatever the skills and dedication of the plane makers and of those who flew them, Britain's slowness in recognising the significance of airpower made it imperative that other committed individuals would help to develop an influential air lobby. One such man was Claude Grahame-White (b. 1879). By his mid-thirties Grahame-White, the audacious second son of a prosperous Hampshire family, would prove an outstanding pilot, a committed advocate for aviation in Britain and a superb salesman for what he termed London's airport, alongside which he would build and manage an aircraft factory.

Always mechanically inclined, following his early education at Crondall House School, Farnham, Grahame-White attended Bedford Grammar School before persuading his parents to let him be apprenticed to a Bedford Engineering firm. At this time he built and raced his own bicycle, following which he bought his first car, a small Bollée three-wheeler, and became a founder-member of the Automobile Club of Great Britain and Ireland. As a teenager he displayed rare confidence and ability when, after joining his uncle's textile business, he instigated great change by installing a new steam powerplant and replacing the shire horses with lorries. Having managed a 20,000-acre estate, he established his own motor business at No. 1 Albermarle Street in London's West End when he was

Claude Grahame-White. (*Author's Collection*)

twenty-six. He quickly made it a successful company and in his spare time sought adventure in the air, initially with balloons and then with aeroplanes. Like other pioneers, his chief inspiration came during the autumn of 1908 with Wilbur Wright's flight at Camp d'Auvours near Le Mans. After watching Wilbur, Grahame-White realised his true life's work lay in aviation rather than the motor industry. In 1909 therefore, following Blériot's flight across the Channel, he ordered one of Blériot's type XII aeroplanes, which he helped to assemble, and then taught himself to fly.

In Blériot's more amenable Type XI aircraft he qualified as a pilot with the Aero-Club de France, following which on 4 January 1910 he gained brevet Certificate No. 30 from the British Royal Aero-Club. By the end of the month Grahame-White founded the first British flying school at Pau, equipped with six Blériot monoplanes and a staff of instructors and mechanics, which he planned to transfer to Britain. Such aeronautical schemes required more capital however, and he set his sights on winning the massive £10,000 prize offered by Northcliffe's *Daily Mail* (which had been unclaimed since 1907) for flying the 185 miles from London to Manchester. Having received good reports about a French Voisin aircraft modified by Henry Farman he bought one for £1,500 with a loan provided by his mother, and on 23 April 1910 he set out for Manchester, coming second to the famous French flyer Louis Paulhan, also flying a Farman. Grahame-White flew the final leg by night (unheard of in those days) and he might well have won had the arrangement for Paulhan to send a message before his projected take-off reached Grahame-White in time.

In addition to his competitive flying Grahame-White took every opportunity to publicise the importance of the aeroplane to the British authorities. Although he had been heavily involved in the pioneering British Aviation meetings of 1910 at Wolverhampton (commencing 24 May), Bournemouth (10 July) and Blackpool (28 July), in August he gave a demonstration of the aeroplane's use in a reconnaissance role which helped lead to official trials being held during the British army's autumn manoeuvres on Salisbury Plain.

By late August Grahame-White was aboard the liner *Cymric* bound for Boston where he would enjoy immense success at America's Harvard/Boston meeting attended by some 250,000 people, where he won its Gordon Bennett Trophy for the speed race at Belmont Park. In all, he won an amazing £6,500 in a French aircraft powered by a French engine. One of his most remarkable achievements during the competitions was the accurate dropping of bombs on a target representing a warship, while the most flamboyant was his decision to pay his respects to President Taft by landing in Executive Avenue.

Together with the excitement of competition, Grahame-White believed passionately in the need to drive home the enormous potential of aviation, not only in terms of civilian travel but for military needs and to have it more extensively recognised in Britain during the early years of the twentieth century. He forecast that,

> with a well-trained Corps of military airmen Commanders-in-Chief will no
> longer grope in the dark. They will sit, so to speak, on either side of a

chessboard, which will represent the battlefield. Each will watch the other's moves; nothing will be concealed[1] ... At present [the war aeroplane's] work has been confined to scouting but it has other and grimmer possibilities. It can, and without doubt will, be used as an engine of destruction – not by means of the bomb-dropping attacks of a few aeroplanes, but by the organised onslaught of large squadrons of weight-lifting machines, which will be able to rain down tons of missiles on any given spot.[2]

While Grahame-White took the opportunities open to him as a pioneer pilot and then as a flying impresario, constructor and businessman, he never lost sight of the grave dangers to British security if the country did not embrace the cause of aviation on a similar scale as France and Germany.

On 1 January 1911 he signalled his intention of becoming a constructor and publicist when he persuaded Louis Blériot and Sir Hiram Maxim to join him in establishing 'a London Aerodrome' on 207 acres of marshland at Hendon. When the other two withdrew, he continued independently and with the help of his uncle, Sir Arthur du Gross, took on the whole enterprise. In August 1911 the Grahame-White Aviation Company was established and a ten-year lease taken on Hendon aerodrome with the right of purchase, together with more land if required. The transfer of his flying school from Pau to Hendon marked the initial stage of ambitious plans to make Hendon, rather than Brooklands, Britain's foremost aerodrome through which he believed he could popularise aviation for both the social elite and ordinary Londoners.

By March 1911 the Grahame-White Aviation Company had taken a stand at the British Aerial Exhibition at Olympia, where it displayed a copy of the Farman which he had used in competitions together with a new 50hp pusher aeroplane called 'Baby' for air enthusiasts of moderate means. In addition to developing Hendon and continuing with his competitive flying, Grahame-White still found time to mount a military flying display on 12 May 1911 for the Prime Minister, the Secretary of State for War and over 300 members of Parliament. At this he demonstrated the military possibilities of aircraft for aerial reconnaissance, the transportation of machine guns and ammunition and the bombing of a model battleship from 2,000ft.[3] The value of reconnoitring was shown when two aircraft, carrying Captain Sykes and Captain Evelyn Wood as military observers, located troops and guns posted under cover between Hendon and St Albans. The outstanding feature came when Grahame-White gave an accurate demonstration of bomb dropping using 100lb sandbags suspended on ropes below the wings of his Farman.[4] A few days earlier he had addressed the Aerial Defence Committee at the Houses of Parliament on the necessity for developing military aircraft. Both initiatives came less than six weeks after the announcement of the War Office's decision to form an air battalion of the Royal Engineers.

During the coming summer, Hendon acted as the first stop for *The Daily Mail* 'Round Britain Race'. The organisers sent their first competitor off at 4.00am on Monday, 24 July and nearly 500,000 spectators spent the night there, with many camping in fields around the aerodrome. Grahame-White's ambitions for

Hendon were boundless, although he was still much involved in flying competitions – as in September 1911 when, together with Tommy Sopwith, he competed in the second Harvard/Boston meeting – although he was less successful than in the previous year.

Hendon's popularity grew and his flying school turned out more pilots during the year than any other in the country,[5] while there was a steady rise in the public attendance at its air displays and when those seeking the experience of flight were taken round the airfield for a fee of £2 2s; although hundreds took part there was not a single accident. Grahame-White built three public enclosures, the one opposite the finishing line cost spectators 2s 6d, that housing the majority cost 1s and those at the rear paid just 6d. The displays at Hendon went beyond pure entertainment, however, for the commercial possibilities of aircraft were demonstrated by means of the first aerial postal service in the United Kingdom, carried between Hendon and Windsor by pilots of the Grahame-White aviation Company.[6]

In 1912 there were other new developments. A four-day flying event was held over Easter and by April regular weekend meetings, including one specially for the army and navy,[7] contributed to a total of thirty during the year. On the first, 22,000 people paid for admission. At these 'there were joyrides, aerobatics and exciting air races often around a closed circuit marked by black and white pylons. What they lacked in speed the pioneer pilots made up for by flying only a few feet above the ground'.[8] The most notable performers were Hamel and Hucks; although Cody had hoped to compete he crashed a few days before and was injured. Another Grahame-White inspiration, an aerial Derby (starting and finishing at Hendon and sponsored by *The Daily Mail*), was held in June. This attracted 45,000 spectators to the aerodrome and thousands more along its 81-mile route. In September 1912 the millionth spectator passed through the Hendon turnstiles, and a clubhouse and thirty-bedroom hotel were opened. On 29 June Grahame-White was married, but on returning from his honeymoon he took part in a 'Wake up England' tour designed to make the country more air conscious in the course of which he visited 121 towns, gave 500 exhibitions and carried 1,200 passengers.[9]

In addition to giving public displays, the Grahame-White Aviation Company built aircraft where it enjoyed mixed success with models designed by J.D. North. These included 'The Popular', a small two-seat biplane marketed at a modest £400, together with a military biplane, which turned out to be a failure. More promising was another biplane, powered by a 120hp Austro-Daimler engine, which had seating for four passengers and went into service in September 1913. The company showed off its 'charabanc' at the 1914 Aerial Exhibition held at Olympia together with a new two-seater pusher with a 100hp Gnome engine. In the last few months before the war, large numbers of aerial enthusiasts continued to visit Hendon to enjoy the thrills, that included parachute descents, joy rides in Grahame-White's 'charabanc' and the aces looping the loop and flying upside down.

At the outbreak of war commercial flying ceased at Hendon and, after Grahame-White's aircraft and aerodrome facilities were requisitioned, it became a naval air station,[10] although its flying school remained in operation which by the end of the war had trained 488 pupils. The factory also continued to operate, chiefly manufacturing aircraft designed by others, and although in the first place Grahame-White left to become a lieutenant-commander in the RNAS, he subsequently resigned his commission and returned to supervise the constructional work there, for which he raised extra capital and increased the work force to some 3,000.

Whatever his successes as a pilot and constructor, Grahame-White's greatest contribution to early flying in Britain came through his unshakeable belief in the future of aircraft and his skills in demonstrating this. *The Times'* obituary of him had no doubt about the message he sent and his methods of communicating it:

> [In 1910] and for many years thereafter, he was an outstanding world personality in aviation. He believed fervently in the future of flying from the outset, and by his own exploits, by organisation, by design of models, by the promotion of meetings and by pen and voice he exercised a powerful influence in making aircraft a practicable,[11] speedy and tolerably safe form of transport.

As *The Times* recognised, Grahame-White's especial endowment to British aviation lay in his inspired attempts to publicise the aeroplane's rich future and to persuade the British Government and the British public about the influential role it would play in any future war and beyond, not to mention the increased levels of investment needed for Britain to hold its own in the technological race with other countries.

*   *   *

Another more inscrutable but genuine early publicist was The Honourable Charles Stewart Rolls (b. 1877), the third son of Lord Llanattock who owned extensive land holdings in both London and Monmouthshire. Rolls quickly became one of the central figures in early British aviation, although his school days gave little indication of what was to come. After an undistinguished time at the Mortimer Vicarage School in Berkshire his three-year-long stay at Eton was more notable for joining the college Volunteers (the ancestor of the Combined Cadet Force) than for anything else. He was already conforming to Thomas Sopwith's later description of him as something of a 'natural solitary', for in 1892 one of his school reports observed that 'Rolls, I regret to say is still forgetful and irregular, sometimes even to vanishing point'.[12]

During Rolls' vacations it was somewhat different, for he supervised the installing of electricity at the Hendré, the family's home in Monmouthshire. At this stage his future was by no means clear and after briefly considering – and rejecting – the army for a career, he attended a 'crammer' run by the legendary Mr Herbert Pigg, following which he was accepted to read engineering by Trinity

Charles Rolls. (*Royal Aeronautical Society* [*National Aerospace Library*])

College, Cambridge, from where he graduated in 1898 with an ordinary Bachelor of Arts degree in mechanism and applied science. At Cambridge he became known as a keep fit enthusiast and was awarded a Half Blue for cycling. Cycling sparked off an enthusiasm for speed and, following a weekend visit to the home of car enthusiast Sir David Salomons, Rolls went over to Paris and purchased a second-hand 3¾hp Peugeot Phaeton which he took to Cambridge. It was notable as the first car owned by an undergraduate.

Two tricycles followed which, together with the car, were repaired in the University's engineering laboratories. In accordance with his fitness regime he avoided alcohol and favoured vegetarian restaurants, although he was not a true vegetarian. At university he also acquired a reputation for carefulness with money that verged on the miserly.[13] Even so, John Brabazon, who on occasion acted as his unpaid mechanic, idolised him. Brabazon called him 'the sweetest, kindest, meanest man I ever met – he was so tight with his cash that he used to join us at lunch at the Aero Club with a packet of sandwiches which he took from his pocket to eat while he ordered a glass of water to wash them down. But I loved him as a brother. We all did'.[14]

Following Cambridge, Rolls spent a further four years acquiring more practical knowledge of engineering, including a period in the railway shops at Crewe. Following this, he made his first ascent in a balloon and began to buy and sell all kinds of motor cars which he drove in motoring events, such as the Thousand Miles Trial of 1900, to demonstrate their reliability.

In 1902, with the support of his father, he decided to go into business as an automobile agent, despite the unfavourable attitude of many of his contemporaries towards trade. It was a financial necessity, for his father's allowance of £500 a year was quite inadequate for the scale of his motoring activities. He soon revealed marked skills as a demonstrator and motor salesman, and acquired the British agency for French Panhard cars. He broke new ground by instituting easy terms for his customers, with a 25 per cent down payment, followed by four quarterly instalments, and he attracted a number of illustrious clients. By 1904 Panhard was losing out to other marques but in May of that year, on meeting the brilliant engineer Henry Royce, Rolls finally found a car which he believed was good enough to be sponsored with his own name. After his first meeting with Royce[15] he dragged his partner, Claude Johnson, out of bed with the excited words: 'I have found the greatest motor engineer in the world'.[16] Even so, it was only after major teething troubles that Rolls, together with Henry Royce and Claude Johnson, produced the six-cylinder Silver Ghost that Rolls so successfully promoted, including driving it to victory in the 1906 Tourist Trophy race held in the Isle of Man, before winning the 15,000-mile endurance trial the following year. By now, however, 'he realised that the motor car had passed from revolution to evolution and he was content to let the affairs of Rolls-Royce settle down to a steady process of consolidation',[17] while his interests turned increasingly to the more exciting challenge of powered flight.

On 8 September 1898, nine years after he had taken his first trip in a balloon, he accompanied Percival Spencer in an ascent from the Crystal Palace, from where they travelled sixteen miles to Epping Forest. In spite of his interests in cars and aeroplanes, Rolls continued ballooning and it was during a flight accompanied by Frank Hedges Butler and his daughter Vera in a balloon called 'The City of York' that they decided to form the Aero Club of Great Britain to 'encourage the study of aeronautics and develop the sciences connected therewith'. From the time of its foundation Rolls remained a committee member, flying the Club's balloons from 1901 to 1905.

In 1905 Rolls decided to enter an international ballooning competition held in Paris sponsored by American publisher James Gordon Bennett, for which he decided he needed his own balloon. Just as his search for excellent cars led him to the highly skilled Henry Royce, for his balloons Rolls approached the Short brothers, with their reputation for quality workmanship, and in his Short balloon he won gold and silver medals for endurance awarded by the Aero Club de France. In 1906, despite the incorporation of Rolls' business into Rolls Royce Ltd, he actually increased his ballooning activity: before the incorporation he made twenty-three ascents in all, but in 1906 he made twenty-nine more, including some with Tommy Sopwith and John Moore-Brabazon.

In June of the same year Rolls was granted his aeronaut's certificate by the Aero Club, although after his motoring successes and with the growing prospect of powered flight, this continuing enthusiasm for ballooning seemed surprising. His colleague Frank Hedges Butler believed it was because, unlike land transport (and powered aeroplanes), 'there is no giddiness, no movement, only a sensation of perfect quiet and restfulness'.[18]

His love of ballooning continued up to the time of his death but, from 1901, he also appreciated the greater importance of airships and aeroplanes. Addressing the Authors' Club in 1909 he acknowledged that 'ballooning is essentially a sport pure and simple'[19] and that future air transportation lay with airships and particularly with aeroplanes. His regard for airships was seen in 1909 when, with his friend Colonel John Capper, Rolls agreed to manufacture the gearing and drive shafts for the propellers of the army airship *Gamma* – much to the anger of his fellow directors at Rolls Royce, who believed such facilities should be restricted to work on motor cars.

Whatever his enduring interests in other forms of locomotion, Rolls was one of the earliest proponents of powered aircraft in Britain. During September 1908, he made his first flight with Wilbur Wright at Auvours in France (Samuel Cody did not fly until 16 October). Watching Wilbur operating his controls Rolls felt sure he could fly such a plane but the Wrights suggested he should start – as they did – with glider trials, which he began on 30 July 1909 in a glider built by the Short brothers to a Wrights' design. He was confident enough in the Shorts' workmanship to order the first of six Wright planes being built on licence by them and follow this with a further order for the sixth. In 1908 he also ordered a French-built Wright plane which had still not arrived the following year. With his reputed knowledge of aviation, Rolls was called as an expert witness before the 1908/9 sub-committee of the Imperial Defence Committee investigating the state of Britain's aerial navigation, when the support he gave to aeroplanes was not well received.

After practising in his glider on 9 October 1909 Rolls flew the Shorts' Flyer, and such was his progress that at Eastchurch on 30 December he set an endurance record for a UK pilot of fifty-five minutes and this was followed by taking up Cecil Grace in a trip lasting twenty minutes, the longest passenger flight made at this time. In March 1910 he received the French Aero Club's Aviation Certificate and the second pilot's licence ever awarded by the Aero Club, the first having been granted a few minutes earlier to John Moore-Brabazon (later Lord Brabazon of Tara) who had briefly flown his Voisin aircraft at Sheppey during May 1909.

By January 1910 Rolls found he could no longer reconcile all his conflicting interests, and during a meeting at Derby he asked his co-directors at Rolls Royce whether he could be relieved of some of his routine work. With their agreement, he no longer had to demonstrate Rolls Royce cars and could transfer his office to the family's London home, thus enabling him to increase his flying activities. During early 1910 he was so busy practising on the Isle of Sheppey that he lived amongst the villagers at Leysdown 'on a diet chiefly of eggs and milk puddings'.

In February Rolls went to France where, although he had still not received his French-built Wright, he was able to pilot one and watch a flying display by Roger Sommer in a modified Farman aircraft. He was sufficiently impressed to place an order.

Rolls continued to emphasise his support of aeroplanes by delivering his Short/Wright No. 1 to the War Office and escorting the Prince and Princess of Wales (the future King George V and Queen Mary) to the Royal Aero Club exhibition at Olympia, where he showed them the third aircraft built by the Shorts, together with his Sommer Farman which had been delivered to him immediately prior to the exhibition. With this, he hoped to take part in aircraft competitions.

In April 1910 Rolls finally received delivery of his French-built Wright, which he also determined to use in his first attempts at competitive flying. He began with the flying meeting at Nice, but missed its opening days because he needed to have a tailplane fitted to make the plane more stable. He told the Wrights that the tailplane was manufactured locally and was mounted on its own outriggers, independent of the rudder. Considering his delayed participation, Rolls did creditably at Nice, although he complained to the Wrights about their system of launching their planes from rails 'during which the Farman fellows won hundreds of pounds in prizes while I am shifting my rails'.[20]

Returning from Nice, Rolls' next objective was to emulate Blériot's feat of flying across the Channel. Between 24 May and 2 June he suffered a number of mechanical problems but on the second day he crossed from Dover to Sangatte, at a moderate speed of around 30mph, where he dropped a message of greeting to the Aero Club of France, before returning to Dover non-stop. For the trip he had special rubberised-fabric flotation bags strapped to the skid chassis of his aircraft in case he came down on water. This was in line with his thorough safety precautions, although his friends 'jokingly said that he wore out his engine by excessive testing in the endeavour to get a few more revs per minute'.[21]

His Channel crossing made Rolls a national hero: he received a gold medal from the Royal Aero Club, the King sent a congratulatory telegram and Madame Tussaud's used him as one of their models. Such was the momentum of his activities that he straightaway resumed testing for the forthcoming aviation week at Dunstall Park, Wolverhampton. Unfortunately, heavy rain reduced its ground to a quagmire and flying was virtually wiped out, although Rolls won a speed prize. As a result he much looked forward to competing at Bournemouth's centenary celebrations where the flying site had been cleared, drained and levelled.

By the time he reached Bournemouth Rolls had several plans in mind, including instructing army pilots on Laffan's Plain, which he hoped would be followed by a visit to America for more air competitions. He had also been making plans to form an aircraft company, with the young pilot Keith-Davies as its secretary. More immediately, he needed to replace his troublesome tailplane with a new one. This did not arrive until 7 July and, although it was fitted three days later, he had no time to flight-test it prior to the meeting. On the opening day, Monday, 11 July, Rolls made a successful slow circuit, and on the second he entered the contest for landing on, or close to, a set circle marked out on the ground. This 'target' had been placed in a hazardous position just sixty yards from the grandstand and the same distance from the judges' box. To make matters more difficult, there was a prevailing crosswind approaching 20mph. Rolls chose to make his attempt by flying into the wind, which required a steep final descent, but as he prepared to pull out of the dive the spectators heard a loud snap and the tailplane disintegrated, bringing the plane down on its nose. As it hit the ground Rolls was thrown clear but he died within seconds from concussion of the brain, the first Englishman to die in a powered flying machine.

With his death Britain lost one of its chief figures in early aviation, someone who had graduated to aircraft following his notable activities in cycling, cars and ballooning. While Rolls' performance fell short of greatness, the best seemed sure to come. That said, his personal limitations worked against him: tall and austere, he seemed incapable of warm human relationships, with his short temper, crude public-school sense of humour and monumental meanness. Those, like Brabazon, who counted themselves his friends, while recognising him as 'curiously unlovable' and 'a natural solitary', seemed prepared to forgive him because of his earnestness and persistence in demonstrating the current mechanical developments on land and in the air.

The crash was the more tragic for, however brave, his courage was always calculated and he never took undue risks (if that were possible with early motoring and flight which were dangerous in themselves). As a result, while undoubtedly successful when driving the best cars, he was not the greatest car driver and, with a flying career that only started in October 1909 and ended in July 1910, not yet one of the greatest pilots nor one of the aircraft industry's outstanding publicists like Grahame-White. He had yet to show any skills as a designer and with his future aeroplane company already in preparation, his aerial exploits could never be divorced from commercial considerations. Notwithstanding, Rolls had shown certain visionary qualities and as a member of the nobility had given powerful support to the further development of cars and aeroplanes where, in the latter case, so many difficulties and prejudices were yet to be overcome.

He was also seen by many as a patriot. In Bedford shortly after his death, the local press published a poem acknowledging his dedication to Britain's need for airpower.

He might have lived at home at ease,
As he had wealth in store
And let his country drift behind
As many did before.[22]

He had certainly joined the army volunteers at Eton and was an early member of the Army Motor Volunteers (later to become the Army Motor Reserve). He also relished conducting members of the royal family around Olympia to witness the air industry's development (and see his own aircraft), while shortly before his death he was planning to train army pilots.

For such reasons this intriguing, contradictory man warrants an undoubted place among those who helped to raise the interest of the British people and the political establishment from dangerous indifference, if not apathy, to the startling mechanical developments of the time, particularly with aeroplanes. In its obituary Northcliffe's *Daily Mail* had no doubts, writing that he was a man 'who assisted in removing the fetters on mechanical invention: Rolls died a martyr to knowledge'.[23]

*   *   *

Another major advocate for aviation in Britain, together with a determination to convert the Liberal government to its importance, was George Holt Thomas (b. 1869). He enjoyed the advantage of having considerable wealth deriving from his position in the newspaper business, for in the year before his birth his father had founded *The Graphic*, an illustrated weekly, and followed it twenty years later with *The Daily Graphic* newspaper. After attending King's College School, London, George went up to Queen's College, Oxford, in 1888, before becoming general manager of his father's newspapers. He went on to found his own illustrated weekly, *The Bystander*, and then *The Empire Illustrated* which championed the production of British goods for British people at home and abroad. He also founded the Association of British Motor Manufacturers, which advocated an import duty on foreign cars.

In 1906 he met Henry Farman, the Anglo-French aircraft designer and flyer, and thereafter he curtailed his newspaper activities to make the promotion of aviation his life's work, convinced it would have momentous civilian and military consequences and in which Britain must become a leading force. To this end Holt Thomas's *Graphic* and *Daily Graphic* offered a £1,000 prize for the first flight of a straight mile by an aircraft.

Holt Thomas spent much time in France watching Farman make the first kilometre flight and Blériot preparing for his own Channel fight in 1909. He was already well aware of the greater emphasis paid to flight in Europe by pointing out in April 1909 that German spending on military aviation was approximately £100,000, French spending totalled £47,000, while the British spent just £5,000.

George Holt Thomas, who
formed the Aircraft
Manufacturing Company
Limited (Airco) in 1912.
(*Royal Aeronautical Society*
[*National Aerospace Library*])

Holt Thomas was so impressed by the aviation meeting at Rheims during the same year where he first flew as a passenger with Henry Farman, and where he saw the markedly improved performance levels of the new French Gnome engines, that he decided to organise similar meetings in England, the first of which was held for the Blackpool Corporation. At great personal expense he brought the French flyer, Louis Paulhan, to Brooklands and Sandown Park to give demonstration flights and in April 1910 he assisted him in his successful attempt on the London to Manchester race, for which his friend Northcliffe offered a huge prize of £10,000. Holt Thomas inspired Northcliffe's own interest in aviation and found accommodation for Paulhan's aircraft with Grahame-White at what became Hendon airfield, before hiring a special train which carried journalists and other interested parties and obtained priority over all traffic to follow Paulhan's flight.

During 1910, as a proud Englishman, Holt Thomas wrote a major article for a compendium on the aeroplane, edited by Claude Grahame-White and Harry

Harper,[24] in which he emphasised the enormous progress made by France during that year in contrast 'to the apathy displayed in this country by the public, the Government and those who should be interested from a commercial point of view'.[25] He went on to point out that with regard to national security 'flying is much more important than motoring, we are no longer an island. The sea is no longer our protection. Flights which are becoming almost daily occurrences, come within the limits of London and Berlin. Paris is an easy flight'.[26]

Holt Thomas asked for 'our great manufacturers (and presumably those constructing motors are the most notable) to share the confidence that I possess, and to enter into the question from a commercial and national point of view'.[27] He proceeded to consider matters of national offence and defence, drawing attention to the vital scouting made possible by aircraft at the French army manoeuvres, and concluded with an appeal for a large military air service.

> We have the men; we need not blush for our aviators. We have as fine aviators as any other nation, but they are not numerous enough. Both in the Navy, and in the Army, volunteers would be forthcoming in their thousands; but machines and schools must be provided for them, and for this we must willingly and cheerfully vote the money – and, after all what a trivial amount is required![28]

Holt Thomas was not only a wealthy and gifted communicator, but he presented a striking figure who, with his trimmed beard, resembled George V, although he was much taller and had a more piercing expression. More importantly, he was quite prepared to use his wealth in the cause of aviation. He was so convinced that Britain needed the resources to build both aircraft and their engines that in 1912 he formed the Aircraft Manufacturing Co Ltd that took over the assets of the Hendon Aeronautical syndicate. Through it, this practical visionary acquired the rights to build the successful French Farman aircraft, which were subsequently used extensively as training machines by large numbers of the RFC, together with the French Gnome and Rhône engines that were installed in British aircraft during the First World War.

Holt Thomas soon demonstrated his business acumen and belief in private enterprise by persuading Geoffrey de Havilland, one of the most gifted designers in aviation history, to join Airco.[29] De Havilland later recalled how glad he had been to work for a brilliantly clever, as well as a kind and likeable man, who was 'far sighted, extremely able and possessed a knowledge of business only equalled by his ignorance of engineering'.[30] Holt Thomas compensated for such ignorance by seeking the advice of another of his friends, Mervyn O'Gorman at the Royal Aircraft Factory, and, of course, by recruiting de Havilland as his designer and test pilot. So influential did De Havilland become, that about 30 per cent of all the fighters, bombers and training aeroplanes used by Britain and the US during the war were his designs and preceded by the letters DH. De Havilland believed that in fairness they should have had the initial DHT involving both his and Holt Thomas's names, but Holt Thomas was quite happy to acknowledge de Havilland's design skills rather than his own position.

Shortly before the First World War Holt Thomas turned his particular attention to the almost total lack of British aircraft engines. He offered to open an engine factory if the British government would guarantee an order for fifty Gnomes. When the Treasury refused, he bought a subcontracting plant run by engineer Peter Hooker to build them, initially on a small scale but with the intention of increasing production as quickly as possible. At the outbreak of war Hooker was still only producing one engine a week and Holt Thomas went to the Daimler Motor Company with a request to build the 80hp Gnomes, 8,000 of which were subsequently produced during the war. He also foresaw the possibility of such engines being made in the USA where over 1,200 were actually built.

During the war Holt Thomas came to head a vast company which by the end employed 7,000 people and produced an aeroplane every three-quarters of an hour. It was the largest of the British aircraft firms (and larger than any other overseas firm) which played a major part in supplying the RFC with the planes and engines that he knew would be required for a massively expanding air arm.[31] His sophisticated test equipment included a wind tunnel and a metal testing laboratory. Shortly after the war Holt Thomas proudly acknowledged that 'Long before the war I was urging on an apathetic Government and country the necessity for developing the aircraft as a weapon; and I may say without boasting that all my predictions have been more than fulfilled by actual experiences of the last few years'.[32]

Holt Thomas was not only shrewd, dedicated and accomplished but he was lucky to see his ideas developed to such practical effect, although at the end of the war he had to sell out to the British Small Arms Company). Holt Thomas was a practical visionary who not only recognised the dangers in neglecting airpower but goaded the British government into taking belated action, and from the beginning of the war personally invested in the remarkable growth of British airpower that took place during the conflict. Although he received no decoration for his work in publicising and sponsoring aviation, in 1925 he was given a major part of the £200,000 from the Commission on Rewards for Inventors 'whose inventions had been utilized during the war'.[33]

*   *   *

In their different fashion, all three men played most influential roles in publicising and furthering British aviation. Graham-White as a brilliant pilot, publicist and oracle, while Holt Thomas' outstanding contribution was in the expansion of the British aircraft industry. But the greatest legacy arguably came from Charles Rolls through his partnership with Henry Royce, legendary engine designer and Engineer-in-Chief of Rolls-Royce Ltd. As early as 1909 Rolls had intended building Wright aeroplanes with engines adapted by Royce from his 20hp car engine, but the more cautious directors of Rolls Royce vetoed it and the project lapsed. In 1914, however, Royce agreed to design an aero engine with 'a weight/power ratio far below anything he had designed before',[34] resulting in his V12

Henry Royce, legendary engine designer and Engineer-in-Chief of Rolls-Royce Limited.
(*Royal Aeronautical Society* [*National Aerospace Library*])

The Rolls Royce Falcon II aero engine that developed 275hp. (*Author's Collection*)

cylinder water-cooled 200hp Eagle engine (with the Falcon Hawk engines of 190 and 75hp developed in parallel).

By 1918 such Rolls-Royce engines had equipped 'five eighths of the aeroplanes and seaplanes we used in the Great War' and the firm delivered 1,500,000 HP to the government during the conflict.[35]

The story by no means ended there, for twenty-one years later the Rolls' legacy continued with Henry Royce's Merlin engine, direct heir to his Eagle that was to prove so important to the RAF in the Second World War.

Chapter 14

Air Publicists –
Parliamentary Voices

Where the air lobbyists were likely to have the greatest effect, of course, was in Parliament, and much the most influential of these was Winston Spencer Churchill (b. 1874), son of the tempestuous Victorian politician, Lord Randolph Churchill. Winston's timing was fortuitous for aviation, with his parliamentary career beginning in February 1901, less than three years before the Wrights' first aeroplane flight on 14 December 1903.

By the age of twenty-six he had already been something of a soldier of fortune who, through his journalistic and presentational skills, had gathered a modest fortune of £10,000 to help support himself in Parliament. With his talents and exceptional industry, it was predictable that Churchill's progress would be rapid. After serving as Under Secretary of State to the Colonial Office, in 1908 he was appointed President of the Board of Trade, becoming Home Secretary two years later. In October 1911 he was made First Lord of the Admiralty which, with the predominance of the Royal Navy and the growing likelihood of war, was a key appointment. It proved to be one that particularly suited Churchill, who had taken the closest interest in military affairs ever since he had manoeuvred his magnificent collection of model soldiers in versions of the great John Churchill's campaigns, and then followed with his own military service.

Churchill was a keen advocate of modern technology. Whilst in the Sudan he had seen the massive advantages brought about by machine guns, breech-loading rifles, artillery and gunboats, which would prove significant when he was First Lord of the Admiralty and also dealing with the infant air forces. As First Lord he pressed for technologically advanced battleships driven by oil-fired engines and equipped with 15in guns, as well as encouraging the development of submarines.

A similar approach was apparent with airborne vehicles, particularly aeroplanes. This became evident during discussions in the Commons about the findings of the 1908/9 Sub-Committee of Imperial Defence on Aerial Navigation that ruled against the development of aeroplanes under army arrangements, declaring itself content for the War Office to receive instruction on an aircraft from Charles Rolls, whose plane had been built by the Wright brothers. Churchill considered such proposals altogether too amateurish: the future role of aeroplanes was so important that the War Office should place itself 'in communication with Mr [Orville] Wright and avail ourselves of his knowledge'.[1] He agreed, however, with the recommendations of the Sub-Committee that the encouragement of private enterprise (for the construction of planes) was a good one.[2]

A young Winston Churchill in military uniform.
(*Author's Collection*)

Churchill's personal enthusiasm for aircraft became evident during the British army manoeuvres of 21 September 1910, when the observations made by Captain Bertram Dickson while flying over the training area proved far more effective than the reconnaissance sweeps by the cavalry of the opposing forces. After the controllers ruled that Dickson's plane had been 'captured', Churchill arrived on horseback to 'inspect' the aeroplane and spent some time discussing its capabilities with the pilot. In addition to watching aeroplanes carry out such tactical roles Churchill had already discussed aviation at length with his confidante, Admiral 'Jackie' Fisher and when Churchill became First Lord, Fisher reminded him of their earlier conversations:

> Aviation supersedes small cruisers and Intelligence vessels. You told me you would push aviation – you are right – but don't take away our splendid young Naval Officers who have been suckled on Gunnery and sea-fighting to do what civilians can do better. The civilian air-man can always carry an expert for observing ...[3]

Churchill disagreed with Fisher on this, believing naval flyers should be serving personnel and following the foundation of the RFC in April 1912 with its Central Flying School and military and naval wings, he attempted to take naval aviation away from the War Office's control. As he wrote later in *The World Crisis*:

> The War Office claimed on behalf of the Royal Flying Corps complete and sole responsibility for the aerial defence of Great Britain. But owing to the difficulties of getting money, they were unable to make any provision for this responsibility, every aeroplane they had being earmarked for the Expeditionary Force. Seeing this and finding myself able to procure funds by various shifts and devices, I began in 1912 and 1913 to form under the Royal Naval Air Service flights of aeroplanes as well as of seaplanes for the aerial protection of our naval harbours, oil tanks and vulnerable points and also for a general strengthening of our exiguous and inadequate aviation. In consequence I had in my own hand on the eve of the war fifty efficient naval machines, or about one third of the number in possession of the Army.[4]

In 1912 Churchill had pressed for his 'various shifts and devices' for purchasing aeroplanes to be replaced by Treasury support, but was rebuffed three times before writing to the Treasury in the strongest terms.

> I had rather hoped from our talk the other day that your objections were removed. I could not be responsible for the conduct of the Admiralty business unless this most vital subject of naval aeronautics received the attention and study it requires. The organisation proposed is absolutely necessary and is already in being. It is most modest in scale and I should certainly not agree to its being broken up. I am very much distressed by these repeated refusals of the Treasury, which are injurious to the public service.[5]

Churchill obtained his Treasury approval and he appointed naval Captain Murray Sueter as Director of the Naval Air Detachments who, by the commencement of the war, had been promoted to Commodore. During the first few months of the war the Deputy Director of military aeronautics in the War Office, Colonel Sefton Brancker, had the task of working with Sueter concerning the allocation of available contractors, aircraft and engines between the army's and navy's air departments, where the navy had already taken an earlier initiative. Brancker wrote:

> I endeavoured to co-operate thoroughly with him and I think he was anxious to meet the wishes of the War Office in every way possible; but he was not his own master, for the vigorous and enthusiastic personality of Mr Winston Churchill had come into play. He believed in aviation. Even at that time he had realised the enormous possibilities of the attack on hostile territory by an independent air force, and had grasped the necessity of some central control over all aeronautical matters. But the Admiralty conceived that this control should be vested in the Admiralty, with the independent force part and parcel of the Navy, his particular responsibility at the moment; and to this end he worked assiduously during the last months of 1914.[6]

In 1912 Churchill made his first flight in a seaplane and was more knowledgeable about the naval wing, which he had transformed into the RNAS, than many of its own officers. He required seaplanes to be of uniform design with standard wireless equipment, interchangeable engines and good visibility for both pilots and observers, while arguing that the objectives of land aeroplanes could never be so definite nor important as seaplanes, 'which when they carry torpedoes may prove capable of playing a decisive part in operations against capital ships'.[7]

Churchill seemed capable of moving effortlessly from considering the role of seaplanes to the minutest details of facilities at the navy's training school at Eastchurch, including whether its accommodation should include a squash court rather than a second tennis court (Minute of February 1914); the extent of visibility required for its landing places; and whether its members' uniforms should sport an eagle instead of an anchor on buttons, cap badges and epaulettes. Among the seemingly endless stream of memoranda flowing from Churchill's pen was one on the need for eight planes to be standing by at Eastchurch, always ready to fly.

In 1913 Churchill gave Murray Sueter a relatively loose rein over the types of aircraft required for the navy, and Sueter was able to demand greater size and power for his seaplanes – needs which were subsequently met by private contractors, notably Shorts, Sopwith and AVRO. Although the army was far less enthusiastic for specialist aeroplanes, it would also benefit from the navy's initiatives and ultimately follow Churchill's example. Under Churchill's probing, by the beginning of the war the navy already saw an aeroplane as a fighting machine with possible additional functions, such as bomb-dropping and machine gunnery, rather than the army's greater concentration on reconnaissance and artillery spotting. In late 1914 the navy gained a publicity coup when it undertook a remarkable series of air raids on German Zeppelin sheds at Cologne and Friedrichshafen, and for a time under Commander Samson it operated with armoured Rolls-Royces and a handful of aeroplanes in support of the BEF. One could argue that the planes might have been as well, or better, used by the RFC elsewhere on the Continent, although by encouraging money to be spent freely with the civilian constructors, Churchill undoubtedly helped them to expand their production facilities to include some outstanding aircraft.

During these years Churchill insisted on flying between naval stations where experienced pilots were given the privilege of carrying him, but were forbidden to let him fly solo in case of a crash.[8] His penchant for risk-taking was well known and on 12 March 1913 his cousin, the Duke of Marlborough, took issue with him about it: 'Really I consider that you owe it to your wife, family and friends to desist from a practice or pastime – whichever you call it – which is fraught with so much danger to life. It is really wrong of you . . .' The risks were made apparent on 2 December 1913 when Churchill's favourite pilot, Captain Gilbert Wildman-Lushington of the Royal Marines, was killed when he side-slipped and crashed as he came in to land at Eastchurch.[9]

Apparently Churchill had earlier promised his wife that he would not fly until she had recovered from the birth of their son, Randolph (b. 28 May 1911), but he could not resist, arguing that it was important for morale, as when he made an inspection of the Oxford Yeomanry on Salisbury Plain and a week later (1 June 1914) flew to make an inspection of Portsmouth dockyard.[10] (During 1917 when, as Minister of Munitions, he was required to make frequent visits to the Continent he did so by air, experiencing a number of hair-raising incidents in which he was preserved only by his remarkable good luck.)

When in 1918 the RNAS was absorbed into the RAF it was an impressive and efficient formation, much of which was due to Churchill who, through his active encouragement and forthright methods, was said to have cut red tape, dispelled mistrust and helped to produce miracles.[11]

Beyond this his contribution, both as determined politician and publicist, towards the development of Britain's air forces was as one might expect, both powerful and individualistic. He quickly appreciated the many military roles open to technically advancing aircraft and their likely influence on war and although the separation of the RNAS from the Royal Flying Corps was bound to be viewed with disfavour by the War Office, he insisted on their close co-operation (between equals) which at times included the loan of aircraft.

Churchill has rightly been called 'a helpful and enthusiastic parent of air-power',[12] an assessment supported on 17 May 1916 during his attack on the current government for its failure to create an air ministry.

> At sea the increased power of the defence in mines and submarines has largely robbed the stronger Navy of its rights. On land, we are in a position of having lost our ground before the modern defence was thoroughly under-stood and having to win it back when the offensive has been elevated into a fine art. But the air is free and open. There are no entrenchments there. It is equal for the attack and defence. It is equal for all comers. The resources of the whole world are at our disposal and command. Nothing stands in the way of our obtaining the aerial supremacy in the War but yourselves. There is no reason, and there can be no excuse, for failure to obtain that aerial supremacy …[13]

Churchill's right to make such an eloquent and highly optimistic conclusion about the opportunity offered by air power had surely been earned by his support of the aeroplanes made by private contractors during the last four years before the war.

*   *   *

In contrast to Churchill's far-reaching aerial activities as an air publicist, William Joynson-Hicks (b. 1865) (later First Viscount Brentford) became renowned for a singular occurrence. The son of a London merchant, Joynson-Hicks came from a strict Evangelical background which led him to take the pledge against alcohol at the age of fourteen, from which he never wavered throughout his life. A notably hard worker who took much inspiration from the Bible, he was articled at sixteen to a firm of solicitors in London'sLincoln's Inn Fields and subsequently set up a successful law practice of his own. Hicks married Grace Lynn, daughter of Richard Hampson Joynson, a silk manufacturer who was prominent both in Manchester conservative and evangelical circles. After adding his wife's maiden name to his own, Joynson-Hicks entered politics as one of Manchester's conservative candidates, but was defeated by Charles Swann in 1900 and by Winston Churchill in 1906, after an ill-tempered campaign notable for Joynson-Hicks'

William Joynson-Hicks, fierce critic of the shortcomings in the British Government's air programme. (*National Portrait Gallery*)

Old Testament-like attacks on the Liberals to whom Churchill had shifted his allegiance.

By this time Joynson-Hicks was becoming known as a fiercely evangelical lawyer with an avid interest in the latest technology. His enthusiasm ranged from early motor cars (he was chairman of the Automobile Association from 1911 to 1922) to telephones and aircraft. After defeating Winston Churchill in 1908 at a by-election for North West Manchester – a seat he was soon to lose – he re-entered the Commons when elected unopposed at a by-election in Brentford during March 1911. From then on Joynson-Hicks set about developing a reputation as an expert on motors and aviation where his persistent and trenchant observations became renowned.

From 1912 to 1914 he was the chief critic of the Government's air programme when he constantly raised questions on aircraft design and production figures, together with possible methods of attacking Zeppelins. (By 1916 the latter would form part of his pamphlet 'The Command of the Air' in which he advocated indiscriminate bombing of Germany, especially Berlin, to terrorize the German population.) Hicks was a fiery and unrelenting orator who, with the journalist Charles Grey, was determined to reveal the lamentably small number of aeroplanes available to the British air services prior to the war, together with the Government's attempts to hide the extent of the shortfall.

Hicks began his campaign in late 1912 at a time of widespread alarm following reports on 14 October of an unidentified airship passing over the Isle of Sheppey during the hours of darkness. In November he put forward a succession of questions in the House of Commons about the speed of Zeppelins compared with British aircraft, before moving to the question seemingly never far from his mind, 'whether the Defence Committee has considered the effect upon the defences (of) the country of the development of aeroplanes and airships and, if so, whether, in their opinion, we have a sufficient number of aircraft of both descriptions?'.[14]

Such enquiries brought a cautious response from Prime Minister Asquith.

> The answer to the first part of the question is in the affirmative. As regards the second part, the policy recommended by the Committee of Imperial Defence was explained by the Secretary of State for War on the introduction of the Army Estimates. That policy is being carried into effect. The Air Committee ... keeps the question of aerial navigation constantly under review.[15]

This reply could never satisfy a vigorous interrogator like Joynson-Hicks. In December he was alluding to the temporary ban being imposed on the use of monoplanes by the army pending the report of a committee upon the subject, and this time his questions were directed at the Secretary of State for War, Colonel Seely, who was responsible for setting up the committee on monoplanes. When Joynson-Hicks asked whether its findings could be expedited, Seely replied in superior fashion that 'it is always dangerous to try to hurry a Committee which is dealing with matters of life and death', although he said he believed the committee was on the point of reporting.

In December Joynson-Hicks raised questions concerning the state of naval aviation, which were skilfully parried by Winston Churchill who assured him that a remarkable amount of progress had been made in naval aeroplanes during the year, and that the naval wing had several machines that could exceed the speed of the latest Zeppelin.[16]

However, a week later Joynson-Hicks was again directing his enquiries to the less wily Colonel Seely in the form of a formidable three-part question, namely, 'What is the total number of biplanes, apart from school machines, in use in the Military Wing of the RFC; how many machines, biplanes and monoplanes, are on order, and how many machines have been ordered since 30th September?'[17] Seely chose to answer the question head-on, however unimpressive his answer might appear. 'Fourteen biplanes are in use in the Military Wing, three of which are under repair. Sixteen machines are on order. No machines have been ordered since 30 September, but tenders for eighteen have been invited.' Joynson-Hicks moved on to the question of the RFC's squadrons, asking whether they were on paper or effective? Seely responded unequivocally. 'They are not squadrons on paper, they are very real, and have made a very great advance.'

Seely did not explain how the squadrons could be efficient with so few planes available and Joynson-Hicks displayed his detailed knowledge by asking about the reasons for the delays in supplying the aircraft, 'whether the aeroplanes stated to be over-due from British manufacturers have been delayed in delivery through the dilatoriness of Government inspectors or through alterations in the official designs after certain parts had been constructed, whether the fifteen machines on order are supposed to be sufficient to supply the RFC with an adequate number of aeroplanes, and, if not, why no further orders have been given?'.[18] Inexplicably, Colonel Seely again refused to give ground or admit to any blame. 'The delay in completion of the aeroplanes due from British manufacturers has not been caused by any dilatoriness on the part of Government inspectors, but the necessity for constant inspection may have caused a portion of the delay in some cases. Further orders are being placed.'[19]

Seemingly satisfied by the answer, Joynson-Hicks switched his questions to the state of the accommodation provided for aircraft, but if Colonel Seely thought he had seen him off with regard to the plane numbers, he was utterly mistaken.[20] With war increasingly likely, the number of front-line planes for the RFC was of ever-increasing importance, and on 12 July 1913 Joynson-Hicks again challenged the Secretary of State for War to produce 120 planes or, failing that, 80 which could fly efficiently. Seely told him, 'We have now got 120 machines – I take only those in first class condition',[21] and he franked this by offering permission for Joynson-Hicks and his friend, Duncan Sandys, to inspect the aeroplanes belonging to the army.

Prior to making their inspection, they asked the War Office to give them a summary of the aircraft presently available. The response was devastating, for it showed that of the 120 only fifty-three were actually ready to fly. (Some were under repair, others were experimental types or ready to be struck off.) Worse still, of the fifty-three some were school machines subject to rough daily use, or monoplanes needing a full overhaul. As a result, during their inspection Joynson-Hicks and Sandys found the number of efficient war machines fell to an utterly inadequate twenty-three.

On 30 July in an open letter to the Press, Joynson-Hicks concluded

> that a Minister holding the responsible position that Col Seely does should have made statements to the House of Commons in regard to so vital a question as our preparations for war, which at the first touch crumble to pieces, is a matter which I can only leave to the judgement of those who have read this statement ... <u>As an effective fighting force at this moment the Royal Army Flying Corps is non-existent.</u>[22]

It was a judgement confirmed by Joynson-Hicks' and Duncan Sandys' detailed inspection.

In the subsequent House of Commons debate Mr Bonar Law for the opposition concluded that Seely 'was rash in the extreme in the statement he made to the House, and if we cannot accept a deliberate statement made in a case of that kind how can we be expected to accept his assurances on other matters in regard to which it was impossible to have such a test'.[23]

The aviation press was equally censorious, apart from the excoriating comments expected from Charles Grey, as editor of *The Aeroplane*, Stanley Spooner, the editor of *Flight*, also pulled no punches.

> It is with more of a sense of shame than with any other feeling that we approach the subject of the recent disclosures made by Mr Joynson-Hicks and Mr Sandys with regard to the hapless state of the Military Wing of the Royal Flying Corps. To our way of thinking anything more shameful, more deplorable than the cynically light hearted manner in which Colonel Seely dealt with the whole question of the Military Wing would be hard to find in the records of British public life.[24]

Joynson-Hicks' publication of these aeroplane figures in the Press not only materially destroyed Colonel Seely's reputation but established the fact that, in order to field 100 aircraft for war purposes, it was necessary to 'buy 300 additional machines or the equivalent numbers of spare parts, each year'.[25] By means of a single public letter (supported by a string of earlier questions on the topic), he revealed that the projected front-line squadrons of the RFC required a much larger budget than had earlier been anticipated.

Although Joynson-Hicks continued with his questions on air matters during the war and headed the inter-departmental committee on aviation, nothing, not even his post-war tenure of four and a half years as Home Secretary, could equal his triumph over a Secretary of State for War, whom he genuinely believed had transgressed Joynson-Hicks' own moral codes, the successful outcome of which led to the RFC's four squadrons receiving their full establishment of planes.

*　*　*

Noel Pemberton-Billing (b. 1881) was the most belligerent, restless and self-opinionated of the early air publicists, seemingly ever ready for a fight but lacking the appetite to see through many of his schemes. His agitations in Parliament took place at a time of war, although by then he had already gained publicity for the number of far-seeing ideas he had put forward regarding aviation.

Given his temperament, Billing's life was destined never to be short of incident. The son of a Birmingham iron-founder, he was born in London and attended Hampstead High School where, after a characteristic clash, he burned his headmaster's papers before running away. By the age of thirteen he was working his way aboard a sailing cargo boat bound for South Africa, where he enlisted in Natal as a mounted policeman before becoming their boxing champion. Following this he joined the British army and served in the Boer War; after being wounded twice he was invalided out before returning to England where he married the half-German Lilian Maud Schweitzer, and opened one of the country's first garages at Kingston-on-Thames. It was not however a success and he returned to South Africa, where he dealt in horses and established the country's first motoring paper.[26]

As a fearless advocate for aviation Noel Pemberton-Billing was never free of controversy. (*National Portrait Gallery*)

By 1906 Billing was back in England, where a new-found interest in aviation – including its military significance – finally appeared to give purpose to an otherwise chaotic life. His commitment always led to rapid action: as early as 1908 he found a backer who put up £150 for him to build an aeroplane,[27] and in that year he established the country's first aerodrome and flying ground at Farnbridge in Essex, where he erected a large hanger with twenty bays which aspiring aircraft builders could hire from him at £1 a week.[28] A number of early pioneers, including Howard Wright, José Weiss and Robert McFee, took advantage of these facilities, but Pemberton-Billing's own two monoplanes failed to achieve genuine flight and he was injured when one crashed. Having recovered, he went to Monte Carlo in an attempt to gain more capital at the tables but, like others both before and after him, he failed. He went on however to found Britain's first aeronautical newspaper called *Aerocraft*, the first edition of which appeared on 1 January 1909, but it folded after a while primarily from the lack of current interest in aviation.

During 1908 Billing proposed the establishment in Britain of the world's first air force which he dubbed the Imperial Flying Squadron, an idea to which he would return later, and forthrightly presented his case to a board of distinguished officers at the War Office[29] – without success. During this time his abundant energy also saw him engaged in land speculation, passing his examinations in law and starting brokering in steam yachts from a site he acquired at Shoreham-on-Sea.

By 1913 such activities had brought him enough money to be able to revive his interest in aviation and found an aircraft factory, after purchasing a site next to Woolston Ferry on the River Itchen at Southampton, where it was his intention to construct flying boats. Like Sopwith and de Havilland, Billing had the gift of attracting other men with similar ideas, and at Southampton he was joined by Hubert Scott-Paine, initially in a general capacity but subsequently Billing's works' manager. From 1913 work commenced on fast launches and flying boats and Billing registered the company's telegraphic address as Supermarine, Southampton, the name by which his firm came to be known.

Billing could never avoid seeking the spotlight. With typical bravado he not only qualified as a pilot but at the same time acquired some money by striking a public bet for £100 with fellow constructor Frederick Handley Page that within four hours of getting into an aeroplane he would pass the test for the Aero Club's Aviator's Certificate. (He won his bet although John Ledeboer, editor of *Aeronautics* and no friend of Billing, later attempted to demolish the worth of his claim by dismissing the test as childishly simple and capable of being accomplished by 'any averagely intelligent and active schoolboy'.)[30] Whatever Ledeboer's criticisms, Billing did succeed in passing the recognised flying test.

Supermarine was soon to make its presence felt by displaying a handsome biplane flying boat at the Olympia Aero Show in March 1914, for which Billing had commissioned the marine architect Linton Hope. Despite its good looks, it failed to fly. By now the company was experiencing serious financial difficulties and it was only through heroic efforts by Billing's partner, Scott Paine, that fresh capital was found to keep the firm alive.[31] This did not stop Billing producing a stream of ideas for aeroplane designs, including one relating to a single-seater scout, the PB9 which he dubbed the 'Seven Day Bus' because he avowedly did the drawings in a day and built the machine from scratch within seven days. However, aviation writer Philip Jarrett subsequently discovered the truth about PB9, for which Billing purchased a set of wings from E.C. Gordon England and adapted drawings made by C. Vasilesco.[32]

Although the 'Seven Day Bus' performed relatively creditably on its first flight, no orders resulted. Philip Jarrett made an additional study of Pemberton-Billing's plans for building flying boats up to the beginning of the war. Jarrett found that logically enough all were given the letters PB preceding their numbers but any attempt to codify them were thrown into confusion by Billing's belief that odd numbers were lucky, with the result that he left gaps to avoid the even ones. Even so, by 1918 Supermarine, which had already been joined by R.J. Mitchell, had designed a successful series of flying boats, the last of which, *Seagull V* was, by the Second World War, to become the legendary small flying boat the Walrus.[33]

Other designs emerging from Woolston at the commencement of the war included a small 'pusher' Scout (PB23E) with its engine behind the pilot, and an ungainly quadraplane designed to attack the German Zeppelin airships. Such work was interrupted when, in 1914, Billing joined the RNAS, where he became closely involved in the operation to bomb the large Zeppelin base at Friedrichshafen on Lake Constance.

After more than a year in the RNAS, during which time he became a squadron commander, Billing resigned to lobby against the way the war in the air was conducted. Elected to Parliament as an independent MP and self-styled 'first air member' he gained considerable notoriety. Uniting with Charles Grey he cited the RFC's BE2 aircraft as being no match for the new German Eindekker with its synchronised machine gun, coining the term 'Fokker Fodder' for RFC pilots. His agitation resulted in a Royal Commission to examine his charges, which recommended setting up an Air Board that ultimately became the Air Ministry.[34] It also resulted in two government committees, the first of which brought about the dismissal of Mervyn O'Gorman, the Royal Aircraft Factory's Superintendent, and the end of the factory as a manufacturing establishment for aeroplanes. The second committee followed Billing's lead in advocating reprisal raids against German cities.

By 1918 Billing had lost focus by broadening his criticisms of air policy with fantastical claims that 47,000 lesbians and homosexuals had been identified by German intelligence among leading public figures. This led to him being sued for criminal libel by the dancer Maud Allan, but he ably conducted his own defence and through his use of political adventuress, Eileen Villiers-Stuart (who had become his mistress) he was able to confirm that leading figures in the government, judiciary and other offices of state were vulnerable to German blackmail. Amidst popular acclaim, Billing won his case, although the head of the Special Branch expressed his belief that Eileen Villiers-Stuart had lied in court; by the end of the war she acknowledged that her evidence in the Maud Allan trial was completely fictitious and had previously been rehearsed with Billing. Billing resigned his parliamentary seat, officially on the grounds of ill health, and from then on his position became increasingly marginalised.

Billing's influence as a publicist for air power is not easy to assess and, although his agitation in Parliament occurred during the war rather than before it, there is no denying that prior to 1914 he came up with a number of futuristic and sweeping proposals, including the establishment of a national air force. He was ahead of his time with the first aeronautical newspaper and in masterminding a devastating aerial attack against a German Zeppelin base. Billing also conceived a number of genuinely novel ideas relating to aircraft design, although he failed to develop them. He was often his own worst enemy, for though a powerful and accomplished orator, he could be unscrupulous and selective with his facts when engaged on one of his self-chosen campaigns. It was such conduct that prevented him from being much more than 'a massive gadfly to the current political establishment',[35] and reduced the extent of his influence in the development of British aviation. Nonetheless, when in full flow in the House of Commons he was still an awesome enemy and his attacks on the Royal Aircraft Factory, intemperate as they were, helped to curb its power in relation to the private aircraft constructors and thereby speed up the introduction of planes that would be effective in meeting the German challengers.

*   *   *

In their contrasting ways, both within and outside the House of Commons, Churchill, Joynson-Hicks and Pemberton-Billing played significant parts in helping to evoke and extend public interest in early aerial weapons.

PREPARATIONS
FOR WAR

Chapter 15

Emergence of Aviation for War

Developments in British military aviation, as elsewhere, owed much – particularly in its early stages – to a group of remarkable individuals. Following the decision by the Committee of Imperial Defence (CID) in 1909 to suspend British aeroplane trials, Charles Rolls not only seized the opportunity to place his Short/Wright aircraft at the government's disposal but to instruct selected officers in flying. As a result an aircraft shed was erected for him at Larkhill on Salisbury Plain. Following his death this instructional responsibility was assumed by four notable early pilots who showed themselves willing to spend both their time and resources in demonstrating the aeroplane's remarkable military qualities: three were artillery officers and the fourth a civilian with close service connections. To achieve their purpose these precursors of the Royal Engineers Air Battalion and the RFC required a measure of independence not normally enjoyed by usual army officers.

The first was Captain Bertram Dickson who, although a regular officer in the Royal Horse Artillery, was currently enjoying an extended leave after a long period overseas and was thus able to attend a flying school at Mourmelon in France founded by Henry Farman, son of an English journalist residing in that country. Farman built a much-improved version of a Voisin biplane in which, during 1908, he flew the first circular kilometre and won the Grand Prix d'Aviation worth 50,000 francs. This helped him set up his own flying school where Bertram Dickson (by this time no longer on the army's active list) showed himself to be a natural and gifted student pilot. On 11 May 1910 Dickson qualified for pilot's licence No. 71 from the French Aero Club, following which, on 3 August of the same year, he retired from the (British) army on half-pay,[1] thereby becoming a free agent.

After buying an aircraft from Henry Farman, Bertram Dickson became so skilled that he excelled as an exhibition performer against the famous French aviators of the time, winning first prize at the aviation meeting held at Tours in late May 1910, so becoming the first British pilot to qualify for an international flying prize.[2] By July Dickson was back in Britain to take part in the British flying meeting at Bournemouth that was overshadowed by the death of Charles Rolls,

Dickson then went on to Lanark for Scotland's first flying meeting. There his skills so impressed Sir George White of the Bristol and Colonial Aeroplane Company that he appointed him as the company's flying adviser, and went on to offer him one of their new Bristol Boxkite aeroplanes to use at the British army's manoeuvres that coming autumn on Salisbury Plain. While generous enough, Sir George White's offer had the additional motive of helping to forge an early

Captain Bertram Dickson in his Farman aircraft. (*David Dickson*)

partnership between his company and the military authorities. This also suited Dickson who was anxious to demonstrate the aeroplane's relevance to the military authorities and to put it forward 'as a weapon into the hands of his country'.[3] Dickson was joined on Salisbury Plain by two other artillerymen, Captain John Fulton, like Dickson in the Royal Horse Artillery, and Lieutenant Lancelot Gibbs, an officer with a part-time militia regiment, the Isle of White Garrison Artillery.

By no stretch of the imagination were either of them typical artillery officers. When Captain Fulton, a gifted engineer, was stationed at Bulford camp close to Larkhill, in 1909 he attempted to build his own plane, but finding his rate of progress too slow, he bought a Blériot-type monoplane which he financed in part with £250 awarded to him by the War Office for improvements to the sighting apparatus for field guns. Fulton experimented with it on Salisbury Plain until he gained Pilot's Certificate No. 27 from the Royal Aero Club, the first regular officer to do so. He would subsequently become a founder member of the RFC and an instructor at the Central Flying School before being appointed Chief Inspector of the Military Wing of the RFC in 1914. By 1915 Fulton had become Assistant Director of Military Aeronautics, but tragically he died from influenza that same year.

In 1908 the third officer, Lieutenant Gibbs, had already demonstrated his outstanding flying skills during the Balloon Factory's trials of John Dunne's aeroplane at Blair Athol, which enabled him to qualify for the French aviators' certificate at Mourmelon. As a militia officer Gibbs could aspire to a full-time career in aeronautics and after purchasing two aeroplanes, a Farman and a Sommer, from Charles Rolls during 1910, he formed his own company offering flying instruction and exhibition flying. Sadly his career was also prematurely cut short by a recurrent spinal injury sustained in a flying accident during 1910.

However motivated and resourceful, Dickson, Fulton and Gibbs could never have taken part in the 1910 army manoeuvres without the help of a fourth air enthusiast and supporter of service aviation, George Cockburn, a Scottish rugby international who, after Rolls' death undertook the task of instructing selected army officers to fly. For this purpose he was allocated Rolls's shed at Larkhill, the use of which he offered to the other three.[4] Cockburn had qualified at the Farman School in June 1909 and in his Farman III biplane was the only British participant at the 1909 Air Meeting at Rheims (where the senior British officers who attended came away convinced that there was no scope for contemporary aircraft). Cockburn not only helped to train early army flyers but at the request of the Aero Club – and at no cost to the Admiralty – he was appointed tutor to the first four naval officers who, from among 200 unmarried volunteers, had been chosen for pilot training.

On 1 March 1910 Naval Lieutenants R. Gregory, C.R. Samson and A.M. Longmore, and Lieutenant E.L. Gerrard from the Royal Marines subsequently started their training at Eastchurch on the Isle of Sheppey under Cockburn in two Short-Sommer biplanes gifted to the Admiralty by the wealthy aviation enthusiast Frank McClean. Working out of Cockburn's shed at Larkhill (which by June 1910 had been joined by three sheds erected for the Bristol Aeroplane Company's Aviation School) Dickson, Gibbs and the aviator Robert Loraine (who succeeded in sending some wireless messages to a temporary receiving station a quarter of a mile away) offered enthusiastic, if somewhat amateurish, services to military formations manoeuvring on Salisbury Plain.

Dickson was the most prominent of the flyers who, in his Bristol Boxkite, carried out a thirty-mile reconnaissance at dawn along the Wylye Valley on 21 September 1910. Following this, he landed and from a neighbouring house telephoned his report on enemy locations, but after being 'captured' by the enemy forces his report was disallowed. Two other sorties were made before dusk, with Lieutenant Gibbs supplementing Dickson's sweeps. Cockburn, who was watching, said the results 'could not be said to be striking' for engine trouble, bad weather and the inexperience of the directing staff weighed against the results achieved by the enthusiastic pilots.

The 1910 manoeuvres were still considered important enough for Northcliffe to send the journalist and entrepreneur George Holt Thomas to report on the merits of the use of aircraft and to point out the difficulties experienced by Dickson and Gibbs.[5] Holt Thomas explained how they had undertaken things largely on their own initiative, with little or no support from the War Office.[6]

In contrast, during the French manoeuvres held in Picardy a fortnight before, aircraft were employed for the control of artillery fire and for aerial photography, as well as for reconnaissance. Even so, in Britain attempts by individual flyers acting largely in a private capacity to introduce aviation into the autumn manoeuvres were not without effect. How far they influenced the Chairman of the 1909 CID committee is not clear, but soon afterwards Lord Esher retracted his earlier recommendations and wrote that it was imperative that the British services acquired their own aeroplanes, and set about forming an air corps.[7]

Whatever the cause, attitudes towards the military role of aeroplanes were undoubtedly changing and the new climate saw discussions in the War Office about changing the army's Balloon School into something more resembling an air arm while, by the end of 1910, aircraft trials were resumed at the Balloon Factory under its new Superintendent, Mervyn O'Gorman. Finally with the Army Order of February 1911 dependence on pioneering individuals ended with the creation of an Air Battalion of the Royal Engineers 'entrusted (with) the duty of creating a body of expert airmen, that would consist of a Headquarters and two companies where selected military candidates would attend a six months probationary course and, if successful, officers from any regular arm or branch of the service on the active list would be appointed to the Battalion for four years'. The warrant officers and men, however, would still be selected from the Corps of Royal Engineers.[8]

In spite of such aspirations, the Air Battalion was planned to be very small, consisting of just fourteen officers, including some who had worked earlier with Colonel Capper, together with representatives from the current military aeroplane enthusiasts. Only six of the officers were scheduled to come from outside the Royal Engineers and the selection of pilots from other corps or regiments depended upon them first paying for their training at one of the emergent civilian flying schools to qualify for a pilot's certificate from the Royal Aero Club, after which the War Office agreed to pay them £75.

The War Office's lack of urgency regarding aeroplanes, together with its residual loyalty towards airships, was seen in the Air Battalion's staff. Its commander was Major Sir Alexander Bannerman, a forty-year-old engineer officer whose aviation interests had always centred on airships, while No. 1 Company, commanded by Captain E.M. Maitland of the Essex Regiment, remained an airship company. Fortunately No. 2 (Aeroplane) Company had Captain John Fulton as its commander who could be relied on to sponsor aeroplanes at every opportunity. Captain P.W.L. Broke-Smith, who had previously been an instructor at the Balloon School, was appointed Adjutant and Captain Carden, Assistant Adjutant under Colonel Capper, became the battalion's experimental officer.

With aircraft certain to become predominant, Major Bannerman and Captains Broke-Smith and Carden were required to take the Royal Aero Club's pilots' certificate, although Major Bannerman did not qualify until April 1912, with Captain Broke-Smith joining him during the same month and Captain Carden not succeeding until the following June.

The staff's reluctance to fly aeroplanes was not the only curb on the Air Battalion. In the early stages its aircraft, most of which were still owned by its members, were undoubtedly far from impressive. Apart from the four Bristol

The unremarkable – and neglected – memorial marking the first army aerodrome. Its plaque includes an acknowledgement of the Military Air Trials. (*Paul Vickers*)

Boxkites which had been purchased by the War Office but whose delivery had been delayed, there was a Paulhan 'experimental' and a Farman 'Type Militaire' (both long in the tooth), Lieutenant Cammell's own Blériot, Captain Fulton's 'Grahame-White' Blériot, Cockburn's ancient Farman and the Short-Wright flyer acquired from Charles Rolls. Although a Howard-White ENV pusher had been bought by Captain Maitland, it was withdrawn from service in July 1911.

Whatever their planes' undoubted limitations, during the summer of 1911 the pilots of No. 2 Company – still in mufti – had a glorious time practising their cross-country flying, which included occasionally dropping in for tea at hospitable country houses. Things took a decidedly more serious turn however when they were required to fly their assorted aircraft from Larkhill to the flatlands east of Cambridge for the forthcoming military manoeuvres. After a series of serious mishaps 'the military air force of the Empire was reduced to two serviceable aeroplanes; one of the five which started from Larkhill and a second which took off some days later and got to Cambridge'.[9] As a result, aircraft participation in the manoeuvres had to be cancelled.

The Royal Navy's initiatives in the air were also remarkably limited, although by 2 May 1911 at Eastchurch – the navy's equivalent of Larkhill – the navy's four candidates for pilot training had acquired their brevet flying certificates and had joined Lieutenant Wilfred Parke who, like the army's early flyers, had taken his test privately.

The first naval pilots who would assume leading roles in its future air service were undoubtedly enthusiastic, for in August they submitted a glowing report on their training, maintaining that 'few people now deny that the aeroplane has come to stay',[10] and rightly concluding that 'the great value of aeroplanes at the present ... lies in their scouting capabilities'.[11] They also succeeded in recommending the acquisition of McClean's two planes together with acquiring other improved types for experimental purposes. Such initiatives were all the more timely when during September *Mayfly*, the navy's only airship, was destroyed.

In contrast, on the other side of the Atlantic naval aviation was progressing quickly. On 17 February 1911, Glen Curtiss took off from San Diego, California, where he flew out to the USS *Pennsylvania* and landed alongside. His aircraft was hoisted on board then placed back in the water, upon which Curtis took off and flew back to North Island without mishap.[12]

The timid steps taken by both services in Britain so far were illustrated by the statistics for 1911, which revealed that Britain had 19 officer aviators compared with France's 263 flying men and over 200 machines within an efficient aerial corps, while Germany's thirty airships were able to reconnoitre the whole of the German North Sea coastline.[13]

Considering Britain's vast strategic responsibilities and the growing likelihood of war it became imperative for this situation to change and a sub-committee of the Council of Military Defence, including Haldane, Esher, Churchill and Seely, appointed a technical sub-committee to devise a military and naval aviation service. Those selected to take part illustrated the committee's importance: Colonel Seely, who was appointed chairman, was due to take over from Haldane as Secretary of State for War, and its other members included General A.T. Murray, the current director of military training, his assistant, Brigadier General G.K. Scott Moncrieff, and Brigadier General David Henderson (who had recently gained his aviator's certificate), together with two of the navy's original flyers, Commander C.R. Samson and Lieutenant R. Gregory. The sub-committee was joined by Mervyn O'Gorman, Superintendent of the Aircraft Factory and although the army's first flyers were not members, submissions from Captain Fulton and Captain Dickson would play an important part in its conclusions.

Before it assembled, Fulton wrote to Seely about the grievances of aeroplane officers from other corps and arms attached to the Royal Engineers' Air Battalion. He was highly critical about the way it was administered in the interests of the Royal Engineers and its commanding officer, who at the time had no aviator's certificate. He concluded that the army's air service should be separated from the Royal Engineers and that similarly its commander should not be an engineer.[14] Seely forwarded Fulton's comments to Winston Churchill, who strongly agreed that HM's Corps of Airmen should be a new and separate organisation, drawing from civilian as well as military and naval sources.[15]

Dickson's contributions came by way of a memorandum in which he boldly suggested that air forces would play a major part in a future war.[16] 'In the case of a European War between two countries both sides would be equipped with large corps of aeroplanes, each trying to obtain information of the other and to hide its own movements ... The fight for the supremacy of the air in future wars will be of the first and greatest importance.'[17]

Another significant input to the sub-committee came on 5 February 1912 from naval captain Murray Sueter who, after helping to introduce submarines into the Royal Navy, went on to command the navy's airship branch before it was disbanded in January 1912, when he subsequently became Director of the Admiralty's Air Department where he was largely responsible for the creation of a separate naval air service. While not a pilot, he fully appreciated the wide scope of future air operations requiring both airships and aeroplanes[18] and he soon advocated the use of private enterprise in aviation where, for instance, he was confident a seaplane could be devised with the help of civilian manufacturers. When asked by the Committee whether Britain must command the air as well as the sea, he had replied, 'I think it will come to that ... I do not say that we wish to do so but I think we will be forced to do so'.[19]

Impelled by such individual supporters of air power, the Committee worked with remarkable speed. Its report was ready by 27 February 1912 and the RFC was constituted a fortnight later by Royal Warrant on 13 April 1912, which saw the air battalion absorbed within it. The Corps was to consist of a naval wing, a military wing and a Central Flying School to train its pilots. It was to work closely both with Haldane's Advisory Committee on Aeronautics and the Royal Aircraft Factory, and a permanent Air Committee – the predecessor of the Air Board – would be established to deal with 'all aeronautical questions affecting both the

A group of officer pilots at Larkhill with the Royal Engineers' Air Battalion, Spring 1912.
(*The Army Air Museum, Middle Wallop*)

Admiralty and the War Office'.[20] It was agreed that during the summer of 1912 a competition should be held at Larkhill to decide upon the aircraft most suitable for the fledgling RFC.

Late as it was, with the creation of the RFC British military aviation finally came of age, although the committee's acceptance of separate military and naval wings and the subsequent development of their different strategic and procurement policies would enable Winston Churchill, when First Lord of the Admiralty, to state on 1 July 1914 that the naval wing, which depended entirely on private constructors for its planes, 'would henceforth be known as the Royal Naval Air Service'. This became entirely separate from the RFC and, except for their joint attendance at the Central Flying School (CFS), the two services remained independent until they were amalgamated on 1 April 1918 through the creation of the Royal Air Force.

Notwithstanding, much of the ethos for the future RAF was determined by the 1912 sub-committee, to which input from the earliest military flyers was significant. Among his observations to the committee Bertram Dickson's belief that the earliest military aviators were both self-willed and diverse provoked discussion about whether the character required by the RFC should most resemble the army or whether it should be closer to the naval tradition of greater independence. It was decided that individual publicity and self-advancement should be discouraged and when, in July 1912, both Captain Loraine and his observer, Staff Sergeant Wilson, were killed in a flying accident the subsequent order 'flying will continue as usual' created an undying tradition to help sustain the Corps through the dark days to come.[21]

An early Farman aircraft 'Type Militaire' as used by the Royal Engineers' Air Battalion.
(*Author's Collection*)

The committee faced the problem of devising formations appropriate to a flying organisation, and these included the squadron, a new tactical unit with three flights of aeroplanes with four machines to a flight (rather than the French escadrilles of six machines). The aim was for each flight to be homogeneous in its equipment of engines and aeroplanes,[22] and for such squadrons to be elastic and adaptable in order to provide a basis for the corporate spirit and tradition necessary for a new service. It was decided that each squadron should have thirteen machines, its three flights plus an additional one for their commanding officers and pay rates ranged from twenty-five shillings a day plus eight shillings

Captain Bertram Dickson.
(*David Dickson*)

An AVRO G being assembled at Larkhill in August 1912 for the Military Air Trials. (*Royal Aeronautical Society* [*National Aerospace Library*])

Samuel Cody weighing-in for the same aircraft competition. (*Mike Goodall*)

flying pay for squadron commanders (the same as a Royal Naval Captain in command of a battleship) to nine shillings a day for warrant officers.[23]

Whatever its differences from the other two services, the committee still thought in terms of a very small flying corps, consisting of seven squadrons, each with their thirteen machines. Although these totalled just ninety-one aeroplanes, because of the need for spare machines the total number required was expected to be over 200, with two pilots needed for each aeroplane and an equal number in reserve, together with their air mechanics and technical staff.

By July 1912, 249 servicemen (mainly officers) had gained flying certificates from the Royal Aero Club but although others were in the process of qualifying, there was a pressing need for genuine military pilots, men fully capable of assuming duties with the projected squadrons.

With this need in mind the Central Flying School was established at Upavon on Salisbury Plain on 19 June 1912, with three courses planned for each year, although in 1913 the length of each course was reduced to thirteen weeks to allow a sufficient interim between them for aircraft to be overhauled and the permanent staff to take leave. Its capacity was in line with the RFC of that time and the first five courses before the war were attended by 153 officers from both services, of which twenty-four army officers and three naval officers qualified for their flying certificates from the Royal Aero Club during their time there.[24] Thirty army other ranks and thirteen seamen also qualified for flying certificates. With such a proportion of students reporting without flying certificates the aim to train a core number of military (and naval) personnel ready for the coming war was made considerably more difficult.

Central Flying School Course 1912. (*Author's Collection*)

While the students without an RAC pilot's certificate attended a qualifying course before they were able to join students on the main course, those possessing certificates were taught to fly planes with which they were not familiar. On the first two courses indifferent weather and the shortage and unserviceability of the school's aircraft made this latter objective difficult and the students' flying time was reduced to a mere fifteen hours which, however, rose to twenty-four hours by the fourth and fifth courses.

All students had to carry out practical work in workshops, including constructing and dismantling aircraft.[25] They also attended lectures on meteorology, observation from the air, navigation, steering while flying and signalling, and due to the presence of Royal Naval students, everyone, including army personnel were instructed on identifying all types of warships.

The courses proved very effective and due to massive wartime expansion both the staff and students concerned enjoyed remarkable successes in later years (details of which are given in the succeeding chapter). Writing later as 'Charlton', one of the officer trainees wrote of what he called three months of advanced instruction where 'distinctions of rank did not exist. They were all only pupils bound, without rivalry, in a common interest in a nascent weapon of war and able, on that account to submerge the parade manner and neglect the law of seniority', where 'the instruction, both theory and practice, was absorbing in its absolute newness'.[26] In his enthusiasm he hardly noticed their crude and scanty accommodation, and it was his belief that 'even the two fatal accidents in those early days of flying [showed] that inevitably a few must suffer just as a skirmishing line is apt to be thinned in preparing ground for the main attack'.[27]

Much credit here was due to the School's Commandant, Royal Naval Captain Godfrey Payne, 'a man of resolute, even intimidating character and a tremendous organiser and disciplinarian'.[28] It also says much for the rapid professionalism of the fledging Flying Corps that preparation for the coming conflict did not end with training at Upavon, for in June 1914 a dress rehearsal for war was held where all its units were brought together for a month in a so-called concentration camp at Netheravon on Salisbury Plain.[29]

This was conceived and organised by Colonel E.H. Sykes who, although not personally that impressive, was a brilliant staff officer who, on the outbreak of war, became Chief of Staff to Brigadier General David Henderson, the commander of the RFC in France. The concentration camp – as its name suggests – brought all the squadrons together, including their pilots, aeroplanes and motor transport (which, like all other motor vehicles, were subject to a nationwide speed limit of 20mph). The longest journey to Netheravon was by 2 Squadron which had to travel 570 miles from its base at Montrose, in the course of which it suffered a dual fatality when Lieutenant John Empson and his mechanic George Cudmore crashed near York, where Empson's parents were waiting to see their son,[30] although the Squadron's thirty-four vehicles arrived safely. Many valuable lessons were learned about moving to likely battle stations before the Corps' officers and men, together with their aircraft and vehicles, reached Netheravon.

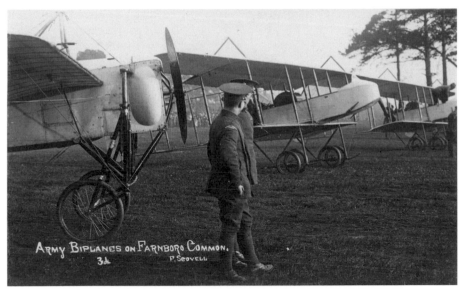

Army biplanes on Farnborough Common. (*Author's Collection*)

There everyone was told officially – if secretly – about the imminence of war with Germany. The mornings were spent flying, which the watching Press noted approvingly took place in any winds, and during which wireless, photography, bombing and reconnaissance exercises were undertaken. In all 630 flights were made, lasting thirty-six hours and covering no less than 21,210 miles, and the training concluded with a flypast before the King and senior military and political officials. Although its numbers were small, by now the RFC had become a viable force.

While it owed its existence to independent flyers and to others in public life and elsewhere who were committed to the development of British aviation, by now both the RFC and the RNAS were developing their own legendary leaders, such as James Burke, Hugh Trenchard and Roland Brooke-Popham for the Flying Corps, and Godfrey Payne, Charles Samson and Arthur Longmore with the Naval Air Service. At the concentration camp the greatest emphasis was on the need to carry out their aerial patrolling whatever the conditions, for Sykes knew flying was what distinguished airmen from land and sea soldiers and which, according to actor Robert Loraine (who gained a DSO and MC in France), 'makes our pulses throb with a zest for life, it points the road to unselfishness, it teaches us to despise the mean'.[31]

Another officer at this time, H.H. Balfour, also stressed the excitement involved in his early days of flying. Writing some time after the war he maintained that even after the passage of the years 'something still remained of that first thrill every time I climb into a pilot's cockpit'. He then gave the experience of flying the ultimate sportsman's accolade, comparing it to 'capturing the same beauty of landscape and the same spice of excitement by fishing in the middle of a

June day, a gin-clear Hampshire chalk stream with the trout rising well to an iron blue ...'.[32]

The RFC, which in a way that is typically British owed its existence and character to those who first supported the cause of air against continuing scepticism, would soon reassemble – not for an exercise this time, but for war. Here their crews' resolution would be tested to the limit.

Chapter 16

The Royal Flying Corps' Move to France

In the event, the outbreak of the First World War came even sooner than Britain's airmen had anticipated. The murder on Sunday, 28 June 1914 of Archduke Francis Ferdinand, heir to the Austrian throne, by Serbian extremists evoked rapid and extreme threats by Austria against Serbia, following which the mobilisation of Europe's armies seemed unstoppable. As a result of Germany's invasion of Belgium on 4 August 1914 the British Foreign Secretary, Sir Edward Grey, declared war on Germany. In accordance with Britain's agreement with France, within eight days two infantry corps and a cavalry division totalling 80,000 men began to embark for the Continent, where they concentrated between Mauberge and Le Cateau to flank the assembled French armies, a process completed by 20 August.

British aircraft were committed to support the country's land forces and from the RFC's total complement of 146 officers and 1,097 other ranks, no fewer than 105 officers and 700 other ranks were sent to join the British Expeditionary Force. While this represented by far the largest part of the RFC at the time, it was an undeniably small force to carry out the tasks of observing British artillery fire (a proportion of which would be carried out from balloons) as well as watching out for – and reporting on – the movements of the vast German forces advancing towards them.

Before the RFC could begin such duties, its far flung units in Britain had to assemble then fly across the Channel and move to airfields sufficiently close to the enemy positions. With such small numbers, the need to accomplish this without undue loss of aircraft or pilots was vitally important, especially when the opposing German air forces had under their command 110 dirigibles and 245 rugged, dependable two-seat reconnaissance craft propelled by reliable water-cooled engines, 'with 254 pilots and 271 observers to operate them'.[1] The movement to France was rendered even more difficult with the RFC being divided into seven squadrons, quite apart from its separate headquarters and airfield park containing spare aircraft and major workshop facilities. Its anticipated numbers were reduced further with only squadron Nos 2, 3, 4 and 5 being ready to move,[2] for No. 1 Squadron was just beginning its conversion from dirigibles and 6 and 7 Squadrons were very recent formations.

The chosen assembly point was on Swingate Downs, Dover, conveniently placed for crossing the Channel and from here the RFC commander, Sir David Henderson, ordered all the squadrons to be ready to fly off for France by 6.00am on 13 August. For the RFC's primitive aircraft, reaching the assembly point intact was in itself no small achievement and crossing the Channel remained a formidable prospect.

The Corps' senior unit was No. 2 Squadron, equipped with the Royal Aircraft Factory's BE2as and commanded by the broad-shouldered and barrel-chested Irishman, Major James Burke, with its airfield at Montrose on the Scottish east coast almost 600 miles from Dover. Burke was a hard taskmaster and he had insisted on strenuous flight training and reconnaissance duties, with the squadron flying an average of 1,000 miles a week. When inspecting officers arrived in Edinburgh by train, they were routinely met 'and flown to Montrose from where they were flown back to Edinburgh the same night'.[3] Such training paid off for when, on 3 August, the squadron set off for Farnborough, from where it would go on to Swingate Downs, it encountered no serious mishaps.

In contrast, No. 3 Squadron, despite the much shorter flight from Netheravon, experienced considerably more problems with its Blériots and semi-obsolescent Henry Farmans. The Farmans lacked power and they were heavily overloaded when carrying full fuel tanks and two men, together with their tools and other equipment. After staggering into the air, one crashed soon after take-off, killing its pilot, Lieutenant Bob Skene, and his air mechanic, Ray Barlow. Another was wrecked and its mechanic injured when landing at Dover.

No. 4 Squadron also had mixed aircraft, two of its flights being equipped with BE2as, while the third had Henry Farmans. It too suffered serious mishaps: during its preliminary move from Netheravon to Eastchurch on 30 July, two planes were badly damaged, one reportedly due to engine failure, the other to pilot error, in which the latter's two-man crew died.

Maurice Farman with a 70hp Renault engine, which was obsolescent by 1914. (*Author's Collection*)

A Henry Farman, ageing but still in extensive use. (*Author's Collection*)

Although No. 5 Squadron, with its AVRO 504s and Henry Farmans and its mixture of regular and reservist pilots, was based at nearby Gosport, it experienced considerable trouble in getting to Dover. One plane collapsed on taxiing out, another crashed at Shoreham and its pilot was concussed, while a third made a forced landing on the South Downs between Brighton and Lewes.

In addition to the squadrons, the aircraft park with nine BE2as, one BE2c, three BE8s and three Henry Farmans (its Sopwith Tabloids were in packing cases and scheduled to go by sea), was also due to fly to France. Its role was to replace any casualties suffered by the squadrons in action, as well as to carry out repairs beyond the capability of the squadrons' workshops. In practice, half its planes were needed to make up the losses incurred by the squadrons in reaching Dover, and as a result it became necessary to scrape up any plane capable of joining the squadrons in France. As a young lad working at Farnborough observed, 'We patched up everything that could stagger off the ground. We sent off a total of seventy aircraft, some of them hardly capable of flying'.[4]

At Swingate Downs at midnight on 12 August, the airmen received a warning order that they were to set off for France at 6.00am the next morning. It was a short night for the pilots bedded down beside their planes, with their rest apparently not much helped by Major Burke's prodigious snoring. As a group they had won their places in different ways – requiring personal initiatives, and possible financial sacrifices, with some training at civilian schools while others were lucky enough to join the CFS.[5] As a result, most were older than the later entrants. Prior to setting off, they received a short briefing about what was expected of them. Both the pilots and navigators were given maps and the name of their destination, together with tyre inner tubes to act as primitive lifebelts –

which had been bought from local suppliers over the preceding few days. The pilots carried additional stores, including a revolver or Verey pistol, field glasses and a spare pair of goggles; for mechanics there was a roll of tools.[6] With no sea rescue organisation in place, pilots were also required to carry a remarkable survival kit, including a water bottle containing boiled water, a miniature stove and a haversack containing biscuits, cold meat, a bar of chocolate and a package of soup concentrate.[7]

As for the flight itself, the pilots were told not to set their course before reaching a height of 3,000ft, following which in the event of engine failure they were expected to be able to glide across the Channel. (No parachutes were available at this time.) After reaching Boulogne they were ordered to follow the coast and move south-east along the Somme river before reaching Amiens. During his briefing to his crews Major Burke raised the possibility of meeting a German Zeppelin head-on whilst crossing the Channel. Due to their lack of armament, he ordered them to use their planes to ram it. While this was a good indication of his belligerent state of mind, since their BE2as could not normally reach the airships' altitudes, his pilots had little chance of carrying out his orders.

Charles Burke was undoubtedly one of the distinctive characters of those early days. A Boer War veteran, he was older and larger than most and, while gruff, uncompromising and renowned for his heavy landings, he was respected for his courage and loyalty. He was promoted to lieutenant colonel as commander of the RFC's second wing before being appointed Commandant of the Central Flying School. (Always a land soldier at heart, when he learned of his previous regiment's heavy losses in France he rejoined the infantry and was subsequently killed on 9 April 1917 while commanding a battalion of the East Lancashire Regiment at Arras.)

On the conclusion of the briefings, the order for take-off was given at 6.25am on 13 August 1914, just one day after the first contingent of the British Expeditionary Force crossed the Channel. It was a beautiful morning on the Downs and a crowd of townspeople had risen early to see the aeroplanes off. Heavily laden as they were they battled to gain height, before turning towards their target. All No. 2 Squadron made the crossing safely, although the first to arrive, pipping Charles Burke for the privilege, was the debonair Lt Harvey-Kelly who had ignored orders and flown cross-country from Boulogne to Amiens. At 8.15am No. 3 Squadron took off in its mixture of BE2as, BE8s and Henry Farmans. After suffering engine trouble one of its pilots was to follow five days later, but the rest succeeded and were fêted by the people of Amiens on their arrival.

No 4 Squadron was the last to leave that day, with its two flights of BE2as and one of Henry Farmans. One flight of BE2as made an unscheduled landing in a ploughed field, although after repairing minor damage they got away again the same day. All eventually arrived at Amiens, although Lieutenant Patrick Playfair (destined to become an air marshal) decided to land a second time to ask the way. By nightfall forty-nine planes were parked in the open at Amiens, where there were just two small sheds.

No. 5 Squadron flew to Amiens on 15 August without its stragglers. After being given replacement planes they rejoined it within a few days including Lieutenant R.M. Vaughan who, although he flew over with the squadron, had had to make a forced landing at Boulogne where he had been arrested and held as a prisoner for nearly a week.

As the aircraft set off from Dover, the RFC ground personnel, including its headquarters, set sail from Southampton, while those attached to the aircraft park went from Avonmouth. A number of commercial vehicles that had been requisitioned also travelled by sea. The RFC enjoyed a comparatively low priority, and these vehicles were somewhat bizarre: one van had an external roof rack for Peek Frean biscuit tins; another sported a massive blue-black splash for Stephens Ink, while there was a green Maples pantechnicon, a large black Carter Paterson lorry and even a dustcart. The assorted cars included a Mercedes Tourer and a Rolls-Royce, and there was a two-seater coupé, together with its owner/driver (a Mr Weeding from Guildford in Surrey). Most distinctive of all was a large scarlet lorry with gold letters proclaiming HP (Houses of Parliament) Sauce as 'the World's Appetiser', which was used as No. 5 squadron's ammunition and bomb lorry and later acted as a landmark for disorientated pilots during the coming withdrawal.

Such equipment was unorthodox but at least it was available. Back in England, with the RFC administrative wing at Farnborough, Major Trenchard found his was limited to 'one clerk and one typewriter, a confidential box containing a pair of old boots and a lot of unpaid bills incurred by various officers in the Flying Corps during the rush to the Front'.[8]

The RFC still needed to reach its forward base at Mauberge, ten miles behind the BEF front-line units. On 16 August low cloud delayed their departure but after it cleared they set off and all went well until a BE8, newly acquired from the aircraft park, crashed on take-off killing its pilot, Second Lieutenant Evelyn Copeland Perry, and his mechanic, Herbert Parfitt. This was an unpopular and dangerous make of aeroplane and on 18 August on the way to Mauberge another BE8 suffered a control failure, severely injuring its pilot Robert Smith-Barry and killing his mechanic Corporal Frederick Geard. A third replacement BE8 crashed soon afterwards but without causing serious injury to the crew.

The hazards facing the flyers before they reached Mauberge were not yet over, for on their approach they were greeted by a fusillade of fire from the neighbouring French forces, to be joined later by the British. Fortunately only one aircraft suffered significant damage. Although the crews worked all night painting Union Jacks on the underside of their wings and on their fuselages, these were still mistaken for the German cross and fired at enthusiastically. (It was not until October, after the death of a pilot and observer, that the roundel markings were adopted.) On their road and rail journey from Boulogne through Amiens to Mauberge the RFC ground parties fared much better, being showered with flowers and gifts at every stopping place.

In this fashion the RFC moved to support the BEF in the main theatre of the war. By any standard its numbers were small for the observation duties during the

BE8, 'The Bloater', with a 80hp Gnome engine – an aircraft with a poor reputation. (*Author's Collection*)

BEF's rapid withdrawal, while both its aircraft (and transport) were of a decidedly mixed nature. Apart from the reliable but distinctly slow BE2as and a few AVRO 504s, there were the 'death trap' BE8s and the semi-obsolescent Maurice and Henry Farmans and Blériots. As yet the only planes capable of mounting weapons effectively were the Henry Farman 'pushers' with their engines at the rear, and all aircraft still depended on French engines (and German dynamos).

The RNAS, with its ninety-one officers and 700 other ranks, thirty-nine aeroplanes, fifty-two seaplanes and seven airships, was given far wider responsibilities. Its aeroplanes had more powerful engines and wireless facilities, with bomb-dropping and fighting equipment superior to that used by the military Corps,[9] while for fleet support it had developed deck landing and a range of functions for its kite balloons and seaplanes.[10] Its responsibilities included defending the east coast and the Channel, and a forward strategy was adopted on the continent of Europe against the German Zeppelins that included a successful bombing raid on 22 September 1914 against Zeppelin sheds at Friedrichshafen. In spite of this, from the time of the great German offensives the land war took precedence and the caucus of the RFC in France represented the chief focus of military air operations, a predominance that it would retain throughout the war

Whatever their mishaps before reaching Mauberge, there were remarkable opportunities to be taken for those capable of doing so, defining them as a golden generation. Out of 105 officers (including attached personnel) at Mauberge a remarkable eighty-five would survive the war. During it, five would at some stage hold the army rank (and air force equivalent) of general, six of brigadier general, six of colonel, thirty-two of lieutenant colonel, twelve of major, seventeen of captain and six of lieutenant.[11] A proportion, including Geoffrey Salmond and

Patrick Playfair, would go on to reach elevated rank in the Royal Air Force both between the wars and during the Second World War. That they succeeded as they did owed much to their personal qualities, enthusiasm and training, but also to the rapid growth of the RFC during the war, and its translation into the RAF, which by 1918 had become the world's largest air force.

Many of the Mauberge veterans were also fortunate in having served as young officers during the early days of observation and artillery spotting before the development of aerial combat. On their arrival in France they could not have been aware of such advantages, their main sensation probably one of relief at finally being able to face down the earlier scepticism, even ridicule, of their fellow land soldiers[12] – although some, like James Burke, would always retain a visceral loyalty to their parent regiments.

In spite of the future dangers and the weight of expectation laid on them as heirs of Charles Rolls, Grahame-White, Bertram Dickson and the others who had supported the aerial lobby against the sceptics, such young men could not be expected to dwell overmuch on the world they had left behind, nor have any undue sense of tragedy from the increasing destructive capacity of the air weapon. It was enough for most of them that theirs was a marvellous life, a sport, a game where they were invulnerable,[13] doing what they wanted to and so lucky not to be part of the ground war. Whether or not they were, in fact, 'the best brainpower of the nation'[14] and whether they wore the distinctive slate-blue tunics (with inside fastenings for sitting in aircraft) or stayed loyal to their original uniforms, what mattered now was their first aerial reconnaissance just three days after arriving at the front.

Aftermath

While our story of those who gave us wings by establishing British aviation and helping to shape the future of British air policy ended at the outbreak of the First World War, their influence would be expected to continue throughout the conflict.

Whatever the restrictions on the pre-war air budgets that led to relatively small numbers of aircraft going to France, once the war started earlier proposals for a larger air establishment were bound to find favour and, during the course of a prolonged and costly war, British air formations not only experienced rapid expansion but became increasingly influential as a result of the patterns of leadership and the fighting doctrine already established, together with the constructive genius present within the industry.

The performance of the British air forces in France was also subject to those of its French ally and their German opponent. In the case of the first, during 1912 Stanley Spooner, editor of the British air publication *Flight*, had made the startling suggestion that France's (aerial) inventiveness seemed to have peaked and 'for the moment, at least, evolution is stagnant on the other side of the channel. While we have undoubtedly progressed quite substantially the French constructor seems to have been marking time'.[1] With France's monumental achievements so far in both aeroplane and engine design this seemed a premature, if not wishful, conclusion, for when looking at national expenditure figures for air in 1914, France still spent US$9,181,513 compared with Britain's US$4,926,108, although both were significantly outspent by Germany and Austro-Hungary with US$15,155,033.[2]

Aside from expenditure, Spooner's reservations seemed more justified by the number of major bureaucratic blunders that affected the performance of the French Aviation Militaire during the war. General Bernard, their chief of aeronautical services, was so confident of a short war and France's inevitable victory that he stopped all aircraft production, ceased pilot training, demobilised the factories and sent many of the best designers and their employees to the front line. Before the end of 1914 the decision had been reversed, although by then there were only 192 (French) aircraft in service.[3]

Another damaging decision which jeopardised initial French superiority was to specialise in certain types of aircraft and aero-engine production to prepare for the anticipated air campaign in 1915.[4] Although the development of large productions runs for a few types of aircraft was rational enough – and practised by the British Royal Aircraft Factory – it was adopted at a time when aeroplane types obsolesced in months and aeroplane designs underwent frequent major modifications which led in early 1916 to the Aviation Militaire having a considerable portion of its aircraft inferior to the Germans.[5] This was most unfortunate when during 1915 the French raised their aircraft production figures to 4,900 compared with Germany's 4,532 with Britain still lagging well behind at 1,700.[6]

While during the summer of 1915 the French air arm retained its supremacy on the Western Front, acquitting itself well in the traditional roles of reconnaissance, artillery-spotting, local bombing and the restricted aerial combats of the time, by the autumn many of its bombers were out of date or obsolete and delays had occurred for instance with the proposed building of replacement Sopwith 1½ Strutters under licence. During late 1915 the French encountered German E planes with machine guns firing through their propeller arcs, and in 1916 over Verdun, when they faced the German Albatros DII and the Halberstadt DII and DIII, aerial supremacy see-sawed from one side to the other.

The French aviation writer Georges Huisman, writing after the war, believed that, in fact, 'administrative anarchy had lost France aerial mastery and what was needed was an autonomous air arm with an Air Ministry and the High Command's aviation commander as the arm's chief',[7] when what they had was an 'Under Secretary with insufficient prestige and power whose commands lacked the authority which those of a full Minister of State would have carried'.[8] Huisman was undoubtedly a harsh critic, but among the French administrative shortcomings was their decision to produce armoured planes which were unduly heavy, their failure to decide upon aircraft armament and the delays in building genuine bombers. As a result their bombing attacks were restricted to railway stations, camps and supply depots supporting front-line troops.

By early 1917 German planes, working in large formations, succeeded at times in dominating air space over the French lines, although by the end of the year, with the arrival of fresh aircraft such as the Breguet 14 bomber, the Salmson

Halberstadt DII. (*Author's Collection*)

Salmson 2. (*Author's Collection*)

Spad 7 with 180hp H-Suiza engine. (*Author's Collection*)

two-seater reconnaissance vehicle and their SPAD 7 fighter, and by increasing their aircraft production, the French regained superiority over their areas of the Front.

Even so, shortcomings in the French command structure led to their forces achieving rather less than might have been expected at the opening of the war – which required the British to take the initiative beyond their areas of the Front.

* * *

In 1914 the German air forces were far larger than Britain's, with wide strategic responsibilities. In pride of place came their massive airships (twelve of which were on strength at the beginning of the war) whose duties (together with long-

Gotha bomber. (*Author's Collection*)

range aeroplane bomber units shortly to be formed) included attacking the British homeland, while their 228 aircraft, mostly slow Taube monoplanes, were assigned to reconnaissance duties on the Western and Eastern Fronts.

During the war their bombing raids succeeded in frightening the British civilian population and provoking a massive counter-response, but neither the airships (which proved remarkably vulnerable) nor their limited number of Gotha and Giant bombers carried enough destructive capacity to change the balance of the war. What was more on the dominant Western Front the balance of strength was against them, where they faced both the French and British (and the Americans in the final stages).[9]

The German High Command appointed a Chief of Field Aviation (Feld-flugchef) to direct all their aviation affairs, including industrial production, but they could never equal the entente's aeroplane construction levels, especially in the final stages when British production surged ahead. In 1915 they succeeded in gaining a tactical advantage by introducing their Eindecker aeroplanes, although until 1916 numbers of these were relatively limited.

By 1916 at the Battle of Verdun, when the air war began in earnest, they had to meet large concentrations of French aircraft and by mid-July 1916 during the Allied build-up for the Somme offensive they were facing a 3:1 superiority. By the autumn they had responded by introducing new aircraft like the Albatros D2 fighter which, under the admirable leadership of Oswald Boelcke and others using 'permanent groups',[10] were able to inflict heavy losses on their opponents.

However, by now the British were introducing formidable new aircraft of their own, such as the Sopwith 1½ Strutters and Camels, together with the Royal Aircraft Factory's SE5s, and the German air units had increasingly to face the allies at a severe disadvantage, both numerically and in the vital field of fighter planes. Even so they succeeded in building up their numbers to support the great land offensive planned for the spring of 1918, which it was hoped would end the war. Following its failure, during which both sides suffered heavy losses, the Allies mounted counter-offensives in which the German air forces were comprehensively outnumbered – although concentrated attacks with Halberstadt

Albatros D2. (*Author's Collection*)

Oswald Boelcke.
(*Author's Collection*)

Halberstadt CV. (*Author's Collection*)

CVs and their new Fokker D7 biplanes were still capable of inflicting major local reverses upon their opponents.

*   *   *

British air operations on the Western Front differed from both France and Germany, due in large part to the principles established by their early flyers. From the beginning they were distinguishable by high levels of aggression. Although in the early stages the small numbers of their machines (in 1915 they still had only 152 aircraft in France) limited their operations and reconnaissance remained vitally important, one flight per squadron was already assigned for bombing duties, although at this early stage 'of the 141 attacks mounted on railroad junctions and stations only three were judged successful'.[11]

For such aggressive tactics Hugh Trenchard, commander of British air operations in France, favoured pilots in the public school tradition, independently-minded individuals who viewed aerial combat in terms of deadly sport, rather than the more circumspect approach of non-commissioned pilots and others used extensively elsewhere. Such commitment and relish for flight had been demonstrated earlier by flyers such as Captain John Fulton and Bertram Dickson, but under Trenchard it became the British method of air warfare complementing Douglas Haig's tactics on land. Trenchard's tactics were bound to be costly – arguably needlessly so – from the time his stately Royal Aircraft Factory's BE2s encountered the German Fokker aircraft.

For the British, aerial warfare started in earnest with their Somme offensive beginning on 1 July 1916, for which the RFC assembled 410 aircraft and 426 pilots in twenty-seven squadrons, when their pusher-engined fighters (the single-

Trenchard and Longmore in a Maurice Farman prior to the war. (*Royal Aeronautical Society* [*National Aerospace Library*])

seat DH2 and the two-seat FE2 with their forward-mounted guns) were expected to be a match for the German Fokkers.[12]

From the outset Trenchard planned to follow the German planes over their own territory and force them onto the defensive. Such tactics resulted in high numbers of casualties, although Trenchard, convinced that his forces could survive a war of attrition, persisted with his offensive policy. According to Cecil Lewis, the doyen of young pilots at the time, the RFC attracted 'the adventurous spirits – men who were not happy unless they were taking risks',[13] although Trenchard's tactics led to the horrific situation where pilots were lasting an average of just three weeks and Cecil Lewis himself had to return to the UK to regain his nerve. During the Battle of the Somme, up to 17 November 1916, 782 British planes were destroyed or missing and 576 pilots had been killed or struck off strength, while in return the RFC destroyed 164 enemy aircraft and drove down 205 damaged planes.[14]

Such losses brought a radical expansion and revision of pilot training under Major Robert Smith Barry, when pioneer constructor A.V. Roe's AVRO 504 came into its own with its responsiveness and dual control facilities. Unsurprisingly, the losses of 1916 aroused widespread anger in Britain and as a result a rampant Pemberton Billing (now in Parliament) declared that Britain's pilots were being murdered for lack of better planes. In the tradition of other air publicists Billing sought to exploit Britain's long-standing democratic traditions to arouse public opinion and, in conjunction with others such as the Air League, bring about changes in a way not possible in other European countries.[15] His agitation led to the strengthening of the Air Board and to the resignation of

Mervyn O'Gorman, the Superintendent of the Royal Aircraft Factory. However unfair personally, O'Gorman's removal freed the private contractors from official competition with regard to both aircraft and engine developments, thereby releasing 'the commercial-technological dynamic through which the (country's) bicycle, automobile and aircraft industries had sequentially developed'[16] and opened service procurement to the free market in a way already carried out by Winston Churchill's RNAS. Although a strengthened Air Board still lacked the powers of an Air Ministry it succeeded in bringing about the transfer of procurement from the two services to the Minister of Munitions. This was badly needed for, in December 1916, the army and navy had 9,483 aircraft on order 'of no fewer than 76 varieties and 20,000 engines of all kinds'.[17]

Whatever the relatively incoherence in British aerial affairs during 1916, the aviation industry was by now achieving remarkable results: Sopwith's successful string of aircraft culminated in his Camel in December, while the Bristol fighter underwent successful trials in September and the Royal Aircraft Factory's SE5 appeared in late November. The bombers, the Airco DH4 fighter/bomber and the massive Handley Page 0/100 also became available during the late autumn.

During 1917 Trenchard's determination to give vigorous support to the BEF's offensives at Arras and Cambrai brought continuing heavy casualties, with the RFC losing 365 aircraft to the German's 176, although by now British aircraft production had doubled to make good the losses. The strong sense of commitment and patriotism inherited from the early flyers helped Trenchard retain the support of his pilots, but not all his commanders were in agreement: a future leader of the RAF, Philip Joubert de la Ferté, was for one highly critical of his tactics of trying to maintain strength all along the Front.

Sopwith Camel. (*Author's Collection*)

Bristol Fighter F2B. (*Author's Collection*)

A golden opportunity for a further massive increase in the British air establishment, and its full recognition as an independent service, came on 13 June and 7 July of 1917 with the German Gotha raids on London. Ex-Boer General Jan Smuts was appointed to examine the position and he advocated the establishment of a large independent air service to end, once and for all, the differences between military and naval aviation. The Royal Air Force Bill for a single service passed through the British parliament and came into operation on 1 April 1918, together with the creation of a powerful Air Ministry. By such means Britain acquired an air arm with greater independence and power than the air forces of either France or Germany.

By 1918 the scale of British air operations on the Western Front reached remarkable heights under a new commander, General John M. Salmond, who remained true to Trenchard's policy of vigorous battlefield support, while Trenchard himself went to command an independent bombing force. On 21 March 1918, at the time of the final German offensive on the Western Front, the British had 1,232 planes – but by 29 April they had lost 1,302 (including replacements).[18] During April, in support of the British Fourth Army the RAF lost 847 aircraft – 100 of them on the first day of its offensive – and from 1 August to 11 November the RAF lost 2,692 planes, although they received 2,647 replacements from British manufacturers.[19]

By now Britain had the world's largest aircraft industry, supplying the world's largest air force numbering 291,175 officers and men with some 22,000 aircraft, including independent elements committed solely to the bombing of German cities.

In spite of the personal antagonisms that seemed inseparable from parliamentary and public agitation on behalf of air, the nature of the British civil/military command over its air forces proved capable of overseeing enormous expansion. In fact, after the gross over-estimate of German bombing capability, its share of scarce resources exceeded its capabilities, although this was understandable with a new weapon, the limitations of which were not fully appreciated.

Whatever the predominance gained by the Royal Air Force in 1918, its largest debt was unquestionably to that special band of aeronautical devotees who from the beginning of the nineteenth century had conceived, built, developed, publicised and supported the aeroplane against all doubters and opponents.

Central Flying School Upavon – First Course

Course Members

(Front Row)	Captain R.N. Corder
	Major Eugene Louis Gerrard
	Lt Arthur Murray Longmore
	Lt Colonel H.R. Cook
	Captain Godfrey Marshall Paine
	Captain John Duncan Bertie Fulton
	Engineer Lt C.J. Randall
	Asst Paymaster John Henry Lidderdale
	Lt Quartermaster Frank Howard Kirby
(Middle Row)	Lt E.V. Anderson
	Major John Frederick Andrew Higgins
	Lt R. Cholmondeley
	2/Lt Robert Raymond Smith Barry
	Captain John Harold Whitworth Becke
	Lt G.B. Stopford
	Lt K. Atkinson
	Lt Stephen Christopher Winfield Smith
	2/Lt Thomas O'Brian Hubbard
	Major H.M. Trenchard
(Back Row)	Lt Rutter Barry Martyn
	2/Lt R. Abercromby
	2/Lt D. Young
	Lt P.A. Shepherd
	Lt Francis Fitzgerald Waldron
	Lt Gilbert Vernon Wildman-Lushington
	Lt D. Allen
	Lt I.D. Courtney
	Lt J.W. Pepper
	Captain Charles Erskine Rusk

(Seven other individuals joined the course once it had begun)

The Staff members, some of whom also attended the course, were Paine, Trenchard, Lidderdale, Corder, Kirby, Cook, Randall, Longmore, Gerrard and Fulton (Captain Philip William Lilian Broke-Smith was also on the Staff.)

Programme of Training Schemes for Squadrons

	Aircraft	*M.T.*
Tuesday, June 2nd	–	Convoy run by flights, 1 flight per squadron
Thursday, " 4th	–	Ditto
Friday " 5th	–	Ditto
Monday, June 8th	No. 1 – Aeroplane reconnoitre given area; troops on ground stationary	Convoy run by squadrons
Tuesday, " 9th	No. 2 – Ditto	Convoy night run by flights, 1 flight per squadron
Thursday, " 11th	No. 3 – Ditto	Convoy run by squadrons
Friday, " 12th	No. 4 – Ditto	Convoy night run by flights, or squadrons
Monday, June 15th	No. 5 – Aeroplanes reconnoitre a given area; troops on ground partly in motion	Participation in aircraft schemes
Tuesday, " 16th	No. 6 – Ditto	Ditto
Thursday, " 18th	No. 7 – Aeroplanes seek a named object in a given area	Ditto
Friday, " 19th	No 8 – Aeroplanes seek a free balloon despatched earlier, and when found circle round it	Ditto
Monday, June 22nd	No. 9 – Field Day – each squadron using one temporary landing ground	Participation in aircraft schemes
Tuesday, " 23rd	No. 10 – Ditto	Ditto
Thursday, " 25th	No. 11 – Field Day – each squadron using two temporary landing grounds successively	Ditto
Friday, " 26th	No. 12-Ditto	Ditto
Monday, June 29th	Reserved for special exercises	Reserved for special exercises
Tuesday, " 30th	Ditto	Ditto

Appendix B

Officers and Men of the Royal Flying Corps stationed in France prior to the Battle of Mons

HEADQUARTERS

Brigadier-General Sir David Henderson, K.C.B., D.S.O.; Commander, Royal Flying Corps.

Lieutenant-Colonel F.H. Sykes, 15th Hussars; General Staff Officer, 1st Grade.

Major H.R.M. Brooke-Popham, Oxfordshire and Buckinghamshire Light Infantry; Deputy Assistant Quartermaster-General.

Captain W.G.H. Salmond, Royal Artillery; General Staff Officer, 2nd Grade.

Lieutenant B.H. Barrington-Kennett, Grenadier Guards; Deputy Assistant Adjutant and Quartermaster-General.

Attached

Captain R.H.L. Cordner, Royal Army Medical Corps
Captain C.G. Buchanan, Indian Army
Lieutenant the Hon. M. Baring, Intelligence Corps
2nd Lieutenant O.G.W.G. Lywood, Norfolk Regiment (Special Reserve); for Wireless duties.

NO. 2 SQUADRON

Squadron Commander

Major C.J. Burke, Royal Irish Regiment.

Flight Commanders

Captain G.W.P., Dawes, Royal Berkshire Regiment.
Captain F.F. Waldron, 19th Hussars.
Captain G.E. Todd, Welch Regiment.

Flying Officers

Lieutenant R.B. Martyn, Wiltshire Regiment.
Lieutenant L. Dawes, Middlesex Regiment.
Lieutenant R.M. Rodwell, West Yorkshire Regiment.
Lieutenant M.W. Noel, Liverpool Regiment.
Lieutenant E.R.L. Corballis, Royal Dublin Fusiliers.
Lieutenant H.D. Harvey-Kelly, Royal Irish Regiment.
Lieutenant W.R. Freeman, Manchester Regiment.

Lieutenant W.H.C. Mansfield, Shropshire Light Infantry.
Lieutenant C.B. Spence, Royal Artillery.
Captain A.B. Burdett, York and Lancaster Regiment.
Captain A. Ross-Hume, Scottish Rifles.
Lieutenant D.S.K. Crosbie, Argyll and Sutherland Highlanders.
Lieutenant C.A.G.L.H. Farie, Highland Light Infantry.
Lieutenant T.L.S. Holbrow, Royal Engineers.
2nd Lieutenant G.J. Malcolm, Royal Artillery.

Supernumerary

Major C.A.H. Longcroft, Welch Regiment; Squadron Commander
Captain U.J.D. Bourke, Oxfordshire and Buckinghamshire Light Infantry;
   Flight Commander.
Captain W. Lawrence, 7th Battalion, Essex Regiment (Territorial Force);
   Flight Commander.

Attached

Lieutenant K.R. Van der Spuy, South African Defence Forces.

NO. 3 SQUADRON
Squadron Commander

Major J.M. Salmond, Royal Lancaster Regiment.

Flight Commanders

Captain P.L.W. Herbert, Nottinghamshire and Derbyshire Regiment.
Captain L.E.O. Charlton, D.S.O., Lancashire Fusiliers.
Captain P.B. Joubert de la Ferté, Royal Artillery.

Flying Officers

2nd Lieutenant V.H.N. Wadham, Hampshire Regiment.
Lieutenant D.L. Allen, Royal Irish Fusiliers.
Lieutenant A.M. Read, Northamptonshire Regiment.
Lieutenant E.L. Conran, 2nd County of London Yeomanry.
Lieutenant A. Christie, Royal Artillery.
Lieutenant A.R. Shekleton, Royal Munster Fusiliers.
2nd Lieutenant E.N. Fuller, Royal Flying Corps, Special Reserve.
Lieutenant W.C.K. Birch, Yorkshire Regiment.
Lieutenant G.F. Pretyman, Somerset Light Infantry.
Lieutenant W.R. Read, 1st Dragoon Guards.
2nd Lieutenant A. Hartree, Royal Artillery.
Lieutenant V.S.E. Lindop, Leinster Regiment.
Lieutenant G.L. Cruikshank, Gordon Highlanders (Special Reserve).
Lieutenant W.F. MacNeece, Royal West Kent Regiment.
2nd Lieutenant L.A. Bryan, South Irish Horse.
Major L.B. Boyd-Moss, South Staffordshire Regiment.
2nd Lieutenant E.W.C. Perry, Royal Flying Corps, Special Reserve.

NO. 4 SQUADRON
Squadron Commander
Major G.H. Raleigh, Essex Regiment.

Flight Commanders
Captain G.S. Shephard, Royal Fusiliers.
Captain A.H.L. Soames, 3rd Hussars.
Captain F.J.L. Cogan, Royal Artillery.

Flying Officers
Lieutenant P.H.L. Playfair, Royal Artillery.
Lieutenant K.P. Atkinson, Royal Artillery.
Lieutenant R.P. Mills, Royal Fusiliers (Special Reserve).
Lieutenant T.W. Mulcahy-Morgan, Royal Irish Fusiliers.
Lieutenant R.G.D. Small, Leinster Regiment.
Lieutenant W.G.S. Mitchell, Highland Light Infantry.
Lieutenant G.W. Mapplebeck, Liverpool Regiment (Special Reserve).
Lieutenant C.G. Hosking, Royal Artillery.
Lieutenant H.J.A. Roche, Royal Munster Fusiliers.
Lieutenant I.M. Bonham-Carter, Northumberland Fusiliers.
2nd Lieutenant A.L. Russell, Royal Flying Corps, Special Reserve.

Wireless Flight
Lieutenant D.S. Lewis, Royal Engineers.
Lieutenant B.T. James, Royal Engineers.
Lieutenant S.C.W. Smith, East Surrey Regiment (Special Reserve).

Attached
Captain D. Le G. Pitcher, Indian Army.
Captain H.L. Reilly, Indian Army.

NO. 5 SQUADRON
Squadron Commander
Major J.F.A. Higgins, D.S.O., Royal Artillery.

Flight Commanders
Captain D.G. Conner, Royal Artillery.
Captain G.I. Carmichael, Royal Artillery.
Captain R. Grey, Warwickshire Royal Horse Artillery (Territorial Force).

Flying Officers
Lieutenant H.F. Glanville, West India Regiment.
Lieutenant F.G. Small, Connaught Rangers.
Lieutenant R.O. Abercromby, Royal Flying Corps, Special Reserve.
2nd Lieutenant C.W. Wilson, Royal Flying Corps, Special Reserve.
Lieutenant H. le M. Brock, Royal Warwickshire Regiment.
Lieutenant R.M. Vaughan, Royal Inniskilling Fusiliers.
Lieutenant L. da C. Penn-Gaskell, Norfolk Regiment (Special Reserve).

Lieutenant A.E. Borton, Royal Highlanders.
Lieutenant Lord G. Wellesley, Grenadier Guards.
Lieutenant C.G.G. Bayly, Royal Engineers.
Lieutenant C.E.C. Rabagliati, Yorkshire Light Infantry.
2nd Lieutenant A.A.B. Thomson, Royal Flying Corps, Special Reserve.
2nd Lieutenant L.A.Strange, Royal Flying Corps, Special Reserve.
2nd Lieutenant R.R. Smith-Barry, Royal Flying Corps, Special Reserve.
2nd Lieutenant D.C. Ware, Royal Flying Corps, Special Reserve.
2nd Lieutenant V. Waterfall, East Yorkshire Regiment (Special Reserve).
Captain R.A. Boger, Royal Engineers.
Captain B.C. Fairfax, Reserve of Officers.

Attached
Lieutenant G.S. Creed, South African Defence Forces.

AIRCRAFT PARK
Squadron Commander
Major A.D. Carden, Royal Engineers.

Flight Commanders
Major Hon. C.M.P. Brabazon, Irish Guards.
Captain W.D. Beatty, Royal Engineers.
Captain R. Cholmondeley, Rifle Brigade.
Lieutenant G.B. Hynes, Royal Artillery.

Flying Officers
Lieutenant G.T. Porter, Royal Artillery.
2nd Lieutenant C.G. Bell, Royal Flying Corps, Special Reserve.
2nd Lieutenant N.C. Spratt, Royal Flying Corps, Special Reserve.
Lieutenant R.H. Verney, Army Service Corps.

(Walter Raleigh, *The War in the Air*, Vol. 1, 288–92.)

Notes

Prologue
1. Hansard, 29 April 1909, Vol. 4, 478–80. Lloyd George speaking about the Naval Debate.
2. Hansard, 29 May 1911, Vol. 26, 702–3. Questions of Mr Byles to Lloyd George.
3. At the outbreak of war, Russia had 500 aircraft of all types and a significant aerial industry of its own. David Divine, *The Broken Wing, A Story of the British Exercise of Airpower* (1966), 46.
4. Germany's production already exceeded Britain's, while by 1910 America's production had grown to 80 per cent of all Europe's. Hugh Driver, *The Birth of Military Aviation* (1997), 3.
5. Notably by D. Edgerton, in *England and the Aeroplane, an essay on a militant and technological nation* (1991).
6. Lord Birkenhead, *Rudyard Kipling* (1978), 24.
7. Peter King, *Knights of the Air* (1989), 88.
8. Air Commodore J.A. Chamier, *The Birth of the Royal Air Force* (1943), 2.
9. King, 87.

Chapter 1: The Father of Flight
1. J. Laurence Pritchard, *Sir George Cayley, The Inventor of the Aeroplane* (1961), 89.
2. Letter of Sir Antony Carlisle to Cayley, 12 November 1809 in Pritchard, 57, 58.
3. This publication set itself to offer a novel combination of original research papers, reviews and summaries on the contents of provincial and foreign journals.
4. Pritchard, Appendix III, 225.
5. *Oxford Dictionary of National Biography* (2004), Vol. 40, 838–40.
6. J. Laurence Pritchard, 'The First Cayley Memorial Lecture', *Journal of the Royal Aeronautical Society* (February 1955), 82–3.
7. Ibid.
8. Op cit, 83. Cayley suggested the Adelaide Gallery (later the London Polytechnic) as he had a controlling interest in it.
9. Ibid.
10. Ibid.
11. Charles H. Gibbs-Smith, *Sir George Cayley's Aeronautics 1796–1855* (1962), ix.
12. John D. Anderson, *A History of Aerodynamics and its Impact on Flying Machines* (1998), 28.
13. Gibbs-Smith, *Sir George Cayley's Aeronautics*, 4.
14. These are held in the National Aerospace Library at Farnborough.
15. Pritchard, *Sir George Cayley*, 220.
16. Op cit, 221.
17. J.A.D. Ackroyd, 'Sir George Cayley, Inventor of the Aeroplane', *Aeroplane* (December 2003), 93.
18. Gibbs-Smith, *Sir George Cayley's Aeronautics*, 17–18.
19. Ibid.
20. Op cit, 24.
21. National Aerospace Library, Cayley Notebook, 95–7.
22. Op cit, 121–5.
23. Op cit, 137–8.
24. Theodore von Karman, *Aerodynamics, Selected Topics in the Light of their Historical Development* (1954), 7.

25. Ackroyd, 'Sir George Cayley, the Father of Aeronautics, Part 2, Cayley's Aeroplanes', *Notes Rec. Royal Society* (2002), 333.
26. Gibbs-Smith, *Sir George Cayley's Aeronautics*, 4.
27. Op cit, 43.
28. Op cit, 70.
29. Pritchard, *Sir George Cayley*, 189.
30. Gibbs-Smith, *Sir George Cayley's Aeronautics*, 114.
31. Op cit, 127.
32. Op cit, 128.
33. Op cit, 149.
34. Cayley Papers, letter of Mrs George (Dora) Thompson of 2 November 1921 to J.E. Hodgson.
35. Ackroyd, 'Sir George Cayley, The Father of Aeronautics, Part 2, Cayley's Aeroplanes', 347.
36. Walter Raleigh, *The War in the Air: Being the Story of the Part Played in the Great War by the Royal Air Force*, Vol. 1 (1922), 42–3.
37. Pritchard, 'The First Cayley Memorial Lecture', 105.
38. J. Sproute, 'Making Flying Replicas of Sir George Cayley's Gliders', *Aeronaut Journal*, 78 (1974), 315–19.

Chapter 2: Shape of Things to Come
1. Harald Penrose, *An Ancient Air, A Biography of John Stringfellow of Chard* (1988), 42.
2. M.J.B. Davy, *Henson and Stringfellow, Their Work in Aeronautics. The History of a Stage in the Development of Mechanical Flight* (1931), 15.
3. National Aerospace Library. Stringfellow Papers, Copy of Aerial Steam Carriage Prospectus.
4. Penrose, *Ancient Air*, 48.
5. Ibid.
6. Op cit, 52.
7. Letter of John Chapman to Sir John Guest, Penrose, *Ancient Air*, 49.
8. This was the forerunner of Cayley's London Polytechnic.
9. Stringfellow Papers, Copy of Draft Agreement between Henson and Stringfellow of 1843.
10. Penrose, *Ancient Air*, 68. Letter of Stringfellow to Brearey, *Popular Science Review* (1869).
11. Op cit, 70.
12. Ibid.
13. Davy, 56 (Account of F.J. Stringfellow, John Stringfellow's son).
14. National Aerospace Library. Copy of the Agreement between Mr John Ellis and John Stringfellow.
15. Davy, 87.
16. National Aerospace Library. Report of the First Exhibition of the Aeronautical Society of Great Britain, 25 June 1868 and ten following days, 15.
17. Ibid.

Chapter 3: Multi-Wings, Wind Tunnels and Tethered Planes
1. Edward M. Nelson, 'Obituary of Francis Wenham', *Journal of the Royal Microscopical Society*, Vol. 2 (16 December 1908), 693–7.
2. F.H. Wenham, 'Lecture on Aerial Locomotion', *Transactions of the Aeronautical Society of Great Britain* (1956), 19.
3. Op cit, 32.
4. Meeting of the Aeronautical Society, 1 July 1868, 40, 41.
5. Concluding Remarks by Mr Brearey, Hon. Secretary to the Aeronautical Society at its Meeting of 3 July 1868, 60.
6. John D. Anderson, *Inventing Flight, The Wright Brothers and their Predecessors* (2004), 47.
7. Aerial Locomotion, *Transactions of the Aeronautical Society of Great Britain*. Fourth Annual Report for the year 1869, 84.
8. National Aerospace Library, Wenham Papers, Chanute–Wenham Correspondence, Letter of Wenham of 24 September 1892.

9. Op cit, Letter of Wenham, 6 June 1896.
10. Op cit, Letter of Wenham, 17 January 1905.
11. Op cit, Letter of Chanute, 24 November 1905.
12. Letter of A.H. Phillips (Horatio's son) to the Secretary of the Royal Aeronautical Society, dated 6 October 1929.
13. N.H. Randers-Pehrson, *Pioneer Wind Tunnels* (1955), 3.
14. W. Hudson Shaw and Olaf Ruhen, *Lawrence Hargrave, Explorer, Inventor and Aviation Experimenter* (1977), 68.
15. Charles H. Gibbs-Smith, *Aviation, An Historical Survey from its Origins to the end of the Second World War* (2003), 97.
16. Op cit, 98.
17. National Aerospace Library. Hargrave Papers, Introduction by A.E. Berriman, 15.
18. Shaw and Ruhen, xvii.
19. Gibbs-Smith, *Aviation*, 99.
20. National Aerospace Library. Unpublished Account by A.V. Stephens on the Life and Work of Lawrence Hargrave, 4.
21. Op cit, 17.
22. Iain McCallum, *Blood Brothers, Hiram and Hudson Maxim, Pioneers of Modern Warfare* (1999), 49.
23. Op cit, 7.
24. Hiram S. Maxim, *Artificial and Natural Flight* (1908), 31.
25. Hiram S. Maxim, *My Life* (1915), 297.
26. Maxim's tunnel was a wooden box, 12ft long and 3ft by 3ft inside its cross-section, connected with a shorter box 4ft square. It was in operation by 1896 (Randers-Pehrson, 7).
27. Maxim, *Artificial and Natural Flight*, 41
28. Hiram S. Maxim, 'Experiments in Aeronautics', *Journal of the Society of Arts* (Friday, 30 November 1894), 29–30.
29. *The Daily Graphic*, 5 November 1894.
30. Octave Chanute, 'Aviation at the Present Day. The Conclusion of Mr Maxim's Experiments', *Industries and Iron* (10 August 1894), 126–7.

Chapter 4: The British Troubadour

1. Philip Jarrett, *Another Icarus. Percy Pilcher and the Quest for Flight* (1987), ix.
2. Philip Jarrett, *Percy Pilcher and the Challenge of Flight* (1999), 2.
3. T.O.B. Hubbard and J.H. Ledeboer (eds), *The Aeronautical Classics, edited for the Aeronautical Society of Great Britain* (1910–11), Gliding, viii.
4. National Aerospace Library, Pilcher Papers, Notebook No. 1.
5. Jarrett, *Another Icarus*, 10 (Paper read by Pilcher before the Military Society of Ireland on 21 January 1897).
6. Op cit, 21.
7. Pilcher Papers, Lecture to the Royal Military Society of Ireland, Dublin 21 January 1897, 6.
8. Hubbard and Ledeboer, xii–xiii.
9. Jarrett, *Another Icarus*, 55. Letter of 25 June 1896 from Pilcher to Hargrave.
10. Pilcher Notebook No. 2. *Practical Engineer*, 6 March 1897.
11. Pilcher Papers, Lecture to the Royal Military Society of Ireland, Dublin 21 January 1897, 16.
12. Raleigh, 49.
13. Jarrett, *Another Icarus*, 113.
14. Pilcher Papers, Letter of Pilcher to Baden-Powell, 30 January 1899.
15. Op cit. Letter of Pilcher 9 June 1899.
16. Jarrett, *Another Icarus*, 122.
17. Op cit, 133.
18. Pilcher Notebook No. 2, Octave Chanute, 'The Present State of Aerial Navigation', 43.
19. King, 21.

Chapter 5: Lift off in America

1. Simone Short, *Locomotive to Aeromotive, Octave Chanute and the Transportation Revolution* (2011), 239.
2. Tom Crouch, *A Dream of Wings, Americans and the Aeroplane, 1875–1905* (1981), 262.
3. John D. Anderson (Jnr), *Inventing Flight, the Wright Brothers and their Predecessors* (2004), 74.
4. S P. Langley, *Experiments in Aerodynamics* (1891), 3.
5. National Aerospace Library, Chanute correspondence. Letter of Chanute to Francis Wenham of 13 September 1892
6. Short, 238.
7. Crouch, 177.
8. National Aerospace Library, Letter of O. Chanute to A.M. Herring of 31 December 1894.
9. Crouch, 190.
10, National Aerospace Library, Letter of Chanute to Langley of 11 June 1899.
11. Memo of Langley to Charles D. Walcott of March 23, 1899 (Crouch, 257).
12. National Aerospace Library, Langley Correspondence, Letters of Langley to Octave Chanute of 7 December 1902 and to Orville and Wilbur Wright of 24 November, 1902
13. Crouch, 287.
14. Op cit, 288.
15. Op cit, 291.
16. Fred Keller (ed.), *Miracle at Kitty Hawk* (1951), 4.
17. Fred Howard, *Wilbur and Orville, The Story of the Wright Brothers* (1987), 9–10.
18. Letter of Wilbur Wright to the Smithsonian Institution of 30 May 1899. *Papers of William and Orville Wright* edited by Marvin W. McFarland, Vol. 1, 1899–1905 (1953), 4–5
19. Notebook of Wilbur Wright 1900–01, 1–16.
20. Ibid.
21. Brian Riddle and Colin Sinnott (eds), *Letters of the Wright Brothers* (2003), 77.
22. The McFarland Papers, Vol. 1. Letters of Wilbur Wright and Octave Chanute between 17 May and June 1900, 19–22.
23. Op cit. Letter of Joseph S. Dosher from the Weather Station Kitty Hawk to Wilbur Wright, 16 August 1900, 21 n.9.
24. Op cit. Letter of 16 November 1900 of Wilbur Wright to Octave Chanute, 40–4.
25. Keller, Diary of Wilbur Wright 30 July, 1901, 42
26. The McFarland Papers, Deposition of Orville Wright of 2 February 1921, Vol. 1, 551.
27. McFarland Papers, Letter of Orville Wright to George A Spratt at Dayton on 7 June 1903, Vol. 1, 310.
28. Keller, Letter of Orville of 1 November 1903 to his sister Katharine, 105.
29. Ian Mackersey, *The Wright Brothers, The Remarkable Story of the Aviation Pioneers who Changed the World* (2003), 213.
30. Orville Wright (editor Fred C. Kelly), *How We Invented the Aeroplane* (1953), 1.

Chapter 6: Rejecting the Wrights' Offers

1. Alfred Gollin, *No Longer an Island, Britain and the Wright Brothers, 1902–1909* (1933), 4.
2. Op cit, 72.
3. Wright Brothers' Papers; English Negotiations, 8 February 1907, Gollin, *No Longer an Island*, 69.
4. Gollin, *No Longer an Island*, 71–2.
5. Capper was not over-generous financially towards Cody. Although he was extended in post from July 1905 for a further three months, his salary was actually reduced from £65.00 a month to £33.6s.8d a month: Peter Reese, *The Flying Cowboy, Samuel Cody, Britain's First Airman* (2008), 79.
6. Cody lived in Patrick Alexander's former house Pinehurst in Mytchett, Surrey until 1911.
7. HMSO 1906 Patents for Inventions, Aeronautics 1901–4. Patent no. 6732, 45.
8. Library of Congress, Wright Brothers Papers, General G.L. Gillespie to Hon. R.M. Nevin of 24 January 1905.
9. McFarland Papers, 495, Letter of Wilbur Wright of 1 June 1905 to Octave Chanute.

10. Wright Brothers' Papers, Letter of Colonel Foster to the Wrights of 7 December 1905 (written from Fort Leavenworth).
11. Percy B. Walker, *Early Aviation in Farnborough, Vol. II, The First Aeroplanes* (1974), 46.
12. Ibid.
13. Percy B. Walker, *Early Aviation at Farnborough, Vol. I, Balloons, Kites and Airships* (1971), 133.
14. Walker, Vol. II, 47.
15. War Office Papers 32/8595. Gleichen to Sir M. Durand, 17 August 1906.
16. Walker, Vol. II, 60–1.
17. Ibid.
18. Gollin, *No Longer an Island*, 313.
19. Walker, Vol. II, 232.
20. Reese, 115.
21. National Aerospace Library. Report of Colonel Capper of 16 October 1908.

Chapter 7: Thumbs Down for the Aeroplane

1. Charles H. Gibbs-Smith, *The Aeroplane, An Historical Survey* (1960), 62.
2. *The Daily Mail*, 10 September 1908.
3. Walker, Vol. II, 327.
4. Gollin, *No Longer an Island*, 398
5. Letter of Charles Rolls to Lord Esher of 11 December 1908: Walker, Vol. II, 307.
6. Evidence of C.S. Rolls to the 1909 Committee on Aerial Navigation, Tuesday, 8 December 1908: Walker, Vol. II, 304.
7. Evidence of Major B.F.S. Baden-Powell to the Committee on Aerial Navigation, Tuesday, 8 December 1908: Walker, Vol. II, 304.
8. Evidence to the Committee on Aerial Navigation on Tuesday, 15 December 1908: Walker, Vol. II, 314.
9. S.W. Roskill (ed.), *Documents relating to the Naval Air Service, Vol. I, 1908–1918* (1969), 11.
10. Walker, Vol. II, 329.
11. Roskill, 16.
12. Ibid.
13. Walker, Vol. II, 331.
14. *The Morning Post*, 24 May 1911.
15. Sir Geoffrey de Havilland, *Sky Fever* (1961), 69.
16. Robert F. Grattan, *The Origins of the Air War. The Development of Military Air Strategy in World War I* (2009), 1.

Chapter 8: Challenging the Doubters

1. *Oxford Dictionary of National Biography* (2004), Vol. 25, 341–2.
2. Louise Owen, *The Real Lord Northcliffe* (1922), 12.
3. Ibid.
4. *The Times*, 24 February 1909.
5. Letter of Northcliffe to R.B. Haldane, 19 February 1909: Gollin, *No Longer an Island*, 441–2.
6. *The Times*, 6 April 1909.
7. Alfred Gollin, *The Impact of Air Power on the British People and their Government, 1909–16* (1989), 46.
8. Harry Harper, *Ace Air Reporter* (1944), 66.
9. Gollin, *The Impact of Air Power*, 92–3.
10. *The Times*, 30 August 1909
11. Raleigh, 3.
12. James Thurstan, 'Charles Grey and his Pungent Pen', *The Aeronautical Journal of the Royal Aeronautical Society*, Vol. LXXIII (January–December 1969), 841.
13. Ibid. Grey's correspondents included such worthies as General Smith-Dorrien, Hugh Trenchard, Sir George White, Joynson Hicks, Octave Chanute and Griffith Brewer.
14. *The Aeroplane*, 8 June 1911.

15. *The Aeroplane*, 5 June 1911.
16. *The Aeroplane*, 28 September 1911.
17. *The Aeroplane*, 16 November 1911.
18. *The Aeroplane*, 14 December 1911.
19. *The Aeroplane*, 7, 21 March 1912.
20. *The Aeroplane*, 18 April 1912.
21. *The Aeroplane*, 23 May 1912.
22. *The Aeroplane*, 20 August 1912.
23. *The Aeroplane*, 12 December 1912.
24. *The Aeroplane*, 2 January 1913.
25. *The Aeroplane*, 26 June 1913.
26. *The Aeroplane*, 17 July 1913.
27. *The Aeroplane*, 7 August 1913.
28. *The Aeroplane*, 4 December 1913.
29. *The Aeroplane*, 11 December 1913.
30. *The Aeroplane*, 1 January 1914.
31. *The Aeroplane*, 2 April 1914.
32. *The Aeroplane*, 5 August 1914.
33. *Flight*, 4 May 1912.
34. *Flight*, 31 January 1914.
35. *Flight*, 17 July 1914.

Chapter 9: Early Flyers – Flying for the Hell of It

1. Reese, 203.
2. John Barfoot, *Essex Airmen 1910–1918* (2006), 16.
3. National Aerospace Library. Undated, un-numbered autobiography of Robert Blackburn, written in the third person.
4. *Flight*, 9 April 1910, 272–3.
5. Barfoot, 19.
6. R. Dallas Brett, *History of British Aviation 1908–14*, 1987, 59–60.
7. Brett, 95.
8. Barfoot, 20.
9. G.G. Manton, 'Hucks – master pilot', *Aeronautics*, Vol. 43, No. 1 (November 1961), 30–1.
10. Harry Harper, *Lords of the Air* (1940), 114.

Chapter 10: First Flyers – Pushing the Margins

1. 'Gustav Hamel, an appreciation', *Aeronautics* (June 1914), 159–61.
2. Henry Serrano Villard, *Blue Ribbon of the Air, The Gordon Bennett Races* (1987), 122.
3. Harry Harper, *Conquerors of the Air, Hamel, The First Flying Postman* (1948), 106–7.
4. Harper, *Lords of the Air*, 112.
5. *The Times*, 30 September 1912.
6. Brochure on Flying Impressions and Notes, Whitchurch Cycle Parade and Floral Carnival, Wednesday, 11 September 1912.
7. John Goodwin, 'The Intrepid Gustav Hamel', *WW1 Aero* 183 (February 2004), 83.
8. Op cit, 81.
9. Gustav Hamel and Charles C. Turner, *Flying, some practical experiences* (1914), 7.
10. Op cit, 288.
11. Mary Busk, *E.T. Busk, A Pioneer in Flight with a short memoir of H.A. Busk, Flight Commander RNAS* (1925), 26.
12. Ibid.
13. *The Aeronautical Journal*, Vol. XX (1915), 5.
14. Busk, 61.
15. Op cit, 67.
16. Op cit, 69.

17. Advisory Committee for Aeronautics, April 1914, Reports and Memoranda No.132, 2–3.
18. Advisory Committee for Aeronautics, April 1914, Reports and Memoranda No.133, 4–5.
19. Advisory Committee for Aeronautics, April 1914. Reports and Memoranda No.134, Longitudinal Stability by Mervyn O'Gorman CB, Superintendent of the Royal Aircraft Factory and R.H. Mayo with experiments by E.T. Busk of the Staff of the Royal Aircraft Factory, April; 1914, 4–5.
20. Busk, 67.
21. Op cit, 92.

Chapter 11: The Constructors 1908–1914: Going it Alone

1. The cost of new balloons at this time was between £120 and £400.
2. C.H. Barnes, *Shorts Aircraft since 1900* (1989), 3.
3. Michael J.H. Taylor, *Shorts* (1984), 10.
4. Barnes, 6.
5. National Aerospace Library. Notebook of Horace Short compiled at Pau, February 1909.
6. Michael Donne, *Pioneers of the Skies, A History of the Short Brothers PLC* (1987), 28.
7. Op cit, 28–9.
8. Barnes, 16.
9. A.J. Jackson, *Avro Aircraft since 1908* (1990), xi.
10. Sir Alliott. Verdon-Roe, *The World of Wings and Things* (1939), 28.
11. Jackson, xiii.
12. Philip Jarrett, *Trials, Troubles and Triplanes, Alliott Verdon-Roe's Fight to Fly* (2007), 5.
13. Op cit, 5, 6.
14. *The Times*, 6 January 1958.
15. Jarrett, *Trials, Troubles and Triplanes*, 43.
16. Op cit, 46.
17. J. Laurence Pritchard, 'Sir Alliott Verdon-Roe OBE Honorary Fellow 1877–1958', *Journal of the Royal Aeronautical Society*, Vol.LX11 (January–December 1958), 235.
18. Jarrett, *Trials, Troubles and Triplanes*, 61.
19. Op cit, 3.
20. National Aerospace Library, unpublished account by Robert Blackburn.
21. Harald Penrose, *British Aviation, The Pioneer Years* (1967), 298.
22. Sir Geoffrey de Havilland, *Sky Fever, An Autobiography* (1961), 55.
23. C. Martin Sharp, *D.H.* (1982), 21.
24. De Havilland, 72.
25. Raleigh, 165.
26. Review on G. de Havilland, *Hawker Siddeley Magazine*, Vol.1, No.2 (1965).
27. *The Times*, 22 May 1965.

Chapter 12: The Constructors 1908–1914: Born Winners

1. Alan Bramson, *Pure Luck, the Authorised Biography of Sir Thomas Sopwith 1888–1989* (2005), 32–3.
2. Op cit, 58.
3. Op cit, 62.
4. Op cit, 63.
5. Op cit, 66.
6. *The Independent*, 25 January 1989.
7. Bramson, 163.
8. Harry Harper, 'Bristol Flash-back', *Bristol Review Christmas Issue* (1952), 10.
9. Derek N. James, *The Bristol Aeroplane Company* (2001), 11.
10. Ibid.
11. Ibid.
12. The British and Colonial Aeroplane Company Ltd, Minute Book No.1. Minutes for a meeting held on Tuesday 24 May 1910

13. Andrew and Melanie Kelly, *Take Flight, Celebrating Aviation in the West of England since 1910* (2010), 63.
14. King, 156.

Chapter 13: Air Publicists – Practical Visionaries
1. Claude Grahame-White and Harry Harper, *The Aeroplane in War* (1912), vi.
2. Op cit, vii–viii.
3. *Journal of the Royal Aeronautical Society*, No. 588 (December 1959), 681.
4. Penrose, *Pioneer Years*, 148–9.
5. Graham Wallace, *Claude Grahame-White, A Biography* (1960), 67.
6. *Journal of the Royal Aeronautical Society*, No. 588 (December 1959), 682.
7. Official Programme of London Aerodrome for 14 September 1912.
8. Bramson, 53.
9. National Aerospace Library, A.C.B. Ashworth unpublished biography of Claude Grahame-White, 14.
10. Peter Wright, 'Wings to Wheels', *Cross and Cockade International*, Vol. 38 (2007), 47.
11. *The Times*, 20 August 1957, Obituary of C. Grahame-White.
12. Lord Montagu of Beaulieu, *Rolls of Rolls-Royce. A biography of the Hon. C.S. Rolls* (1968), 14.
13. This did not stop him from continuing the family tradition for charitable works, in his case adding a carpentry ward for the Hermitage Cripples' School at Chailey, Sussex: Bruce Gordon, *Charlie Rolls, Pioneer Aviator* (1990), 12.
14. Penrose, *Pioneer Years*, 116.
15. Montagu of Beaulieu, 107.
16. Op cit, 136.
17. Op cit, 139.
18. Bruce Gordon, *Charles Rolls, pioneer aviator*, Rolls-Royce Heritage Trust Historical Series, No. 16 (1990), 16.
19. Penrose, *Pioneer Years*, 113.
20. Bruce, 42.
21. Montague of Beaulieu, 224.
22. *Oxford Dictionary of National Biography* (2004), Vol. 54, 324.
23. Op cit, 325.
24. Claude Grahame-White and Harry Harper, *The Aeroplane; Past, Present and the Future* (1911), 235–45.
25. Op cit, 237.
26. Op cit, 238.
27. Op cit, 241.
28. Op cit, 245.
29. King, 126.
30. Op cit, 125–6.
31. *Oxford Dictionary of National Biography* (2004), Vol. 54, 325.
32. G. Holt Thomas, *Aerial Transport* (1920), v.
33. *Oxford Dictionary of National Biography* (2004), Vol. 54, 325.
34. Derek S. Taulbut, *Eagle, Henry Royce's first aero engine*, Rolls-Royce Heritage Trust Historical Series, No. 43 (2011), 33.
35. Op cit, 243.

Chapter 14: Air Publicists – Parliamentary Voices
1. Randolph S. Churchill, *Winston S. Churchill, Young Statesman, 1901–14* (1967), Vol. II, 688.
2. Percy B. Walker, *Early Aviation at Farnborough, the First Aeroplanes* (1974), 329.
3. Letter of Lord Fisher to WSC of 10 November 1911: Churchill, 688.
4. Op cit, 687.
5. Letter of WSC to Sir Robert Chalmers, 24 August 1912: Churchill, 687.
6. Norman MacMillan, *Sir Sefton Brancker* (1935), 75.

7. Churchill, 690–1.
8. Statement of Captain Ivan Courtney: op cit, 697.
9. Op cit, 701.
10. *The Times*, 30 May 1914.
11. P.W. Gretton, *Former Naval Person* (1968), 128.
12. Philip Guedalla, *Mr Churchill, A Portrait* (1941), 153.
13. Martin Gilbert, *Winston Churchill*, Vol. III, 1914–16 (1971), 769.
14. Hansard, 27 November 1912.
15. Ibid.
16. Hansard, 4 December 1912.
17. Hansard, 11 December 1912.
18. Ibid.
19. Ibid.
20. Hansard, 30 December 1912.
21. 'Our Service Aircraft and the Government', *Flight*, 9 August 1913, 876–7.
22. Op cit, 878.
23. Op cit, 880. Discussion in Parliament, 30 July 1913
24. Op cit, Editorial Comment, 863–4.
25. Letter of Joynson-Hicks to the Press dated 30 July 1913.
26. *Oxford Dictionary of National Biography* (2004), Vol. 5, 721.
27. King, 71.
28. Noel Pemberton-Billing, *Defence Against the Night Bomber* (1941), ix, x.
29. Op cit, xi.
30. 'Those Magnificent Mags', *Aeroplane Monthly* (January 1983), 49–50.
31. Juniper Dean, 'Noel Pemberton-Billing', *RUSI Journal*, Vol. 150, No. 4 (August 2005), 61.
32. C.F. Andrew and E.B. Morgan, *Supermarine Aircraft since 1914* (1987), 16.
33. Philip Jarrett, 'Boats that Flew', *Air Britain Digest*, Vol. 31 No. 5 (September–October 1979), 100–3.
34. *Aeroplane Monthly* (January 1983), 49.
35. Juniper Dean, 'Noel Pemberton-Billing', *RUSI Journal*, Vol. 150, No. 4 (August 2005), 65.

Chapter 15: Emergence of Aviation for War

1. Hugh Driver, *The Birth of Military Aviation* (1997), 109.
2. This information is given on a monumental plaque close to Dickson's grave at Achanault in the Scottish Highlands.
3. Raleigh, 137.
4. Driver, 251.
5. Reminiscences of G. Holt Thomas, *The Aero* (28 September 1910), 14.
6. Driver, 255.
7. Committee on Aerial Navigation, note by Lord Esher.
8. Raleigh, 142.
9. Chamier, 6.
10. National Archives, AIR 1 1609/204/85/56.
11. Driver, 71.
12. Patrick Bishop, *Wings. One Hundred Years of British Aerial Warfare* (2010), 24.
13. Chamier, 6.
14. Driver, 269, 270.
15. Minute to sub-committee by Winston Churchill, First Lord of the Admiralty, 9 December 1911.
16. Tragically Dickson's flying activities were now seriously curtailed. Shortly after the 1910 army manoeuvres he had been involved in a mid-air collision while taking part in an international air meeting in Milan. His recovery had been in large part due to his sister, Mrs Will Gordon, who had taken over his nursing but although he flew again he died in September 1915.
17. Raleigh, 175–6.

18. At the time of writing his memorandum a confrontation had developed between Italy and Turkey where aerial bombardment had been used for the first time.
19. Raleigh, 175.
20. Op cit, 108.
21. Chamier, 10.
22. *Training Manual, Royal Flying Corps* (1913) Part II, Military Wing, 4.
23. *Royal Warrant, Pay etc of the Royal Flying Corps (Military Wing)*, 1, 4.
24. *Royal Aero Club Year Book 1915–16*, Numerical List of Aviators' Certificates, 194–247.
25. John Taylor, *CFS: Birthplace of Airpower* (1958), 30–3.
26. L.E.O. Charlton, *Charlton* (1931), 216.
27. Op cit, 217.
28. Penrose, *Pioneer Years*, 369.
29. Royal Flying Corps Concentration Camp, June 1914.
30. *Cross and Cockade*, Vol. 43 (Autumn 2012), 185.
31. Winifred Loraine, *Robert Loraine, Actor, Soldier, Airman* (1938), 256.
32. H.H. Balfour, *An Airman Marches* (1933), 147.

Chapter 16: The Royal Flying Corps' Move to France
1. John H. Morrow, Jr., *The Great War in the Air, Military Aviation from 1909 to 1921* (1993), 39.
2. A list of all the officers and men of the Royal Flying Corps who were stationed in France prior to the Battle of Mons is given in Appendix B.
3. Raleigh, 256.
4. King, 125.
5. Ralph Barker, *The Royal Flying Corps in France* (1994), 22.
6. Raleigh, 283–4.
7. Barker, 14.
8. R.H. Kiernan, *The First War in the Air* (1934), 25.
9. Chamier, 18.
10. Ibid.
11. Prince Consort's Library, Aldershot Army Lists, 1914–18.
12. King, 22.
13. Cecil Lewis, *Sagittarius Rising* (1993), 79.
14. Ministry of Reconstruction, *The Resettlement of Officers (Army and RAF)* (1919), 2.

Aftermath
1. *Flight*, No. 259 (13 December 1913), 1341.
2. *Die Militarluftfahrt bis zung Beginn des Werkrises, 1914* (1941), 592.
3. Dr James J. Davilla and Arthur M. Soltan, *French Aircraft of the First World War* (1997), 3.
4. Morrow, *The Great War in the Air*, 86.
5. Op cit, 102.
6. John H. Morrow, *German Airpower in World War 1* (1982), 47.
7. Georges Huisman, *Dans les Coulisses de l'aviation* (1921), 123–9.
8. J.M. Spaight, *The Beginnings of Organised Air Power* (1927), 234–5.
9. Morrow, *German Airpower*, 190.
10. Op cit, 61–2.
11. Malcolm Cooper, *Birth of Independent Air Power* (1986), 21–3.
12. Morrow, *The Great War in the Air*, 168.
13. Cecil Lewis, 137.
14. Morrow, *The Great War in the Air*, 173–4.
15. Aerial League of the British Empire, Pamphlet No. 1 (1909).
16. Driver, 273–4.
17. Morrow, *The Great War in the Air*, 184.
18. Cooper, 142.
19. Op cit, 149–51.

Select Bibliography

Primary Sources
National Aerospace Library
Cayley Papers, Diaries and Correspondence.
Hargrave's Papers, including Unpublished Pamphlet on The Life and Work of Lawrence Hargrave by A.V. Stephens.
Maxim Papers.
Report of the First Exhibition of the Aeronautical Society of Great Britain held at the Crystal Palace on 25 June 1868 and ten following days. Printed by Henry Richardson.
The Air League Journal, Centenary Edition 1909–2009. Robert Owen, Forming the Air League – 14–16.
C.G. Grey Papers.
Catalogues of Aero and Marine Exhibition, Olympia, March 1909, 1910, 1911, 1914.
Minute Book No. 1 of The British and Colonial Aeroplane Company, February 1910 – 8 March 1920 prior to it becoming Bristol Aeroplane Company Ltd.
Catalogs Exposition Internationale de Locomotion Aerienne 1909.
Offizieller Katalog Internationale Luftschiffahrt Ausstellung Frankfurt 10 juli to 10 oktob 1909.
Programmes of the Hendon Air Shows 1912–14.
Unpublished Autobiography of Robert Blackburn (written in the third person).
Sixth Sir George Cayley Memorial lecture to Brough Branch of the Royal Aeronautical Society on 11 November 1959 by Sir George Gardner. 'The Royal Aircraft Factory, Farnborough and the Early History of the Aeroplane'.

Prince Consort's Library, Aldershot
Army Lists 1902–45.
Air Force Lists 1916, 1918.
Navy Lists 1917, 1919.

Magazines and Periodicals
The Aero, 1910.
Aeronautics, Vol. 43, November 1900–April 1901.
Aeronautics, 1909–14.
The Aeronautical Annual, by James Means 1895–7.
The Aeroplane, edited by Chas. G. Grey (Aero Amateur) 1911–14.
Aeroplane Monthly.
Flight, 1909–14.
Journal of the Royal Aeronautical Society, Vol. 65, No. 601 (April 1961), 236–51.
RUSI Journal, 2005.
WW1 Aero.

Articles
Ballantyne, A.M. and Pritchard, J.L., 'The Lives and Work of William Samuel Henson and John Stringfellow, First Henson and Stringfellow Memorial Lecture', *Journal of the Royal Aeronautical Society*, Vol. LX (January–December 1956).
Hodgson, J.E., 'Sir George Cayley's Work on Aeronautics', *Aviation Magazine* (17 December 1923).

Pritchard, J.L., 'The First Cayley Memorial Lecture', *Journal of the Royal Aeronautical Society* (February 1955), 79–109.
Pritchard, J.L., 'The Dawn of Aerodynamics', *Journal of the Royal Aeronautical Society*, Vol. LXI (January–December 1957).
Sturtivent, Roy, 'British Flying Training in World War One', *Cross and Cockade International Journal*, Vol. 15 (1994), 18–28.

Newspapers
Daily Graphic.
Daily Mail.
Daily Telegraph.
Hansard.
Morning Post.
The Independent.
The Times.

Books
Ackroyd, J.A.D., Axcell, B.P. and Ruhan, A., *Early Developments of Modern Aerodynamics*, 2001.
Adkin, F.J., *From the Ground Up. A History of RAF Ground Crew*, 1983.
Anderson, John D. (Jnr), *A History of Aerodynamics and its Impact on Flying Machines*, 1998.
Anderson, John D. (Jnr), *The Airplane, A History of the Technology*, 2003.
Anderson, John D. (Jnr), *Inventing Flight. The Wright Brothers and Their Predecessors*, 2004.
Andrews, Allen, *Back to the Drawing Board. The Evolution of Flying Machines*, 1977.
Baker, David, *Flight and Flying, A Chronology*, 1994.
Balfour, H.H., *An Airman Marches*, 1933.
Barfoot, John, *Essex Airmen 1910–1918*, 2006.
Baring, Maurice, *RFC HQ 1914–18*, 1920.
Barker, Ralph, *The Royal Flying Corps in France from Mons to the Somme*, 1994.
Barnes, C.H., *Shorts Aircraft since 1900*, 1989.
Benbow, Tim, *British Naval Aviation, The First 100 Years*, 2011.
Biddle, Wayne, *Barons of the Sky, From Early Flight to Strategic Warfare*, 1991.
Birkenhead, Lord, *Rudyard Kipling*, 1978.
Bishop, Patrick, *Wings, One Hundred Years of British Aerial Warfare*, 2010.
Blackmore, L.K., *Hawker, A Biography of Harry Hawker*, 1993.
Bloor, David, *Enigma of the Aerofoil, Rival Theories in Aerodynamics 1909–1930*, 2011.
Bramson, Alan, *Pure Luck, the authorised biography of Sir Thomas Sopwith*, 2005.
Brett, R. Dallas, *History of British Aviation 1908–1914*, 1987.
Broke Smith, P.W.L., *History of Early British Military Aeronautics*, 1968.
Bruce, Gordon, *Charlie Rolls – Pioneer Aviator*, 1990.
Busk, Mary, *E.T. Busk, A Pioneer in Flight*, 1925.
Chamier, Air Commodore J.A., *The Birth of the Royal Air Force*, 1943.
Charlton, L.E.O., *Charlton*, 1931.
Churchill, Randolph S., *Winston S. Churchill, Young Statesman*, Vol. II, 1967.
Cooper, Malcolm, *The Birth of Independent Air Power*, 1986.
Crouch, Tom D., *A Dream of Wings, Americans and the Airplane*, 1981.
Davilla, Dr James J. and Soltan, Arthur M., *French Aircraft of the First World War*, 1997.
Davy, M.J.B., *Henson and Stringfellow, their Work in Aeronautics. The History of a Stage in the Development of Mechanical Flight 1840–1868*, 1931.
De Havilland, Sir Geoffrey, *Sky Fever. An Autobiography*, 1961.
Dee, Richard, *The Man who Discovered Flight, George Cayley and the First Airplane*, 2007.
Demetz, Peter, *The Air Show at Brescia 1909*, 2002.
Divine, David, *The Broken Wing. A Story of the British Exercise of Airpower*, 1966.
Donne, Michael, *Pioneers of the Skies. A History of Short Brothers plc*, 1987.
Driver, Hugh, *The Birth of Military Aviation*, 1997.

Edgerton, David, *England and the Aeroplane*, 1991.

Elliott, Brian A., *Blériot, Herald of an Age*, 2000.

Gibbs-Smith, C.H., *The Aeroplane, An Historical Survey*, 1960.

Gibbs-Smith, C.H., *Sir George Cayley's Aeronautics 1796–1855*, 1962.

Gibbs-Smith, C.H., *Aviation, An Historical Survey from its Origins to the End of the Second World War*, 2003.

Gilbert, Martin, *Winston Churchill*, Vol. III, 1971.

Gollin, Alfred, *No Longer an Island. Britain and the Wright Brothers 1902–1909*, 1983.

Gollin, Alfred, *The Impact of Air Power on the British People and their Government 1909–14*, 1989.

Grahame-White, Claude and Harper, Harry, *The Aeroplane; Past, Present and the Future*, 1911.

Grahame-White, Claude and Harper, Harry, *The Aeroplane in War*, 1912.

Grahame-White, Claude and Harper, Harry, *Heroes of the Air*, 1925.

Grattan, Robert F., *The Origins of the Air War. The Development of Military Air Strategy in World War I*, 2009.

Guedella, Philip, *Mr Churchill, A Portrait*, 1941.

Hall, Malcolm, *Images of Aviation*, 1999.

Hallion, Richard, *Taking Flight*, 2003.

Hamel, Gustav and Turner, Charles C., *Flying, some practical experiences*, 1914.

Hamilton, James E., *The Chronic Inventor. The Life and Work of Hiram Stevens Maxim*, 1991.

Harper, Harry, *Lords of the Air*, 1940.

Harper, Harry, *Ace Air Reporter*, 1944.

Harper, Harry, *Conquerors of the Air, Hamel, The First Flying Postman*, 1948.

Hawkey, Arthur, *The Amazing Hiram Maxim. An Intimate Biography*, 2001.

Heinz, J. Nowarra and Duval, G.R., *Russian Civil and Military Aircraft 1884–1969*, 1971.

Henshaw, Trevor, *The Sky their Battlefield. Air Fighting and the Complete List of Allied Air Casualties from Enemy Action in the First World War*, 1993.

Heppenheimer, T.A., *First Flight, The Wright Brothers and the Invention of the Aeroplane*, 2003.

Holt Thomas, George, *Aerial Transport*, 1920.

Howard, Fred, *Wilbur and Orville, The Story of the Wright Brothers*, 1987.

Hubbard, T.O.B. and Ledeboer, J.H. (eds), *The Aeronautical Classics edited for the Council of The Aeronautical Society of Great Britain*, 1910–11.

Hudson, W, and Ruhen, Olaf, *Lawrence Hargrave, Explorer, Inventor and Aviation Experimenter*, 1977.

Huisman, Georges, *Dans les Coulisses de l'aviation*, 1921.

Hurren, B.J., *Fellowship of the Air. Jubilee Book of the Royal Aero Club 1901–1951*, 1944.

Hurst, Ernst Heinrich Hirschel, Horst Prem, Gero Madelung, *Aeronautical Research in Germany from Lilienthal until Today*, 2001.

Jackson, A.J., *Avro Aircraft since 1908*, 1990.

James, Derek N., *The Bristol Aeroplane Company*, 2001.

Jarrett, Philip, *Another Icarus. Percy Pilcher and the Quest for Flight*, 1987.

Jarrett, Philip (ed.), *Pioneer Aircraft, Early Aviation to 1914*, 2002.

Jarrett, Philip (ed.), *Puttnam's History of Aircraft, Pioneer Aircraft, Early Aviation before 1914*, 2002.

Jarrett, Philip, *Trials, Troubles and Triplanes, Alliott Verdon-Roe's Fight to Fly*, 2007.

Karman, Theodore von, *Aerodynamics*, 1954.

Keller, Fred (ed.), *Miracle at Kitty Hawk*, 1951.

Kelly, Andrew and Kelly, Melanie, *Take Flight, Celebrating Aviation in the West of England since 1910*, 2010.

Kiernan, R.H., *The First War in the Air*, 1934.

King, Peter, *Knights of the Air: The Life and Times of the Extraordinary Pioneers who first Built British Aeroplanes*, 1989.

Langley, S.P., *Experiments in Aerodynamics*, 1891.

Langley, S.P., *Langley Memoir on Mechanical Flight, Part I*, 1911.

Lewis, Cecil, *Sagittarius Rising*, 1933.

Lewis, Peter, *British Aircraft 1809–1914*, 1962.

Longmore, Sir Arthur, *From Sea to Sky 1910–1945*, 1946.

Loraine, Winifred, *Robert Loraine, Actor, Soldier, Airman*, 1938.

MacCarron, Donal, *Letters from an Early Bird, The Life and Letters of Denys Corbett Wilson 1882–1915*, 2006.

Mackersey, Ian, *The Wright Brothers. The Remarkable Story of the Aviation Pioneers who changed the World*, 2003.

Mackersey, Ian, *No Empty Chairs. The Short and Heroic Lives of the Young Aviators who Fought and Died in the First World War*, 2012.

Manly, Charles M., *Langley Memoir on Mechanical Flight, Part II*, 1911.

Maxim, Hiram S., *Artificial and Natural Flight*, 1908.

Maxim, Hiram S., *My Life*, 1915.

McCallum, Iain, *Blood Brothers, Hiram and Hudson Maxim, Pioneers of Modern Warfare*, 1999.

Means, James Howard, *James Means and the Problem of Manflight during the period 1882–1920*, 1964.

Middleton, Edgar C., *Aircraft by an 'Air Pilot'*, 1916.

Montagu of Beaulieu, Lord, *Rolls of Rolls-Royce. A Biography of the Hon. C.S. Rolls*, 1966.

Morrow, J.H., Jnr, *German Airpower in World War One*, 1982.

Morrow, J.H., Jnr, *The Great War in the Air, Military Aviation from 1909–1921*, 1993.

Mousseau, Jacques, *Conquering the Skies 1903–1933* (translated from the French by Phillippa Wehle), 2004.

Munson, Kenneth, *Fighters 1914–19*, 2012.

National Aerospace Laboratory NLR, *75 years of Aerospace Research in the Netherlands*, 1994.

Officers Died in the Great War 1914–1919, new enlarged edition, 1988.

Owen, Louise, *The Real Lord Northcliffe. Some Private Recollections of a Private Secretary 1902–1922*, 1922.

Paterson, James Hamilton, *Empire of the Clouds*, 2010.

Pemberton-Billing, Noel, *Defence Against the Night Bomber*, 1941.

Penrose, Harald, *British Aviation, The Pioneer Years*, 1967.

Penrose, Harald, *An Ancient Air, A Biography of John Stringfellow of Chard*, 1988.

Petit, Robert, *How to Build an Aeroplane* (translated from the French by T. O'B Hubbard and J.H. Ledeboer), 1910.

Pritchard, J. Laurence, *Sir George Cayley, The Inventor of the Aeroplane*, 1961.

Pugh, Peter, *The Magic of a Name, The Rolls-Royce Story, The First 40 Years*, 2000.

Raleigh, Walter, *The War in the Air, Being the Story of the Part Played in the Great War by the Royal Air Force*, Vol. 1, 1922.

Randers-Pehrson, N.H., *Pioneer Wind Tunnels*, 1955.

Reese, Peter, *The Flying Cowboy*, 2008.

Richthofen, Manfred Freiherr von, *The Red Air Fighter*, 1918.

Riddle, Brian and Sinnott, Colin (eds), *Letters of the Wright Brothers*, 2003.

Rolt, L.T.C., *The Aeronauts*, 1966.

Roskill, Captain S.W., *Documents Relating to the Naval Air Service, Vol. I, 1908–1918*, 1969.

Saunders, Hilary St George, *Per Ardua. The Rise of British Air Power 1911–1939*, 1944.

Scott, Phil, *The Shoulders of Giants, A History of Human Flight to 1919*, 1995.

Sharp, C. Martin, *D.H.*, 1982.

Shaw, W. Hudson and Ruhen, Olaf, *Lawrence Hargrave. Explorer, Inventor and Aviator Experimenter*, 1977.

Short, Simone, *Locomotive to Aeromotive, Octave Chanute and the Transportation Revolution*, 2011.

Spaight, J.M., *The Beginnings of Organised Air Power*, 1927.

Steel, Nigel and Hart, Peter, *Tumult in the Clouds. The British Experience of the War in the Air 1914–1918*, 1997.

Sueter, Rear Admiral Murray F., *Airmen or Noahs, Fair Play for our Airmen*, 1928.

Taylor, John C.F.S., *Birthplace of Airpower*, 1958.

Taylor, Michael J.H., *Shorts*, 1984

Tobin, James, *First to Fly, The Unlikely Triumph of Wilbur and Orville Wright*, 2003.

Turner, C.C. (Major), *My Flying Scrap Book*, 1947.

Verdon-Roe, Sir Alliott, *The World of Wings and Things*, 1939.

Villard, Henry Serrano, *Blue Ribbon of the Air, The Gordon Bennett Races*, 1987.
Vivian, E.C. and Marsh, W. Lockwood, *A History of Aeronautics*, 1921.
Walker, Percy B., *Early Aviation at Farnborough, Vol. I, Balloons, Kites and Airships*, 1971.
Wallace, Graham, *Claude Grahame-White, A Biography*, 1960.
White, Claude Grahame and Harper, Harry, *The Aeroplane, Past, Present and the Future*, 1911.
Wohl, Robert A., *A Passion for Wings, Aviation and the Western Imagination 1908–1918*, 1994.
Wolko, Howard S., *In the Cause of Flight. Technologists of Aeronautics and Astronautics*, 1981.
Wright, Orville, *How we Invented the Airplane, An Illustrated History*, 1953.

Index